Singing on the
Heavy Side
of the World

Singing on the Heavy Side of the World

A Peace Corps Ukraine Story

John Deever

Copyright © 2002 by John Deever.

ISBN :	Softcover	1-4010-4861-7

All rights reserved. No part of this book may be reproduced or transmitted in any form or by any means, electronic or mechanical, including photocopying, recording, or by any information storage and retrieval system, without permission in writing from the copyright owner.

This book was printed in the United States of America.

To order additional copies of this book, contact:
Xlibris Corporation
1-888-795-4274
www.Xlibris.com
Orders@Xlibris.com

Contents

Prologue
Singing on the Heavy Side of the World 9
Chapter One
Mr. John and the Day of Knowledge 13
Chapter Two
"To You!" 29
Chapter Three
Ukraine Has Not Died Yet 43
Chapter Four
Endings 63
Chapter Five
Lost in the Classroom 81
Chapter Six
Our Own Michael Jackson 100
Chapter Seven
Secondary Project: "Where Is Pinky?" 113
Chapter Eight
Friendship and Then Some 128
Chapter Nine
Here to Stay 147
Chapter Ten
Baranivka—In the Village 170
Chapter Eleven
Bread, the Soul of Our Motherland 193

Chapter Twelve
If You're Happy and You Know It 205
Chapter Thirteen
Now We Have Twenty-Eight 230
Chapter Fourteen
Falling 241
Chapter Fifteen
A Summer Day Is Like a Year 260
Chapter Sixteen
The Spy Corps 276
Chapter Seventeen
Borderland 295
Chapter Eighteen
Stayers, Leavers 312
Epilogue 329
Related websites, as of February 2002 339

TO MY PARENTS AND MY FRIENDS WHO SENT ME OFF,
TO LIZA WHO BROUGHT ME BACK,
AND TO THE TEACHERS AND CHILDREN OF UKRAINE
WHO GOT ME THROUGH IT.

Prologue

Singing on the Heavy Side of the World

I'll always think of Ukraine as the heavy side of the world.

Like the more-familiar Russian, the Ukrainian soul is characterized by "heaviness" in all the word's connotations: weighty, difficult, serious, massive, important, monumental, solemn, soul-wrenching. It's the most valued personal trait in poets, leaders and common people too: "deep-souledness." Living there for two years as a Peace Corps volunteer, I breathed it into me, this "heaviness." For me, it sums up how it feels to live in the former Soviet Union today.

Even the word in Ukrainian for heavy—*tyazhko*—means both greatness of weight and difficulty or painfulness of burden. Ukrainians carry heavy bags and packages everywhere they go, and even the simplest task, from buying groceries to mailing a letter, is more difficult to do than in the United States. Life is difficult and heavy—*tyazhko*.

Ukrainians often *are* heavy, for the diet is heavy. Staple vegetables are the eminently serious: potatoes, beets, and cabbage. The national dish is thick, doughy dumplings smothered in sour cream. An extra special breakfast might include fried pork cutlets, canned sardines on dark rye bread, and a bowl of large curds of cottage cheese sprinkled with sugar. *Salo*, a thick uncooked slice of bacon so fatty that no pink appears at all, is a Ukrainian delicacy.

Look at work: Ukraine was home to 40 percent of the USSR's heavy industry. In a land known for record-setting massive machinery, the level of Ukraine's industrialization is second only to Russia's. Hence every Ukrainian suffers daily from heavy pollution.

Heaviest of all is the weather. Even though it is far south of Moscow and dark northern Russia, in Ukraine the midwinter sun rises at nine and sets at three-thirty. On such short, dark, gloomy days I felt a heaviness of spirit so crushing that every step became an exhausting undertaking. I felt like an orchid in the Arctic, so out of my element I could not thrive. I was a lite potato chip in a ten-pound bag of Idahoes.

Understanding this feeling, Ukrainians taught me about heavy drinking.

Often, foreigners who have visited the USSR describe the relief they experience upon leaving. Why, as their airplanes leave Russian soil, do they so frequently emit long-suppressed sighs? I think those sighs are released once our inner sensors feel the scales tip back. Immediately, perceptibly, there is a lightness as we lift into the air and the sadder, heavier side of the world remains behind. I sometimes imagined a lopsided globe, with a bulbous, massy hump where the former Soviet Union is. Its mammoth scale of proportions, its overgenerous share of human suffering, and the bulky *heaviness* of the Slavic soul caused the globe I imagined to tilt perpetually sideways toward these people, this place, where some strong force of gravity held them in place.

Economic and social conditions in Ukraine are famously, absurdly bad: what pensioners receive in monthly benefits was worth about the price of ten eggs; state salaries of teachers and many other workers went unpaid for eight months straight while I was there from 1993 to 1995. The rampant corruption, the frequent murders of public officials and journalists, the often unbelievable pollution, and the people's declining health standards—every day came more bad news. I wanted to think that conditions since communism's demise were gradually improving, but to say so seemed ridiculous. When I professed optimism, Ukrainians were pleased, but kindly dismissive; when I joked about either my life or theirs growing ever worse, they said: "Now you are coming to understand us."

Living amongst these people, then, what I found—sunk like a rock at the bottom of the well—was not despair but a weird, black humor. Under the heavy burden of daily life lay rare gems of ironic, sad laughter. Many days when my lessons failed disastrously, when my days teaching in a Ukrainian school felt agonizingly pointless, I wanted to cry, give up, go home, forget it. Yet some strangely funny thing would convince me to stay, to try a little harder.

Finally, when even humor would not suffice, there was singing—the pastime of which Ukrainians may be more proud than any other. Late winter evenings, walking the slushy streets of my city, I would first hear them, their voices faint as they approached, and then see them, no more than dark silhouettes under a flickering street lamp: clusters of people strolling arm-in-arm, returning home from some birthday party no doubt, and singing. In deeply beautiful minor-key melodies, whose harmonies merged and then parted in melancholy yet uplifting threads, Ukrainians kept on singing—sadly, resiliently, and with a depth of heart I longed to understand and share.

Chapter One

Mr. John and the Day of Knowledge

I can imagine how a high diver must feel standing at the tip of the board, poised on the balls of his feet. His toes hanging over the edge, he is finally in place, pausing to take one last breath before leaving solid certainty to twist off into the sky and fall, tumbling downward with as much grace and style as he can muster. That's how it feels: the first day of school. Even as a student, but more so as a teacher, at the beginning of a school year I have always been obsessed with the sensation that I'm about to fall and everyone is watching.

I had arrived, just two days before, in the central Ukrainian city of Zhitomir, following only a quick get-organized visit a month earlier and with little preparation for the first week of teaching. It would be my first morning at School 23 with the students whom I would spend the next two years teaching English. I tried to squelch my quiet but nagging fear of failure.

Outside the front doors at least a hundred children milled around, waiting. The boys wore uniforms—brown or navy suits, some with a patch on the arm, all looking faded and worn. Many of them had outgrown the trousers of their school uniforms since the year before; spindly legs poked out beneath their cuffs to reveal white socks. The girls wore brown skirts, brown long-sleeve blouses, and lacy pinafores, some with bows or puffs of lace atop their heads. The youngest looked like Shirley Temple dolls, but teenagers in the same garb looked like hotel maids in movies. In clumps these young women huddled, chattered, and welcomed each other after a summer apart. Playful younger boys ran screaming through the crowd, chasing each other and bumping into other children, who screamed back.

Everywhere moved the blur of rustling flowers. Most children, who customarily brought teachers great bunches of bouquets to show their gratitude for being taught, held droopy yellow daffodils or stiff pink carnations. A few gripped white tulips or a trio of red roses in a cloud of baby's breath and fern, while others held heavy lavender camellias or the occasional dahlia. The solemn drabness of the children's uniforms was hidden in the splash of bright flower colors.

A teacher, visible only as a head and shoulders floating in a mass of children, herded the mob to the schoolyard out back. I slipped into the stream, hoping to see someone I knew. Many of them had heard about me, it seemed—little girls pointed and giggled, covering their smiles with their hands. I heard one boy whisper "*Amerikanets!*" before scurrying into the crowd.

Then a mop-headed boy of maybe eight, bolder than the rest, stopped in front of me and planted his feet apart like a cowboy ready to draw. He held up his hand, waved it wildly, and shouted, "Khhhello!"

I smiled back and said, "Hello."

The children around him squealed with laughter, their eyes as wide as if a man from Mars had spoken. Frozen with panic, the boy stared me in the face a second—then hooted loon-like and dashed off.

September First, the Day of Knowledge, was a national holiday in the former Soviet Union. Now, beginning the second school year since Ukraine's declaration of independence, Soviet rituals had changed little. They had, however, taken on a new tint: the blue-and-yellow bars of the Ukrainian flag waved from the building of this highly-regarded downtown school, which for decades had trained the province's communist officials and later their children.

The principal, a small, stern woman named Nina Volodimirivna, whose whole top row of teeth was pure gold, approached the podium. The mike whistled. In a bold, very loud voice, Nina Volodimirivna proudly welcomed parents, teachers, and children in sentences mostly incomprehensible to me, with my ten weeks of rudimentary language training. I did recognize the Ukrainian words for "glory," "studious," and the "Great Nation of Ukraine."

At the end of the speech the crowd applauded. "Kolya! Annya!" the principal ordered. "Come here." It was time for the annual ritual Ringing of the First Bell, and from the crowd emerged a senior boy holding the hand of a first-grader, a tiny girl of six. After a few more ceremonial words, Nina Volodimirivna handed the girl a large handbell. The young man lifted her onto his shoulder and began to parade around in a space the crowd had made for them. From the loudspeaker above blared a Slavic-sounding march. Held atop the boy's shoulder, the girl used both hands to ring her heavy bell while the crowd cheered.

I looked around for Svetlana Adamovna, my counterpart teacher. According to the official Peace Corps plan, we were to assess the school's development needs together and come up with strategies for improving English education at School 23. On the first day of school, Svetlana Adamovna had told me, I would simply watch.

In the crowd I spotted her tall white beehive of a hairdo. She carried a bundle of flowers bigger than most and was busy welcoming the parents and children. The children congratulated her by shouting *"Z Prazdnikom"*—"greetings on the holiday"—before handing over more big bundles of flowers and dashing off. I greeted her likewise, and her clear blue eyes widened happily when she saw me. "I wish you Happy First Bell," she pronounced in her high, birdlike voice. She was dressed neatly, the pleats in her long skirt carefully pressed, her tanned cheeks streaked with bright rouge. I was glad I had worn a suit and tie.

The ceremony was breaking up, and the children, a few still carrying flowers, pushed and shoved roughly, charging to their first class. When we got inside and out of the crush of small bodies, Svetlana Adamovna invited me to join her for The First Lesson.

The First Lesson had become something of a headache for teachers at this school, she explained. In the past, she said, the lesson covered a few school procedures, but focused mainly on the life of Vladimir Ilyich Ulyanov—Comrade Lenin, or "Grandpa Lenin," as people now joked. The "Lenin lesson," as Svetlana Adamovna called it, began the school year on a patriotic note: it gave students pride in their motherland. I didn't interrupt, although I wondered which motherland she meant—the USSR or Ukraine. I got the impression she felt somewhat lost without the traditional lesson she had taught on this day for more than twenty years. The way Svetlana Adamovna spoke of the Lenin lesson as promoting love of country, a sense of duty, and a commitment to work reminded me of the U.S. Pledge of Allegiance. She still had phonograph records dramatizing legendary episodes in the youth of Lenin, who like George Washington chopping down the cherry tree, could not tell a lie. Now, Lenin would no longer do: in Moscow, St. Petersburg, and Kiev, his statues had been toppled (although his grim statue still stood tall in Zhitomir's central square).

For Ukrainian teachers, not only Lenin but many other Russian images, symbols, and patriotic ideas were now off-limits. The state law that mandated a political First Lesson had not been discarded with Ukrainian independence; only the object of idolatry had changed. Teachers were instructed to glorify the blue-and-yellow flag, the "Tryzub" or trident, and the "Greatness of the Ukrainian People"—nationalist symbols and ideas that, ironically, might have earned jailtime ten years earlier. In a revolution from below, such a moment might have been glorious, as the old power got what it deserved and new leaders were installed on the throne. But not many Zhitomirans had agitated for independence, which had brought them economic disaster.

Svetlana Adamovna, at least, said as much. With a scowl of disgust she winced in scorn at the blue-and-yellow flag. "What greatness of the Ukrainian people?" she snorted. "I don't see this anywhere around me." She found it unbelievably strange and sad that the October Revolution of 1917, Red Square in Moscow, and Cosmonaut Yuri Gagarin (the first man in space) now belonged to the history of a foreign country. So much she had been proud of was Russian. I asked her naively what she planned to teach for The First Lesson instead.

"Oh, I'll teach what I must," she sighed. "What else can I do? I'll play a record."

I followed her to a room on the first floor, where her students were already in their seats. As we entered, they abruptly stood up at their desks. There must have been at least forty, all between the ages of eight and ten. I took an empty seat at the back, hoping to observe quietly, but the children's eyes were on me.

When Svetlana Adamovna said, "Good morning!" in precise Queen's English, the children turned in their desks to face her. In the collective bark of a long-drilled army platoon, they answered loud and clear: "Good morning, Dear Teacher!" If she meant to startle me, it worked.

Svetlana Adamovna welcomed her class of fourth graders to the new school year. She already knew every one, having taught them English the previous two years. In a sunny, energetic voice, she began asking questions about Ukraine, quizzing the children to see what facts they knew. Our capital is Kiev, they told her. The Dnieper River "washes its banks," someone added. The sarcophagus of Yaroslav the Wise is in St. Sophia's cathedral, a boy volunteered. "Raise your hand," Svetlana Adamovna reminded. The children sat up very straight, with arms crossed on their desks; when one wanted to speak, his or her right arm popped up perpendicular like a semaphore's, trembling in eagerness to answer. Our country has 52 million people, a girl noted. The area of Ukraine is larger than France, said another. A boy said: Zhitomir is eleven hundred years old.

Svetlana Adamovna was an excellent teacher. On the first day of school, she subtly shepherded her class back to habits they had lost over the summer, giving reminders of how the game of school is played. Without any notes whatsoever, she let the children supply the material, then combined the knowledge in a few heads to add up to a lesson's worth for all. Without any explicitly scripted lecture—disdaining the subject even!—she directed discussion, generated questions, and conveyed information. I vowed to remember her method.

I also noted how obedient the children were. Maybe it was first-day excitement, I thought, hoping I was wrong. If they were used to that level of discipline, my life would be much easier.

When Svetlana Adamovna put on an old and well-used phonograph record, another Ukrainian march pranced happily along. It occurred to me that this music must have been officially approved in Soviet times (and therefore sanitized of real nationalism) or a teacher like Svetlana Adamovna would never have possessed it. The children listened with some interest at first, but their attention began to wander, and they started whispering, then talking, pointing toward me. Svetlana Adamovna noted the lapse and stopped the record. The period was only half over.

"Now, children," she said in Ukrainian, "you have the special chance to practice your English. You are going to meet and talk to a real American." Then she waved at me to come to the front of the room, switching to English to say, "This is our new teacher of English, Mr. John."

Mr. John was to be my formal title. In Ukraine (and Russia) teachers must be addressed by first name and the patronymic form based on one's father's name: Svetlana Adamovna, Galina Vasilievna, Nina Volodimirivna. As elders and figures of authority, teachers were to be respected; both names had to be used at all times. When I told the staff that my patronymic would be "Davidovich," there were howls of laughter. Too odd-sounding (or too Jewish-sounding?), the name would seem funny to the children, they said. "John" would be too informal, and "Mr. Deever" was difficult for them to say. Thus we settled on "Mr. John." At first my new name sounded silly to me, especially when ninth graders said it, but later even my Ukrainian friends (who normally called me John) addressed me formally in front of my students by saying, "Mr. John, may I speak to you?" "Mr. John" lost its connotations of daycare and became a title I held with pride. It conveyed some of my specialness there, and I liked that. Eventually I caught myself using it in class to refer to myself in the third person: "Mr. John doesn't like when you talk while he's talking." "Mr. John likes to hear *all* of you sing," or "Mr. John has a headache today."

On that first day of school, the pupils were thrilled to try out their English, never mind what my name was. Svetlana Adamovna encouraged them to ask me questions, reminding me to answer slowly and clearly. The first brave boy stood up by his desk and said, "What is your father?"

I momentarily thought this was a philosophical riddle before recognizing it as a question about professions. "A professor of mathematics at the university," I answered. He squinted in confusion, nodded, and sat down. Svetlana Adamovna translated, and then he smiled. "What is your mother?" another asked. "A teacher," I said. They all understood that.

A girl raised her hand and said, "What are you?" I told her I was a teacher, too, and it seemed such a playful question that I asked her back: "And what are you?"

She had already sat down. When she realized my question was directed to her, she stood back up and went pale with fright. She looked to Svetlana Adamovna in helpless panic.

"Irichka, you know this!" her teacher chided. "What . . . are . . . you? I am a . . ."

"Pupil!" shouted a triumphant boy in the back. "Pupil,"

Svetlana Adamovna repeated. Irichka stood back up and said, "I am a pupil."

Many others raised their hands frantically; I called on another boy. He stood up and said loudly, "I am a pupil!" One after another, children stood up and pronounced this phrase, continually repeating that statement of identity for what seemed like ten minutes. I kept pointing to outstretched, waving hands until Svetlana Adamovna cut off one last child who'd been waiting to say, "I am a pupil." She urged the children to ask Mr. John *questions.*

Another boy, whose face had been squinched in concentration all this time, stood up. He said, "Do . . . you . . . have . . . car?"

"*A* car," Svetlana Adamovna reprimanded. "Do you have *a* car." (She pronounced it "caahh" with no audible *r*.) The boy nodded and looked to me eagerly.

"I *did* have a car. I sold it before I came here." Everyone (including Svetlana Adamovna) looked puzzled. I realized that, after my few weeks of language training, I knew enough words to form that sentence into Ukrainian. I repeated "I sold my car," in Ukrainian. At the sound of my flat, American accent—but speaking their language—the children's eyes grew even wider.

A boy in the back shouted out in Ukrainian, "What kind of car?"

I told him a pickup truck, forgetting to make him speak English. The room bubbled with excitement now. I understood a little of their language. What they really wanted was to ask me genuine questions in Ukrainian. But Svetlana Adamovna scolded them and reminded me as well that we were to speak only English.

A child asked, "Do you have a mother?" I smiled and said yes. Perhaps they'd forgotten our discussion of professions already. I called on a pale girl who'd been silent until then, who asked, "Do you have a father?" Yes, I said again, a little impatiently. Thanks to the car question, the class had remembered a new sentence structure: "Do you have a sister?"

"Do you have a grandmother?" "Do you have a cat?" "Do you have a dog?" I smiled like a candidate for mayor and answered each question as sweetly as I could. Until the boy who had asked about my car said, "Do . . . you . . . have . . . girl?" Mischievously I formulated an untactful answer in my head. If I speak quickly, I thought, not a soul in the room will catch what I'm saying.

Fortunately, Svetlana Adamovna interrupted and changed the theme, suggesting they try "Do you like. . . ?" Hands went up everywhere again, and I called on each in turn, giving everyone a chance to speak. The children, as if practicing a substitution drill, asked about every animal, food, and place they could think of. When I answered yes to "Do you like borshch?" they cackled with laughter. Irichka then asked, "Do you like Zhitomir?"

Yes, I answered, yes. I did like Zhitomir.

They hardly cared what I said, so long as Mr. John looked them in the eye and responded. They liked to be called on and to speak English words, and hearing me answer yes or no was enough. The act of speaking to and understanding a foreigner in a foreign language was a magical experience. By the time the bell rang (a whole twenty minutes later), I was exhausted but happy.

For that group of children that year, the First Lesson was not about Lenin, and not even much about Ukraine. Instead, they saw what independence had brought to their school: a person from America who could talk with them. A person who had come to stay for a while.

At least, my plan was to stay. The next day when I met my own students, I wondered if I could even survive the rest of the week.

The first group I would teach was to be 9G. Based on their abilities, students were assigned to groups, or "classes," following the Cyrillic alphabet in descending order, and "G" was the lowest level in ninth grade. I felt comfortable, though, because the school was a Specialized School for the Study of English—something like a foreign language magnet school—and children began learning English from the first grade. Another factor in my favor was small class size. For geography, mathematics, biology, and other subjects, all forty students in the 9G class met together for one lesson. For foreign language lessons, fortunately, each class was broken into three groups, which meant I would only have twelve students at a time. With such a small group, I could give each student more individual attention. Group work and pair work would be easier to monitor, and getting to know each student well would be simple and enjoyable. After a few months of steady work, perhaps the class would be able to engage in discussions about their culture and mine, to write insightful essays and journal entries, and to correspond with penpals in the United States.

The first week I planned diagnostic exercises—ice-breakers and get-to-know-you games designed to show me each student's speaking, listening, writing, and reading skills. My other goals included learning names, setting rules and standards, and determining what levels of material I would teach.

When I arrived at school the next morning, my students were already standing in the hallway on the third floor shuffling their feet, mumbling, and waiting for me to unlock the classroom door. We went in together. The room's desks—long laboratory-style tables—were bolted to the floor beside each other in the shape of a U, facing the front of the room. The desk at the front of the room behind which I was to stand was bolted down too; it sloped up slightly like a podium, separating me from the students. When my students sat in their chairs, looking up at me, they resembled a committee or school board. Nervously, I organized my papers and materials while they whispered among themselves. Finally, like the cue to leap from the high dive, the bell rang.

I introduced myself in English and explained that I wanted to get to know something about them before we discussed the school year. To each student I handed out index cards I had brought from the United States. I instructed them to write "My name is" and four sentences beginning with "I like to . . ." Since these students had studied English for eight consecutive years at School 23, I assumed this would be a modest task. I spoke English as slowly as I could, but sensed their discomfort as they glanced sidelong at each other, whispered again, and looked confused.

"Maybe my accent is hard for you to catch," I said. They had studied British English, and perhaps my vowels differed greatly from what they had learned. They looked absolutely puzzled. "Accent?" I repeated.

At that word, one girl nodded vigorously. I decided to ask in Ukrainian if they had understood me. That time, at least, the whole class shook their heads "no." One young man, large for a ninth grader, sat hunched in a chair too small for him. He fingered the index card with fascination, turning it over again and again, rubbing the paper as if admiring its quality. Then he waved the card and in a deep voice grunted some expression of amazement that I couldn't understand. The boy next to him was playing with the card too but not listening, so the big boy punched him hard in the shoulder to get his attention. The second boy punched him back harder and answered gruffly.

I moved away from the podium and over to the big boy to take the card from his hand. "What is your name?" I asked him in Ukrainian, trying to sound as stern as possible. He had a dark wispy streak over his lip, the soft fuzz of an attempted mustache.

"Serhiy," he said, stressing the second syllable: *SairHEE*. It occurred to me that if Serhiy stood up he would be a head taller than I and fifty pounds heavier. He looked up at me meekly like a scolded puppy.

"OK, Serhiy," I said nicely. In Ukrainian I explained again. "You write your name on this card, then write four things you like to do."

"In English?" he said.

"Of course in English!" said a girl three seats away, laughing mockingly. He snapped something at her I didn't understand and the class burst out laughing. The girls covered their mouths in embarrassment, then whispered to each other, probably noting that I hadn't understood whatever slang or profanity he had used.

I was losing control fifteen minutes into my very first lesson. I decided to ignore this and push on.

"So you understand now?" I asked, turning to the other students. "You all understand?" The girl who had laughed reassured me: "We understand."

They began to write.

All except Serhiy, that is, who sat silently for a few minutes staring at his card. I finally asked him if there was a problem. "I don't know what to write," he told me. I tried not to feel too exasperated, already wondering how I would spend eight hours a week with this boy. But I wanted to give him positive reinforcement, so I gently answered that, for starters at least, he could write, "My name is Serhiy."

"Please," he asked. "Write it on the board?"

It's the first day, I reminded myself. He hasn't used English all summer. After eight years in English class, certainly he managed to learn "My name is" at some point. He couldn't remember it just then, I told myself. "Never mind!" he burst out gleefully in Ukrainian. "I can do it!" When I looked back, he was copying from Ruslan, a small blond boy with crooked teeth who sat on the other side of him. It took him a minute or two to copy each letter. Then he raised his hand politely.

"Would you please show me how to write 'Serhiy'?"

My diagnostic test was proceeding well: I had learned that at least one of my students in 9G knew no English whatsoever.

Other students continued to scribble away slowly, so I didn't give up hope. We spent the whole lesson writing on the index cards, never getting to the other five speaking activities I had planned. Now I knew where to begin: at the beginning. Challenging, perhaps. Beyond me? No way. I would alter my plans for the group and then teach them as best I could. Serhiy I could work with—he was low-skilled but not ornery or vicious. I only had to try harder, with slightly lower expectations.

The bell rang again. I collected the index cards and looked over their writing. "Not slightly lower," I thought. "Way lower."

Before I finished reading the cards, a mob of eight-year-olds stampeded breathlessly into my room. My youngest group of children, the boys and girls of 3D, slammed stacks of books down on the desks and shouted questions in Ukrainian: "Are you our new teacher?" "Are you really from America?" "Where do you live?" "Will you always be our teacher from now on?" Some of them sat down, but others ran up to my desk for a closer look at me. A boy with black hair asked, "Is it true what they say? That you will take us to America this year?"

I couldn't formulate answers fast enough in Ukrainian, so I answered only, "In a minute! In a minute we'll begin!"

When the bell rang, I went through my first-day introduction, and then led the students through some of the same oral drills Svetlana Adamovna had done with her children. After a class with ninth graders, these children looked like little munchkins bursting with energy. I started learning their names. Sasha was the bright-eyed, black-haired boy. Natasha, the blond, smart-looking girl. Vova, the littlest boy with the loudest mouth. Their uncontrollable energy was hard to rein in; it took forever to get them started on simple first-day tasks. But once I did I was surprised at how well they knew English. They had only studied it for two years, but spoke with fearless authority. And when I asked them to read out loud, they pronounced even unfamiliar words carefully, accurately, marvelously.

From her book Natasha read, "Jonathan Bean. Likes ice cream." They translated for me what they read, and I noted which children knew more words, and which words the whole class knew. There weren't very many. The words they did know, however—words like cat, red, apple, family—they knew with total certainty.

As planned, I conducted drills to practice the "th" and "w" sounds, difficult for Slavic-language speakers. I asked them to repeat after me: "Mother, Father, Sister, Brother." They chanted, "Muzzer, Fazzer, Sister, Bruzzer." "No, no!" I said, laughing in the contagion of their spunkiness. "Show me your tongues! *Thh,*

thh, thh. It should tickle!" They stuck out their tongues at me and giggled. Vova exaggerated his grimace, as if he'd eaten something nasty. But they all buzzed, grinning while their tongues vibrated: *"thh, thh, thh.* Mother. Father. Sister. Brother."

After that lesson came the fourth grade class, my last. I felt a little less awkward already, and the lesson proceeded well until at one point I said in Ukrainian, "All students will write three sentences." Everyone giggled. Perhaps I had botched subject-verb agreement or goofed up a case ending. I stopped to ask what was so funny.

A boy named Seryozha stood up. "We're not students," he said politely. *"Studenti*—that's for the older ones." I had been using the word *studenti*—an easy cognate to remember—but that word was restricted to college students. No wonder it sounded silly to nine-year-olds.

Another boy, Andrei, raised his chin proudly and said, *"I'm a student."* He preened and strutted, and the children laughed.

"You're no student," a boy named Nikolai said loudly. "You're a fool." The kids laughed harder.

"You yourself are a fool," Andrei retorted.

"Okay, okay!" I interrupted. "Enough!"

"Okay! Okay!" echoed the class. They waved thumbs-up signs to each other and repeated the word over and over. To them, "okay" was a word from TV, a word that sounded very American and very cool. Their other teachers never said "okay."

"Enough!" I said in Ukrainian. "You're not students. How do I call you?"

"Uchniki," said one. Pupil. I now understood why Ukrainian teachers always said "pupil," and I vowed to learn this word well.

A girl in the corner raised her hand and asked me a long question. Although I listened very carefully, I didn't catch a single word she said. I muttered, "Ummm, I don't know," and sort of shrugged. The class stared back in equal confusion. "Now," I went on. "Three sentences."

I realized I was going to have to learn a lot of Ukrainian, and learn it quickly.

The first week of teaching such young children was a struggle, but on Friday we somehow finished everything I had planned for that day, and several minutes remained before the end of the class. The children had already shown me they liked to sing, and so, improvising as best I could, I decided to teach them a song, right there on the spot. It had to be something simple, catchy, and easily teachable. For some reason, the first song that popped into my head was "Bingo." In a flash I mentally went over the words, happy to find "farmer," "dog," and "name," words the children already knew. I could invent some explanation for "name-O."

"All right, children," I said. "Today we will learn a new song." Several of them shouted out with pleasure. They eagerly read aloud as I wrote the first line on the board. I asked them to repeat it, and, after several successful responses, I wrote the second line, which they also repeated. Straining my voice to stay on key, I began to sing. "There was a farmer had a dog. And Bingo was his name-O." Carefully I wrapped my lips around each word to enunciate as clearly as possible. When I didn't, their responses were nothing but muffled, incoherent mush. My solo voice echoing around the room sounded weird and distant—lonely. The pupils of 3D marveled in delight to hear a goofy American man stand in front of them and sing such a jolly melody. " . . . B-I-NGO, and Bingo was his name-O." When I stopped, they applauded. Together we sang the first verse all the way through. They got it exactly right.

Rushing ahead, I explained (in stilted Ukrainian) that after each verse one letter transforms to a clap. Since I didn't know the verb for "to clap," I clapped once to demonstrate. They all began to clap at once. The period was almost over, and I was afraid that if time ran out they would not sing the song all the way through and we would have to start from scratch the next day.

Hurriedly, I explained again as best I could: "Listen, please! First time: no (clap). Second time: (clap)—I—NGO. Third time: (clap, clap)—NGO."

The brightest girl, Natasha, jumped out of her seat. "I get it! I understand!" she yelled, and breathlessly proceeded to explain (her Ukrainian perfect, of course) how the song should be sung. I listened hard to her explanation, trying to memorize the phrases she used. Natasha unknowingly served as my teaching assistant. If I could only communicate with her, I thought, she would joyfully clarify my instructions to the other pupils.

We sang Bingo all the way to the end. On the last verse, they understood the fun of the song—you don't sing letters at all, you only clap—and I caught a few smiles of recognition. I smiled broadly too, because they had understood and because they liked it. The bell rang, signaling the start of the mad in-between-class rush. My pupils shuffled their books and papers together and stuffed them in their knapsacks, hurrying to be first out the door. As they ran off down the hall, I heard them singing, still chanting "B-I-NGO." I had taught my third-grade pupils something.

The wispy smog that separated us—age, language, the roles of teacher and student—had momentarily parted. Natasha said, "I get it!" and a painfully wide gap was bridged, if only for a second. I kept that small moment tucked in my pocket for a long time—that, and the few others like it that occurred over the next few weeks. I had done little more than teach ten eight-year-olds a simple song, and yet I felt as if I had successfully crossed a desert.

The hardest part of life in Peace Corps for me—then and for two whole years—was the rarity of that kind of communication. I had always taken for granted the ease with which people connected their minds through words, but now no one understood anything I tried to say—either in English or broken Ukrainian. The moment those kids sang "Bingo" was a rare reward, and I walked around humming the song for days.

Chapter Two

"To You!"

When the Peace Corps accepted me and assigned me to newly independent Ukraine, I was thrilled at the opportunity. I had finished a master's degree in English at the Ohio State University in Columbus, where I grew up, and I craved both useful work and international travel. Everything about Peace Corps felt fresh and exciting: as a volunteer teacher, I would be escaping my materialistic culture by teaching English and living in the land of our former enemy! I would live amidst change in a newly opened democracy! Within a few days of arriving at our training site in Kiev, however, I wondered how long my idealism would sustain me.

So much of the former Soviet Union looked and felt like an industrial-strength nightmare: the uniformity of factories, schools, apartment buildings, all of it gray and veiled in bluish haze. Along with the rich, lead-heavy smell of vehicle exhaust, a sour scent of cheap tobacco hung in the air, as well as something like body odor, only more vinegary. The signs along the roads and on stores, written in an alphabet whose letters resembled spiny insects, bewildered me; newer, gaudily-colored signs in English advertised casinos or "investment import-export banks." On my very first day in Kiev, I had seen a drunken man lying on a sidewalk, bleeding. Ukraine's capital, upon first sight a least, had plenty of the tattered grimness of a Prague or Budapest but little of the charm that was supposed to go with it.

Riding the subway underneath the dim and paint-chipped city, I almost expected to find anvils, steam, and the reddish glow of a smelter diabolically churning out endless copies of that one Lada automobile everyone drove. The subway's superfast escalator churned deep down into the earth, like a fast track into hell. Steep and long, it descended into the dark tunnel with no bottom in view—there were hundreds of steps and the ride seemed endless. From the other direction, people rose from the deep hole, their faces nightmarish: squashed noses, dark sunken eyes, hair dyed orangish-auburn but with dark roots and white scalp peeking through. Wrinkled babushkas looked like witches just off the train from fairyland. Stooped and bent like gnomes, their crooked noses peeped from shawls or scarves wrapped over their heads. Even smiling or laughing was eerie down there in the dark.

On the subway platform at the bottom trains zoomed up with a whine before screeching to a stop. Crowds crushed on board and stood nose-to-nose, since the seats were all occupied. I jumped in before the doors slammed shut and the train lurched off. A taped voice over the speaker announced the next stop, but it ran too fast, squealing like a manic chipmunk. The stuffy car stunk of armpit, cabbage, and noon vodka gone stale on the breath. Everyone clutched a plastic bag or sack of some sort; someone, it seemed, was carrying ripe, fresh meat. Young soldiers stood around in olive-drab uniforms and ominous black-billed round hats, looking like dangerous punks. Their slushy-sounding thick-tongued speech came blurting from mouths full of silver-capped teeth, and they laughed menacingly—at me. I always thought.

After a week or two, though, I began to acclimate a little and to understand why Ukrainians were so proud of Kiev's "Metro." In a country where people could depend on nothing—from buses to ballpoint pens—to work right, Kiev's subway was the glistening exception. Punctual and clean, it quickly connected the distant regions of sprawling Kiev to another; without it, most Kievites could not get to work or do their shopping, which took several hours out of every day. The subway reminded me, too, of the recent Cold War past because Soviet subways were built incredibly deep into the ground and designed to double as bomb shelters. Had Americans dropped nuclear weapons on Kiev, its people would have hidden in those subterranean depths.

With some of the other twenty-two Peace Corps trainees, I explored the city throughout the summer, marveling both at Kiev's splendor and grime and talking about the odd triumph of getting to live there. One young woman from California named Liza, who already spoke Russian, showed me around Bessarabsky market in the center of Kiev. She studied the piles of cucumbers and tomatoes and remarked, "There's a lot more to eat here than there was in St. Petersburg." A Russian Studies major, she had spent four late winter months in what was then Leningrad on a semester abroad; she wondered aloud if conditions had really improved or if the abundance of vegetables were typical of summer. She went over to examine flowers and asked the scarfed babushka behind the counter how much one bundle of bright red carnations cost. I admired Liza's ability to communicate; I could only watch the woman's hand gestures as she stroked the flowers and cooed lovingly. I gathered that she was describing how beautiful the flowers were—stalling a bit before giving a price. Liza repeated the question, and to my delight, I understood the answer: six thousand. Liza had been curious, mostly, and didn't want to spend that much (about two dollars). As we walked away, the woman called after us, "Girl! All right! Four thousand!" Over her shoulder Liza smiled back politely, and we left. If only I could learn to talk so well, I thought. Language proficiency was my biggest worry. Here was someone who had that battle won on the first day.

Before long I wondered how I had noticed only the ugly remnants of Soviet rule. Despite its tarnish, golden Kiev was exotically beautiful. A scent of ancient grandeur hung in the air like the incense that wafted up into the gold-domed cupolas of the thousand-year-old St. Sophia's. Kiev's main street, Kreschatik, lined with chestnut trees and towering stone buildings, ran west to the cliffs above the Dnieper River, where a scenic overlook showed the flat expanse of the left bank and its forest of high-rise apartments. In the thirteenth century, from that same vantage point the citizens of Kiev had watched the Golden Horde of Batu Khan (grandson of Genghis) storm its gates not in the expected seven months, but in a single day. The long vista to the east symbolizes that crossroads in time and space—indeed, "Kreschatik" means both crossroads and christening—between the land masses, cultures, and entwined histories of Asia and Europe. Seeing beyond the Soviet in this way depended on having the right eyes, listening carefully, and not letting preconceived expectations get in the way.

However, daily life in Ukraine was obviously going to require more than just having the right eyes. The radio in my room, for example, received only the main state radio station—not because it was broken but because it was built without a tuning knob. A small white box with only a crackly speaker and a volume control, it had no way to be switched off. I turned down the volume until the sound was imperceptible and then later unplugged it, but couldn't get over the feeling that someone might be listening to me through it.

My Peace Corps assignment, as I understood it, would be teaching either college-level courses to English-teachers-in-training or English as a Foreign Language courses to upper-level high school students. In July, a month after my arrival in Kiev and a month before school would begin, I learned that a site had been chosen for me. I was going to live and teach in the city of Zhitomir, the first large provincial town west of Kiev. I was relieved not to have to work in the polluted steel belt of the Donbass in eastern Ukraine—until I checked the map again and saw a Ukrainian word I recognized easily: Chornobyl.

"Don't worry," Peace Corps staffers assured me. "The

quarantined radiation zone is over one hundred miles away from Zhitomir. Every placement has been checked out, and your living situation will be entirely safe. Just remember: a high level of radiation remains in wild mushrooms. Ukrainians love wild mushrooms, but don't you eat any." The simple advice was not altogether reassuring, but I hoped that two years there would not expose me to enough radiation to cause any harm.

On my first site visit to Zhitomir, I had taken the bus west of Kiev, nervously watching the countryside and hoping someone would be there to meet me. T-shaped telephone poles ran in a row alongside the road. Now and then I noticed large clumps of sticks atop some of them. When I saw a huge white stork perched and preening on one, I realized the sticks were nests. Storks were considered a lucky omen, I remembered happily. Superstition or no, I was going to need some luck: the prospect of teaching again both excited and scared me. Teaching American college students Freshman Composition counted as experience—I knew how to behave at the front of a classroom—but working with high-school-aged kids would be challenging and new.

The moment the bus stopped, I knew whom to greet. A heavy-set, very proper-looking woman wearing a neatly pressed blouse and skirt scanned every face on the bus, searching for me.

"You must be John!" she beamed, and the warm greeting made me like her instantly. We shook hands and I dragged my bag from the cargo bay underneath the bus. "You're so young!" she smiled again. I agreed sheepishly, not knowing how to respond. Her snow-white hair was recently styled and whipped up into a cotton-candyish beehive high on her head. Her eyes were bright and wide, a clear blue like melting ice. Maybe it was the combination of her elegant, stern posture and her open, kind face that clinched it. She carried herself like a Teacher with a capital T.

"Galina Vasilievna asked me to meet you here." She enunciated carefully in a very British accent, saying, "aahsked me to meet you heeah." I could tell she had taught English pronunciation for a long time: her absolutely precise phonetics could have put Queen Elizabeth to shame. She told me her name was Svetlana Adamovna.

We boarded a crowded trolleybus, laughing together at my struggle to squeeze my bag through the mass of passengers. She seemed happy and pleasant, if slightly nervous, and promised we would ride only a few stops. Near the center of the city we stepped out. The weather was gorgeous—no clouds, not too hot. People quietly strolled around, enjoying a beautiful Friday in July. Svetlana Adamovna pointed out the central department store at the corner of Kievska and Moskovska streets. "Earlier it was Lenin Street," she said, pointing to Kievska with what sounded like a note of pride. "The more things change, the more they stay the same." We laughed together at the familiar proverb, though I wasn't clear what her point was.

We walked along a tree-lined street to Secondary School Number 23, a block away from the center of Zhitomir. It was really two schools: an older two-story building built just after the war, and a newer more modern-looking building, four stories of concrete and glass. They were connected by a walkway on the second floor, and behind the school was an asphalt playground.

Svetlana Adamovna and I entered the new section and were met in the lobby by a shorter, dark-haired woman who spoke very rapidly in Russian. In this woman's manner I recognized her at once as the principal: unflinchingly strict and skilled at hiding her deep kind-heartedness. Svetlana Adamovna introduced her as Nina Volodimirivna Kupriychuk, and I shook her hand, saying *"Doozhe priemno"*—pleased to meet you.

Her eyes widened and she smiled a terrifying mouthful of gold teeth, not a single white one visible in the whole top row.

In Ukrainian, she answered, "You speak Ukrainian?" She spoke no English.

"A little," I responded.

"Good," she said, turning to Svetlana Adamovna and remarking in Russian, *"He's so young!"* I knew almost no

Russian, but the word for "young" was similar enough to Ukrainian that I understood her.

Translating Nina Volodimirivna's incredibly fast commands, Svetlana Adamovna told me we'd see the school and then meet for a small reception in the teacher's room. Upstairs, when I saw young people scrubbing floors and moving chairs, I thought the school was undergoing some repairs; actually it was getting its yearly cleanup. Then we went up to the third floor of the newer wing (or "the new school" as it was called), where, Svetlana Adamovna explained, all the school's English classes were held. This floor was very neat, the wood floors recently repainted and still smelling fresh and new. On the wall, painted by a moderately talented student, I guessed, was a huge map of England, surrounded by the Tower of London, Nelson's Column on Trafalgar Square, and a Beefeater. Hanging from the ceiling was a sign reading "The Country—The Language We Study." I made a mental note of this Anglophilic focus, wondering what that meant about the school's attitude toward the United States. I decided I would have to wait and see.

We then toured "the old school," which housed the school library and elementary level classrooms. The younger grades remained in one room all day except for their English lesson, which they attended in the new school. From fifth grade on, students changed every period as in our junior high schools. When the tour was complete, Svetlana Adamovna said "Let's see if everything is ready in the Methodology Room."

We returned to the hall of English classes and entered a room whose walls were covered from ceiling to floor with elaborately painted plywood signs. In tiny black letters and diagrams, flowcharts described in very technical Ukrainian the correct structure of a lesson, the correct principles on which to base language learning, and the correct behavior of teachers in the classroom. The displays looked like handouts from the most tedious Theory of Education class in existence, blown up into ten-foot-high permanently affixed murals. In my two years there,

I never saw a single soul pay more attention to them than you would to wallpaper. Though ominous and severe, the effect of these walls was counteracted by the ferns and other plants in wicker baskets all over the room and by the light flooding in through large windows on the south wall.

Against one wall stood a twelve-foot-wide bookcase full of brand-new English workbooks and textbooks. Clearly printed in the West, the shiny covers of the bright blue, yellow, and red books boasted names like "Patterns," "Horizons," and "Discovery." They gleamed beautifully in the sunlight from behind locked glass doors. At a glance it was obvious they had never been used.

In the hubbub around me, I realized we were sitting down to a small reception. The teachers had laid the table with home-prepared food: small meringue pastries, homemade jam, little open-faced sandwiches. Because it was summer we had cucumbers and juicy plums fresh from someone's garden. I realized it was after two and I hadn't eaten lunch yet.

A bottle of cognac and several shot glasses had been placed on the table as well. According to the customs of Ukrainian hospitality, drinking and speeches accompany any meeting with a new acquaintance. When the guest is an American for whom a display of generosity is wanted, alcohol tends to flow even more freely. I wondered about the propriety of drinking in the school building, but the principal was here, and after all it was the middle of summer.

At this point I hadn't yet experienced how Ukrainians sometimes judge a person's capacity for drink as one measure of his hardiness. If I had known how much this one meeting was to affect my two years there, I would have been more on my toes. I might have foreseen my future, or at least picked up hints, interpreted clues, or even simply listened for the underlying messages being transmitted beneath the surface of the conversation. At the time, though, I wanted most of all to get off on the right foot, to make a good impression, and to have my new colleagues like me.

As the food was spread out on desks, I watched Nina Volodimirivna. She had the breezy, regal air of someone long accustomed to authority, a sharp leader whom I guessed it would be unwise to cross. As she waltzed around giving orders, other teachers hustled to follow them, answering with impatient but not impudent replies. Clearly, this routine could happen without her, but everyone responded as if to a general whose commands are anticipated before they are given.

A large black-haired woman with pale skin approached me. She was introduced as the teacher of Russian language. She grabbed my arm and rattled away in a very high singsongy voice. Not understanding a word of Russian, I tried to nod politely. Her thick glasses and patronizing schoolmarmish manner got on my nerves quickly: as she talked to me, she stroked my shoulder with her chubby hand, sticking her face right up to mine.

Another English teacher, Larisa Mikhailivna, greeted me as well. Mousy and prim, her hair steely gray, she was less peppy, less cheerful, and less smiley than Svetlana Adamovna, though just as proper. Larisa Mikhailivna spoke less vivaciously, more thoughtfully: if Svetlana Adamovna was the naturally playful elementary school teacher, then Larisa Mikhailivna was the professor of literature. Her pronunciation too was so perfect I began to wonder if teachers here trained by listening to recordings of the Queen and imitating them for practice. But her eyes were kind and I felt I could trust her.

This made five of us: the principal, the Russian teacher, two English teachers, and myself. We sat down to eat and to discuss the school, my workload, and the details of what was expected from me. I had brought a notepad with a few of my own questions—more about the apartment they were to provide than about lessons. Svetlana Adamovna would translate for me while Nina Volodimirivna spoke.

Everyone insisted that before the meeting began, we would eat. I certainly didn't object. Before you eat, they said, you must have a toast.

Nina Volodimirivna poured each shot glass full of cognac. She made a kind, brief speech welcoming me to School Number 23. She hoped I would enjoy my time there, and she wished me success. In unison we raised our glasses, then drank them to the bottom. An inexpensive but tasty cognac from Odessa, it went down warm and easy. We began to eat.

The first questions were about my educational background, my hometown, and especially my family. "My mother and father are both teachers as well," I said. Glasses were refilled immediately, and we drank the next toast. "To your parents!" Svetlana Adamovna announced. According to tradition, the second toast follows soon after the first, and every toast must be knocked back in one gulp; anything less is a reproach to everyone at the table.

The reception seemed to become more lively, and the line of questioning shifted. The teacher of Russian wanted to know about teacher salaries in the United States. What does the average teacher make? Is it enough to live on? How many hours a week do they teach? I wanted to speak Ukrainian whenever possible and to speak directly to my principal without translation. So I told them that the average teacher makes somewhere around twenty-six thousand dollars.

"A month?" Larisa Mikhailivna cried.

"No, no—a year," I said. "We measure salary by the year."

Nina Volodimirivna calculated a split second, then said in Russian: "Two thousand."

"More!" someone shouted, and they burst into an argument.

I leaped to explain take-home versus net pay, retirement and taxes, the cost of living, and the salaries of other professionals like doctors and lawyers. But it was too late—they had gone off into their own conversation, full of tsk-tsks and knowing nods. Since glasnost and the flood of new information about the West, they were well aware of the gross disparities between East and West. Here, in person, I'd confirmed an ugly truth: their relative poverty.

After a moment, Larisa Mikhailivna summed up the discussion: "You see, our salary is thirty thousand *rubles*." While she went back to the argument, I wondered if I should read something into her calling Ukrainian currency "rubles," the Soviet (now Russian) currency. Was that out of habit or did it betray a dislike for independence? Most people called the money "kupons," the word printed on the bill; the temporary scrip was supposed to be replaced with Ukraine's real currency any day now. Thus distracted by her choice of words, I did my own math more slowly, realizing eventually that the amount she had told me was under ten dollars a month.

Ten dollars a month. All my explanations about relative earnings vanished. The week before I had bought a cheap, Soviet-made used clothes iron in Kiev for about that price. Ten dollars wasn't enough money—even here, where prices were so low—to buy a month's worth of food. Not even close: two pounds of meat would cost their entire month's wages. And here I was, happily drinking cognac, eating food they had probably grown in their gardens, and worrying about the apartment they were going to give me. I hoped they wouldn't ask about *my* salary, paid by the Peace Corps. It would come to fifteen times that.

Svetlana Adamovna interrupted the argument to scold the others in Russian: "Girls, enough. That's enough." In English she said to me diffidently, "You have your problems just the same. Let's drink."

We raised glasses again, this time "to friendship." Friendship between Ukraine and America, and between us. Relieved to defuse a potentially embarrassing issue, I joined in, repeating their toast in Ukrainian.

Returning our glasses to the table, Svetlana Adamovna announced, "It is necessary to remember: East or West, home is best." Even the Russian teacher, who spoke no English, laughed in agreement at this. Apparently everyone knew these proverbs, which popped out even when they didn't quite fit.

Nina Volodimirivna said not to worry, that if the school's salary wasn't enough for me, other teachers would help by giving me home-canned food, meat, and other products. She had assumed the school would be paying me.

"No, no!" I answered. "I can't!" I asked Svetlana Adamovna to explain that I couldn't accept a salary from the school, that it was against Peace Corps rules for me to be paid by the host organization.

"But you're already on the list!" she said. "You must take it." I said that if some bureaucratic appropriation had already been made, the money could go to another teacher or for some other use. After a little more arguing, Nina Volodimirivna agreed and waved that problem away. She wanted to talk about my workload. Svetlana Adamovna translated.

"Of course, sixteen lessons is very few," she said. Peace Corps required that I accept at least fifteen. "Most teachers have twenty-six. And the older pupils study English six to eight hours a week. With sixteen lessons you would have only two groups of students." I considered this for a moment. The more students I could work with, the better. And if other teachers worked that much for so little, I could hardly turn down my principal's request.

"We were thinking twenty, twenty-two lessons a week," she said.

Though it would be a challenge to do that much planning, preparation, and grading, I was determined to work hard and to sacrifice as much time as necessary for my school. I felt fueled by a sense of being useful and important. Or by three snootfuls of cognac. With a warm, soothing glow in my belly, I said yes.

Then Svetlana Adamovna halfway suggested that all the pupils would be very glad to see me. The younger ones especially.

"Actually, I kind of expected older students," I said. "Ninth, tenth, eleventh grade."

"You'll have some older pupils," Nina Volodimirivna reassured me after my response was translated. "Don't worry. Are you against taking on younger pupils?"

"No, no," I said, "It's just that I speak Ukrainian very badly."

"No you don't!" said Svetlana Adamovna, "You speak very well!" Everyone at the table nodded vigorous agreement. Then she promised to help me if I had any problems, adding, "You will have a good practice here."

I wondered what I was getting into. Twelve-year-olds? Ten-year-olds? First graders? I thought back to the daycare job I held during college, babysitting screaming kindergartners. My responsibility as a Peace Corps volunteer was to provide whatever technical assistance the school requested, within my means and abilities. But certainly *this* test of my abilities I wasn't prepared for. Still, my language skills praised and the getting acquainted moving along famously, I felt a surge of pride and confidence. Or maybe it was the cognac again.

"If it doesn't work out, can I switch groups after the first term?" I asked tentatively. Of course! of course! my new principal said. So I agreed to teach some classes of younger grades.

The food was gone, but she insisted on another drink to close the deal. All the faces looked a bit rosy, and my own cheeks felt hot. This time the principal stood up, glass in hand; we all stood up as well. Looking me in the eye, she said solemnly—the first time I was to hear her thickly accented English—"To you." The other teachers burst into hilarious laughter. Svetlana Adamovna quickly explained that the English staff customarily sang "Happy Birthday" on every teacher's birthday and that the only words Nina Volodimirivna could get right were the final ones: "To you." Giggling still, they assured me the toast to me was sincere. They were letting me in on their first inside joke, and they were genuinely happy to have me there. We tossed back one more shot of cognac and sat down.

Just then there was a sudden crash. I looked over to see the Russian teacher sitting on the floor amidst a pile of splinters. Her rickety chair had smashed underneath her as she sat down. In her high-pitched Brunhilda voice she was cackling with laughter, and the other teachers began to howl too. Our earlier tension now vanished, we couldn't help laughing at the sight of this rotund, stately woman on the floor in the wreckage of the chair. She was helped up, the table was cleared of dishes, and Nina Volodimirivna repeated in Russian something about how I was very young. Svetlana Adamovna announced that in the absence of my parents, she would be my "mama."

Nina Volodimirivna nodded wholeheartedly and shouted in Ukrainian, "And I'll be his 'papa!'"

The women burst into giggles again, and once more I laughed with them in agreement. "Yes," I said in Ukrainian, "that's fine." For the third time this morning I had responded "Yes, yes! Good!" without fully understanding what I was getting into.

Chapter Three

Ukraine Has Not Died Yet

Svetlana Adamovna called the nine-story building where I lived a "hostel," a word that for me had other connotations—a cheap hotel where college kids backpacking across Europe crashed for a night or two. A temporary stop on vacation. The word "hostel" represented everything that I, as a Peace Corps volunteer (working, joining, living in the community), hoped to avoid.

My new home, however, combined student dormitory, hotel, and apartment building for teachers. School 23 arranged with the Teacher Training Institute, which owned the building, for me to live on the third floor in a wing occupied mostly by teachers, professors, and their families. College students lived in the other wing.

My first glance inside my apartment evaporated all my concerns about housing. In contrast with some of my Peace Corps comrades in Africa, Latin America, and the Pacific, I had a sink, electric stove, and refrigerator. I had my own tiny shower, with a separate closet for the sink and a toilet that flushed by the push of a plastic button atop the tank. In the horizontal six-inch strip of mirror bolted above the sink I saw the top of my head. So I would shave on tiptoe. I had it easy.

By my reckoning, the tradeoff for the luxury of an electric refrigerator was the school dress code. Unlike volunteers headed for Africa, I had packed a dozen neckties. A dark blue suit and a brown suit with several white dress shirts would be my daily outfits if I were to be taken seriously as a teacher. The white shirts already looked a little yellowish—laundry was an unpleasant chore.

For a few days I ran my fingers along walls and doors like a cat sniffing out the corners of its new dwelling. The walls' chalky paint, I quickly learned, came off on anything it touched. The flimsy, ill-fitting doors were made of unsanded boards rough to the touch, and gave the impression of having been built in haste. Yet with several large closets, my room had generous storage space. It was designed to serve the four, five, or even six students who normally would have inhabited it. Spartan by some standards, my living arrangements were spacious compared to the typical Ukrainian family of four, who often shared one-room apartments that were much smaller.

Back in July on my site visit, the furnishings had included only a bed, a chair, and a table. Svetlana Adamovna had conveyed my request for a desk to the building superintendent, a burly, frowning man whom she identified as "The Komandant." He had answered in Russian.

"There will be a television," she translated. The Komandant had nodded sternly and said, "Da, da, da." Okay, I answered, that would be fine. It might help my language skills. But what about a desk? For grading papers? Lesson plans? The Komandant nodded again.

"The television is here in the building," Svetlana Adamovna said. "He will bring it."

Returning to Kiev, I had resigned myself to doing schoolwork on the kitchen table, but when I moved in I found not only the huge black-and-white television (a school model named "Horizont" built into a trunk-sized cabinet with locking doors) but also a simply-made wardrobe with shelves and a glass front, several more chairs, and—hooray!—a desk. It was small and wobbly, and its drawers didn't close right, but it was nevertheless a desk.

Even as I settled in, I wasn't sure what it meant to be a Peace Corps volunteer in the former Soviet Union. No other teaching volunteers preceded us, so no one could suggest paths to pursue, pitfalls to avoid. "The Peace Corps," had always evoked images of rural villages and intolerable heat—not this nine-story cinderblock high-rise with an elevator. But then, the elevator never worked anyway. I awoke to the sounds of roosters outside my window and on my way to school dodged a tethered goat neatly trimming the grass. Yet this "village" was a European city of 300,000 people. And as for heat, I was about to learn, I could have tolerated quite a bit more.

Despite my snug apartment, my first month in Zhitomir was the most difficult of my life. Everything I ever learned was useless; everything I needed to know was beyond me.

Intending to put myself in the shoes of the average Ukrainian as much as possible, I tried to do everything without help. My teacher friends offered assistance in shopping for food, but I was determined not to be the foreigner in the Soviet Union who receives special treatment and is thus excluded from the reality of its people's lives. I had come to serve, not be served, and any easy way out—foreign currency stores, taxis, translators, and assistants—seemed deceitful.

Quickly I discovered that there were no special stores for foreigners in Zhitomir anyway. In fact, there were almost no foreigners. Until I spoke aloud, Ukrainians thought I was one of them. In my heavy wool coat, bought in a Kiev department store for about six dollars, I passed for a young Ukrainian man, blond-haired and blue-eyed as many others around me. My "disguise," I felt, was my only advantage in a place I comprehended so poorly. Perhaps unnecessarily, I expected to be cheated at every haggle, and thus spoke as little as possible. When I had to use Ukrainian, I practiced and developed an artful mumble. I held my face in a bored, sullen scowl. And I fit right in. I went shopping alone, and the infrequent times people questioned my slurred accent, they assumed I was Polish. Upon learning my nationality, they laughed out loud, shook their heads in amazement that I was somehow in Zhitomir. They asked, "So, how are things in America?" as if they had left it long ago. "Not bad, eh?"

If I had stopped to answer every question, I would never have had time for buying groceries. Even hurrying, shopping took hours. After locating the most promising food stores, I memorized what was sold in each. Basically illiterate at reading Ukrainian (though I could speak quite a bit), I could not identify most of what I saw on the shelves: cans with inscrutable labels or jars of unrecognizable liquids and pulps. I wanted to buy laundry soap but had no idea what it looked like or was called. And because we had learned only the typewritten forms of letters, merely remembering an item's name was not enough; shelf labels handwritten in cursive script appeared to use another alphabet entirely.

I asked questions but couldn't understand the answers. For instance, when I asked a clerk what the bottled, clear fluid on her shelves was—it could have been mineral water, vodka, any number of things—she snapped "Ooksoos." To find out, I bought it. One sniff taught me the word for vinegar. One time I bought a plastic bag of something I thought was beans, but turned out to be puffed rice for babies. Another volunteer blundered even more drastically; he later told me about how he had bought black licorice, and that it tasted bland and awful. Not until he bit down on string did he realize he was eating candles.

Vegetables in the bazaar were recognizable—but there I had troubles with the amounts. For example, how many onions in a kilogram? A kilo is 2.2 pounds, I knew that. Or was a pound 2.2 kilos? Did I want half a kilo or two kilos? I mistakenly bought more cucumbers than I could eat in three weeks because, out of embarrassment, I could not ask the babushka to put some back. For a while after that I stuck to cabbages—one head at a time. I could say "one," and could point to the one I wanted. Useful sign language came naturally: pointing, frowning, head-shaking, more pointing, nodding, holding up fingers—and then probably handing over ten too many bills. That first month I avoided the choosing and haggling that is basic to any farmer's-market shopping. If it had to be weighed, I skipped it.

Shopping in stores was not really easier. To buy milk or sour cream I had to return an empty bottle or jar, which I didn't have. Finally, I found a store that let me make a purchase without exchanging an empty bottle. Instead of milk, though, I bought what turned out to be a product called *ryazhanka*—fermented, boiled milk, too sour to drink. At least now I had a bottle, I thought to myself, pouring the nasty stuff down the drain.

Each dairy product, in fact, presented a new difficulty. The only cheese I found was a tasteless Velveeta-style foil-wrapped brick, easy to find in stores but awful. Butter was available, but rationed. Zhitomir residents were enrolled on a list at their local store, where they waited in line, showed their domestic passports, and waited again while the clerk searched several pages of small print to locate their names. Then the clerk crossed the buyer off the list and sliced two kilos of butter from an enormous chunk melting on the counter. Other lists restricted sales of cooking oil and sugar. Rationing prevented cityfolk from hoarding food and reselling it at a profit in remote villages that lacked the "abundant" goods available in cities like Zhitomir.

Not being a listed resident, I couldn't buy any of these items. For rationed goods, I had to I accept the help of teachers and staff after all. They gave me portions of their butter, sugar, or oil when they hardly had enough themselves; they invited me to dinner. It was difficult to refuse their generosity. They insisted adamantly and I relented after only slight resistance. Even my meals in the dorm were often prepared from their gifts: bags of potatoes, a dozen apples, a box of instant soup, a bottle of cooking oil, a plastic bag of precious sugar, a block of butter wrapped in greasy brown paper. Food was not scarce—the market was full of products my living allowance enabled me to afford easily—but difficult to locate and to buy. I didn't know where to go or what to look for. I stood in all the wrong lines. I wouldn't have starved without my school's help, but I would have been much hungrier.

The meat market, a large open building in the center of the bazaar, was the greatest test of my shopping skills. At the entrance, old women hunched over by osteoporosis sold plastic bags and old men, often with a limb missing, begged for spare change. The warm air gushing out the doors of the building carried the smell of flesh. Inside, dozens of men and women stood behind marble counters covered with great red and white hunks of pig carcass. The butchers used machetes or axes to hack off pieces, and a dull "thunk, thunk" reverberated now and then around the high-ceilinged hall. They wore white aprons smeared with red fingerstreaks, and when they weren't hacking at meat they sat on the great tree stumps that were their cutting blocks, smoking acrid cigarettes and waiting for customers. The smoke drifted up into light that streamed in from closed second-story windows; the air was close, and tinted with blood. Half-horrified, half-fascinated, I wandered around, mulling over the idea of converting right then and there into a vegetarian. With so few food choices to begin with, though, limiting myself to even fewer seemed too daunting a challenge.

Meat being desirable but expensive, the haggling was intense, and I could not guess what were good prices. When I mumbled "How much?" in my sullen, tired voice, the butcher usually grumbled back a number, for example, "forty," which meant 40,000 kupons a kilo. One kilo of pork shoulder for less than a dollar was plenty cheap, but cost more than a month's salary for the average teacher. My own problem was more the selection of a cut. Despite twenty-five years of eating I couldn't tell beef from pork unless it was shrinkwrapped, labeled, and priced in cents-per-pound to help comparison shop. Comparison shopping in Ukraine consisted of rummaging through great piles of meat as if they were socks in a clearance bin at K-Mart. Taking the butcher's long two-tined fork, I poked at heaps of red pork, maroon livers, marbled steaks and ribs, furry hooves, and yellow ears. Wisely, I didn't poke the monstrous decapitated pig heads, which sat on the countertops staring from black eyeholes which mesmerized me. My goal was to focus on what looked vaguely, conceivably consumable: shoulders, loins maybe. I stopped to sniff at something I thought was a pork chop.

The butcher blurted out, "Hey, you! What's wrong?" I maintained my critical face, brows clenched thoughtfully. "It's fresh, fresh!" he bellowed. "Killed this morning, what do you want?" I was too bewildered to actually buy it, and answered, "I don't like it."

Discouraged, but my disguise intact, I wandered over for curiosity's sake to look at salt pork, or *salo*—that thick, outer layer of white fat along a hog's back that is a Ukrainian delicacy. I eavesdropped on a babushka haggling for a chunk of white fat edged with stubbly hog skin. Sighing, I browsed over plucked whole chickens, glanced at some scrawny skinned rabbit carcasses, then despaired at my ineptness and gave up. On my way out I bought sausage. The long reddish-brown links, called *kovbasa* in Ukrainian, still had state-controlled prices. For almost a year, the only meat I managed to buy and prepare was *kovbasa*. I had feared shortages, but found plenty to eat (if one had money). My only obstacle was my ineptness.

Every day on my way home from school, I walked through the bazaar and bought anything that looked good to eat. Before long, I was visiting the bazaar just for the incredible sensory experience. Raucous, colorful, and dynamic, it was packed with people who bustled shoulder-to-shoulder hunting for car parts or fresh eggs, boots or baby strollers. Stepping around the puddles on the uneven asphalt, where pigeons clucked and pecked scraps, I admired the multitude of amazing sights and smells, the people peddling random hodgepodges of goods. Old clothes and scuffed-up boots sat next to stacks of plain white porcelain bowls; bottles of perfume with phony French labels (made in Poland) lay between a fur hat and a motorcycle drive chain. Whisk brooms, plastic shopping bags, and fishing lures stuck into styrofoam pads fell jumbled in with handkerchiefs full of raspberries. The proximity of unlike items made each more odd and interesting: a hairbrush, three tiny dried fish, a miniature of Stalin. A single butterknife, a frilly pair of children's socks, a jar of pink homemade horseradish. Two watch batteries, a packet of instant soup, and a slotted spoon.

Even the people began to look pieced together, like the rotund, toothless woman wearing long ropes of garlic strung around her neck and holding a thick stack of kupons—or the shrunken, thinner one standing in the cold with only three carrots. Almost as a rule, women, young and old, sold things to other women. Bleached-blondes in leather coats bought vegetables from the dirty-smocked babushkas in head scarves, who then exchanged those bills to different bleached-blondes for imported cigarettes or liqueurs. The brown sun-wrinkles at the corners of some women's eyes suggested years of field labor, while those in lipstick and heavy purple eyeshadow unconvincingly affected a cosmopolitan air. Only in contrast to the village women in felt boots and tattered coats did anyone seem well-off.

Men browsed the market too, mainly the area where young men in leather jackets and loafers strolled back and forth on the sidewalk. Like pacing wolves, they chanted a monklike incantation: *"Rubli, dollari, marki. Rubli, dollari, marki."* To their jacket lapels, some had clothespinned cardboard labels reading, "I Buy Gasoline." Nearby, Metallica blasted from the speakers of the cassette-recording kiosks, where a young man in a faded jogging suit recorded tapes in his cramped booth. Teenagers huddled around waiting while the albums they had selected were being dubbed; they had to bring their own blank tapes. Everyone else walked past, ignoring the roar of a thrashing guitar.

It was autumn, so freshly harvested food was sold in abundance. Everywhere were dappled green-and-red apples which, despite overripeness and soft, brown spots, Ukrainian children adored and gobbled up like candy. Radishes, green onions, and fresh parsley lay in bundles, and cabbages were piled like balls of yarn. Along the aisles were plastic-lined barrels of minnow-sized fish and jars of preserved pickles. Brown paper sacks of dried herbs, green and yellow grasses, and other wild plants gathered in the woods were stacked on tables. Nestled among them lay brown and white eggs, with dung flecks and feathers still clinging to their extra-tender shells. White-smocked state farm workers leaned against wire mesh boxes with wheels that held dirty beets or puny onions. They measured them out by adding black milkbottle-shaped weights to a set of scales until the needle dawdled at zero. Across the aisle, for less than a penny I often bought two handfuls of white beans from a withered babushka, who, with a juice glass, scooped them from a pile on her scarf and poured them into my plastic bag, cooing: "That's right, sonny. Eat my good little beans. To your health."

Baskets of kiwis, mandarin oranges, pomegranates, raisins, and dried apricots were sold by dark-skinned central Asians who traveled long distances even to the provincial markets like Zhitomir's. Elsewhere, parked army trucks had their olive-green back doors flung open to display shampoo, housepaint, or flimsy pink tights. People crushed together, shouted, and waved money in the air. The loudest and pushiest were served by women in aprons and headscarves who stood inside the trucks and sighed, hands on hips, before bending over to take handfuls of bills and then hand down a child's dress or a pair of shoes in return.

Young men with cardboard boxes full of loose tobacco called out, "Tabachok, tabachok!" Buyers preferred Marlboro and Camel and Lucky Strike, but usually settled for Chinese packages with names like "Yuangdong" or "World Ball" (all labeled "Mad in USA"). Other fake American brands included "Kennedy," "Clinton," or the straightforward and popular "President." No Ukrainian was fooled by the Mad in USA labels. Even young children could identify whether products came from Germany, Holland, or the United States by decoding the numbers in the Universal Product bar codes. Cigarettes were cheaply available everywhere, and my evil crutch of a nicotine habit was easy to lean on. Every man I knew smoked. Many women did too, although never outdoors in public. Instead, from newspaper scraps rolled into cones they munched small, black sunflower seeds, popping them into their mouths and spitting out the husks—on the sidewalk, on themselves, on me as I walked past.

In the electronics section at other end of the bazaar was my local "Radio Shack" and one of my favorite places to browse, probably because I did not need anything sold there. Old men spread sheets of plastic on the ground and laid out in no apparent scheme their collections of TV tubes, toothed gears, resistors, pipe fittings, beat-up pliers, shrink-wrapped Sony audio cassettes, electronic schematic diagrams, whole electric motors. I watched one old man lift up a scratched Soviet army watch to show it to a potential buyer, who turned it over a few times before handing it back. The man replaced it delicately on his tarp—straightening, adjusting, making his "shop" tidy.

Nearby were the animals. Most days potatoes and carrots were sold in that area, but on Saturdays horse-drawn carts full of hay and grubby people pulled in with loads of eggs, produce, and small livestock. In baskets, huge white rabbits snuggled together. Scraggly chickens flopped about quietly, their feet tied with twine. Once I saw a big, beautiful, squawking white goose. But if I stared and smiled for too long, the seller might growl suspiciously, "What are you playing at?"

The market boasted splendid variety and color in a place predominated by gray sameness. But it could also seem ugly—a ragged, patchwork quilt of plastic tarps, dirty blankets, and sheets of newspaper spread on the ground. It was the oddest of flea markets, or a hundred mini-garage-sales in one, a circus of pressurized desperation. Audible from a distance were the noises of hucksterish price-calling, arguments over cheating or gouging, and the hum of a steady schmoozy pander. I studied the noise, trying to recognize familiar words in that ongoing babble, trying to learn the words I needed to get by. Laughter, too, was everywhere—but a mirthless, greedy sort. People were unceasingly irritable too. Outbursts of bickering made it a heavy, unhappy place. I wondered if the bazaar, with its constant griping and tantalizing, unaffordable goods colored people's impressions of "capitalism" and "open markets."

After scavenging about town those first few months, what I often bought to eat was Snickers bars: the only Western-made food available, the only food I bought with anything resembling calmness or confidence. Though it felt like cheating, I folded anyway. Snickers were sold in every kiosk, so I never had to search. They were easy. That dear, familiar alphabet on the brown-and-white-striped package told me exactly what it was. I purchased them more for the pleasure of knowing what I was purchasing than for the candy bar itself. I pronounced it like Ukrainians—"*Sneakers*"—and kept my disguise too.

Wandering around seeking food drained all my energy. I had never felt so stressed, so stupid, and so incompetent in my life. To accomplish the most ordinary tasks in a poorly understood language, I had to pay attention, listen closely, and think fast. For this reason, I returned home from my after-school shopping exhausted; I collapsed into bed at four in the afternoon, woke briefly to eat a little supper, and fell back to sleep. When tired and grouchy, I told myself that acquiring food was so much simpler for Ukrainians. It was their country, their language, their custom of prowling town for milk and then standing in a long line only to be screamed at by a frustrated store clerk. They had it easy, I thought. They were used to it.

One missing fact, however, disproved those thoughts. One condition of life—a realization every Peace Corps Volunteer in the world probably feels acutely—contradicted those feelings.

I could always leave.

No matter how frustrated I became, I would never feel what a Ukrainian would feel. I had the ruby shoes: with a click of my heels I could be back in Ohio in a matter of days. I tried to remember this every time I stood in a line of thirty people, all silently waiting for the bread lady to finish her conversation and resume work. Smiling slyly, I cherished my delicious secret: a guaranteed airplane ticket out of those troubles. My trials, for that reason, did not compare remotely to what Ukrainians endured and are enduring every day.

In 1991, two days after a failed military coup against Gorbachev, Ukraine declared its independence. In Kiev that autumn, President Bush made what has since been dubbed his "Chicken Kiev" speech, advising Ukrainians to be patient and wait, even as the United States simultaneously encouraged the Baltic states to separate from the USSR. At the time, of course, no one could imagine what a Ukraine divorced from Russia might entail.

Soon, in a vote of 392 to 4, the agonized parliament of Soviet Ukraine chose to split from Russia. Ukraine's communist party chief explained, "Today we will vote for Ukrainian independence, because if we don't we're in the shit." After the vote, one parliament member said, "I don't see why we should be independent. We haven't done anything wrong." Almost 90 percent of the Ukrainian people, however, voted for independence when it was put to a popular referendum. Suddenly, Ukraine became a sovereign nation and the world's third largest nuclear power.

Ukraine has since dismantled those nuclear weapons, but we still haven't recovered from this surprise. Ukraine's desire to be recognized as distinct and separate from Russia was so strongly suppressed that it was easy to underestimate the intensity of the feeling. Like other eastern European states, the country's borders have changed frequently and dramatically, muddying the question of what is Ukraine and who are Ukrainians. Its history reads like a Who's Who of conquering empires: from the Mongol invasion in 1240 to later occupations by Poles, Lithuanians, Swedes, Russian Tsars, and finally Soviet General secretaries. The present era is the longest period of Ukrainian sovereignty in more than 700 years.

The phrase "Ukrainian sovereignty," however, is a loaded one. Kiev is the birthplace of *Russian* civilization, and in the glorious ninth and tenth centuries, the peak of the civilization called "Kievan Rus," no distinction between Russian and Ukrainian existed. Since then, Russians became "Great Russians" and Ukrainians were labeled "Little Russians," to them an insulting term. Still, no matter their disputes, the citizens of Ukraine of Russia are more alike than different and understand each other in ways outsiders will never understand them.

For its first three years of Ukraine's independence, more effort was spent on forging a national identity than on running the country well. The government did little but print money—and lots of it. With privatization still on the drawing board, individuals dismantled state structures and appropriated the pieces for themselves. For anyone without access to hard currency, hyperinflation tore through savings like wildfire. Before independence 7,000 Ukrainian karbovantsi (Ukrainian for rubles) would have bought a small car, if any had been for sale; in just a few years, that same amount bought a box of matches. A loaf of black bread, which once cost five kopecks, now cost 2,500 karbovantsi. Even Russian rubles were bought on the street as hard currency.

The money itself—brightly colored, miniature bills called "kupons"—was actually quite beautiful. At the time I arrived, 3300 kupons equaled one dollar. Higher denominations of bills were printed and distributed in an effort to keep up with inflation—first the red 5000, then the green 10,000, then the purple 20,000. My first summer I saw worthless ones, fives, and tens fluttering in the streets; by the next summer the ripped scraps laying in gutters were 5,000s, 10,000s and 20,000s. Eventually there were 500,000-kupon and even one-million-kupon bills.

What scared people was not only the daunting number of zeros but their drastically decreasing buying power. Amazingly, people withstood frequent government price increases that would have sent Americans into the streets with rocks and bottles. State-paid wage increases barely kept up with the price increases, and brain surgeons, nuclear power plant engineers, military officers (not to mention average workers) earned the equivalent of less than $50 a month. Prices for staple food items soared, not to mention for shoes or car repairs.

Everyone in Ukraine asked: how did this happen? Once the second wealthiest Soviet republic (after Russia) Ukraine was expected to do well after independence. What looked like assets under Soviet accounting, though, turned out to be liabilities—like the 70 percent of Ukraine's industry dedicated to military purposes. Their goods and services already poor and backward by Western standards, Ukraine's enterprises experienced a dried-up market in Russia and began to die slow deaths. When no more orders come from Moscow, what is the plant that manufactures only speedometers to do? Then there was oil. Russia, suffering its own crisis, began early to charge Ukraine near-world prices, and Ukraine's oil debt ballooned until the value of the whole country's exports for a month were spent on what it paid for *one day's* worth of oil.

Waste, inefficiency, and corruption weren't new, but they were never so disastrous nor so visible. The countries of the former USSR, forcibly "developed" under Stalin, must now mold their social structures and personal behavior into shapes that work without the power of Soviet coercion. Ukraine, it seemed, had switched not from a communist system to a market-based system but rather to *no* system whatsoever. No organized society held together by laws, cultural norms, and civic institutions existed. For the average person in Ukraine, independence turned out to mean that the network of social support vanished, and nothing took its place.

Instead of dumping its rulers, Ukraine dumped its symbols, replacing them with those of the formerly outlawed Ukrainian nationalist movement. Only a small percentage of Ukraine's people had been involved in this cause, and thus its flag, its icons, and its songs were alien to most. For example, the national anthem was so new that nobody had learned the words yet. In official ceremonies when the proud new hymn was played, Ukrainians put their hands respectfully over hearts, and listened silently.

Remarkably, that anthem is called "Ukraine Has Not Died Yet." For a people dominated for centuries by others, boasting that they are not destroyed may be a good start. In a minor key, a chorus of deep, Ukrainian basses proclaims glorious triumph in the midst of ruin:

> Ukraine has not died yet, brothers, neither glory nor freedom
> Yet still, young kinsmen, will destiny smile on us . . .
> All our foes will perish like dew in the sun!
> And we too, brothers, will live happily in our own land.
>
> Soul and body we will lay down for our freedom
> And we'll prove, brothers, our native Cossack courage.

Looking around at the collapsing economy, I wondered if courage for battle was the best metaphor, though. If the Soviet Union was the enemy, it was already gone. The remaining disaster needed not vigilant armies, but good hospitals, cleaner industries, and an economy that worked.

Despite the swells of national pride, most of my pupils preferred to speak Russian. Growing up, it had been for them the language to be proud of: cosmopolitan, educated, the lingua franca of the empire. They spoke Ukrainian on official occasions, and some of them spoke it home, but on the streets, with their friends, most spoke Russian. The Russification of Ukraine, a goal of Stalin and the Tsars before him, was so thorough that Russian seemed to be Ukraine's first language—even in Zhitomir, a western, and therefore "more Ukrainian," city. School 23 had always been a Ukrainian language school, and now that a Ukrainian diploma had become more favorable, parents were eager to enroll their children there. But even so, most of the teachers still spoke

Russian on their breaks and outside of class. Ukrainian was not their native tongue.

My English classes, then, became a jumbled mix of three languages. Most frustrating for me was when pupils used Russian words whose Ukrainian equivalent I knew. It was so easy for them to prevent my comprehension when they wanted to. Although the two languages share many words, the most commonly used ones sound nothing alike. The third graders and fourth graders, at least, felt sorry for me and tried to help me, often shouting at one another, "Mr. John doesn't understand Russian—speak Ukrainian!"

Actually I was so deficient in both languages that keeping order in my classroom was an ordeal. Important phrases had not been included in my training—a fact I was to discover from 9G. One day, in the middle of class a girl named Oksana raised her hand and asked sweetly in Ukrainian, "Mister John, may I go out?" Her words, which I understood perfectly, made no sense. Out? Why would I let a student just "go out" of class? I looked shocked and said, "No. No you may not." Out of curiosity, I asked her why.

A boy with spiky hair and a smushed-up nose laughed nastily. Oksana rolled her eyes as if to say, "Do I have to spell it out for you?" In this way I came to learn the euphemism for "May I go to the bathroom?" When my third graders asked the question, they hopped up and down a little—sign language being a helpful giveaway.

Some of my confusion was cultural, however. During my second week of teaching all the boys in my 9B group disappeared. That left a class of six pupils—all girls—hardly enough for the speaking activity I had planned. Halfway hoping the boys had been transferred to another group, I asked the girls where the boys had gone.

They said something I didn't understand and pointed to their biceps. Seeing my confusion, they sighed with impatience, before one of the two Lenas said in English: "Zay go to Army." With her finger she drew on her arm in a gesture I could have taken to mean "The boys went to get tattooed." I still didn't understand. The girls groaned in frustration and made emphatic squeezing motions with their fingers. The other Lena shouted in Ukrainian, "Girls! How do you say 'blood'?" The first Lena then spoke English again: "Blood test. Za boys go to blood test."

"They're only fourteen," I said. "Are they in the army already?" Ukraine still had mandatory military service for all young men, and I knew that in the recent past both boys and girls had taken high school courses on military tactics, first aid, and even grenade-throwing.

"No!" Oksana laughed. "But they will be."

The boys were back soon, some boasting about not flinching before the needle, the more honest ones holding their arms in pain.

In this way, mutual instruction was our norm at first. I had a much more urgent need to learn than they. Also, I reasoned, forcing them to explain things in English would help them. By emphasizing active, genuine communication instead of the rote grammar and translation they practiced so often, I hoped to get them speaking better English. As for the younger pupils, we stuck to practicing what they already knew. Together, we counted to forty. We told time. We listed all the fruits and vegetables we knew, all the animals, and we used those words in sentences: "I like to eat cabbage." "I have a dog." Vova waved his hand and said, "I have an elephant!" The kids giggled, but I was pleased they could invent silly sentences on their own. The ones they made by matching up words from their textbooks were so sensible and dull. So I said, "Very good, Vova!" and he grinned a wide, beautiful smile.

The pupils, I soon learned, were more accustomed to an iron hand. My soft touch drew out their speaking strengths, but also unfortunately seemed to signal that I stood for "anything goes." The pupils talked all the time, got out of their seats whenever they wanted, and soon became impossible for me to control. I wanted them to get up and move, to speak up, and to talk—but not *that* much. I was having trouble striking a medium.

All my vocabulary was too polite. "Would you please sit down, Vova?" worked once or twice, but not after that. My little gang of eight-year-olds was so noisy sometimes that Svetlana Adamovna entered my classroom to see what was wrong. At those moments, the children fell instantly silent and crossed their hands in front of them on their desks. My pupils didn't believe me serious until I raised my voice. Other teachers, even when only mildly displeased, let loose shrill screams, I had noticed. Against my better judgment, I learned to bark out the sharp, stinging commands teachers shouted to regain classroom discipline. "Behave yourself!" and "That's uncultured!" I found myself saying. I heard one teacher scold a young boy with the phrase, "What was that! Are you sick in the head?" but decided to forgo this approach. The phrases didn't work well for me anyway: In Mr. John's flat, twangy accent, they probably sounded hilarious.

Svetlana Adamovna, checking in on my classroom now and then, silently took note of my difficulties and shortcomings. I knew she still saw me as a guest, and I felt like such an incompetent teacher that I could not blame her for wondering about my real purpose. Her solution to my problems was to shower me with generous hospitality.

She invited me to eat with her family so often that I could have visited every night if I had wanted. She would always telephone my dormitory's *dezhurnaya*, the woman at the front desk who guarded the entrance. She knew this woman personally—but then, Svetlana Adamovna seemed to know *everyone* in town personally. Svetlana Adamovna would then ask the *dezhurnaya* to send a student up three floors to fetch me. Svetlana Adamovna lived so close we could have used tin cans on a string to talk; it struck me as pitiful that a country of satellites and space probes had no reliable technology for calling across town.

"Hello? Hello?" I shouted into the receiver, a giant piece of dirty plastic that was as heavy as a dumbbell.

Over the scratchy line came Svetlana Adamovna's high sweet voice, in her regal accent, hollering, "You will visit us for dinner this evening! You will visit us for dinner!"

I tried to speak Ukrainian, but always ended up answering, "Okay! Okay!" I felt self-conscious shouting in English in the dorm lobby. College students in slippers and sweatpants stared curiously at me or whispered behind their hands.

At dinner, Svetlana Adamovna served heaps of food that I knew, with my own cooking in mind, had taken hours to shop for and prepare. Yet she piled my plate high with mashed potatoes and forced me to eat as if an end to the food were inconceivable. Despite my own shopping and worrying about food, here I was living high on the hog like a pampered foreigner after all. My determination to be self-sufficient gave way, and I ate at Svetlana Adamovna's very often that autumn, getting to know her family and speaking more and more Ukrainian.

After one of those meals when I had been stuffed to bursting, I dragged myself home, took my room key from the *dezhurnaya* at the front desk, and headed upstairs. The stairwell and third-floor hallway were both pitch black, all of their lightbulbs burned out or stolen. Outside my door my foot brushed against something. I picked up a Ziploc bag. "A plastic bag that seals!" I thought happily. "A Westerner was here!" The bag contained apple turnovers, mandarin oranges, and a note that read:

> John,
>   Didn't know if you might need a little food. I'm sure you don't, knowing the Ukrainians.
>   —John Maddox

John Maddox, a six-foot-six tall accountant from Rome, Georgia, had been working as a small business development volunteer in Zhitomir for seven months—hence, his accurate guess that I was being treated to Ukrainian hospitality. Even so, I was grateful to have oranges. John had worked for the city administration counseling entrepreneurs, incubating new businesses, and setting up small-business auctions. Whenever I stopped in his office, around the corner from my school, he was always cheerful, patiently determined, and good-natured. We shared a post office box, and I felt lucky to have him for a neighbor. Later that week he came by my dormitory, saying he wanted to check in on me.

When we sat down for instant coffee, he said in his sweet drawl, "Did you enjoy moving desks today?"

"What?" I said. "How did you know?" My principal had asked me to help rearrange a classroom with the physics teacher. I had spent the afternoon hauling desks and chairs up to the fourth floor. Had I failed to notice some strange significance to the event?

"A teacher who saw you," he explained, "told my translator, who told me." The odd feeling of being watched crept over me. I was being talked about.

"Better get used to living in a fishbowl," he added.

Chapter Four

Endings

"Do you know the ending of *Santa Barbara*?"

For two years Ukrainians repeatedly asked me this question, always in the same exact words, as if the ending of *Santa Barbara* was the United States' best-kept secret. Forget about military, politics, economics, culture—they wanted to know the conclusion of a soap opera.

My students grew brave enough to ask me after the first week of teaching; teachers asked right away: how did this "serial film" finish? Had I been cleverer, I would have invented an ending. I should have told the Ukrainians that Cruz *doesn't* marry Eden, that the whole detective squad dies, that the finale is a glorious tragedy of Greek epic proportion, a pastel living room covered in self-poisoned bodies. They would have loved that. But I didn't think of it. Instead I told them the truth: "I don't know the ending, but the last episode will probably look about like every other." They murmured disappointment and disbelieved me.

The most popular TV show in all of Russia (and therefore, in Ukraine) was the American-made 1980s "daytime drama" *Santa Barbara*. Even by soap opera standards the show was so kitschy, cheap, and poorly made that our network canceled it. Then, like every Hollywood reject, it was relegated to the Bad Movie Graveyard of the former Soviet Union. The upshot was that

Russians and Ukrainians adored the show. No obscure daytime drama now, *Santa Barbara* played during primetime. Children, teenagers, women and men young and old—everyone turned to Channel One at seven o'clock to watch desperate love scenes between Cruz and Eden, or overheated threats and counterthreats between Mason and the evil Gina. The following day, in the market, the teacher's lounge, the dormitory where I lived, wrinkled brows, "tsk, tsks," and shocked delight abounded. The whole country behaved like a class of self-indulgent college sophomores. "Did you see *Barbara* yesterday?" they chirped. "No? O, God! Let me tell you what happened."

Ukrainians thought it was a miniseries. From their newspapers they learned that it had over two thousand episodes. "What a country you are from!" a babushka who swept the halls of my dorm told me. "A film with two thousand episodes!" Even on the Soviet scale of grandness, that was tremendous scope, admirable magnitude. She added, "Do you know how it ends?"

It was futile to explain the point they were missing. When translated, the words "soap opera" amounted to nothing meaningful, so I explained that the program's only purpose was to sell advertisements. How does that differ from other shows? everyone asked. All shows have advertisements now. *Santa Barbara* is different, I said: the writers invent the story as they go along. But our newspaper says it is an American film from the 1980s that has ended in your country. Yes, I said, that's true. So there is an ending! Well yes, I admitted, but only because it was worse than other films like it—for instance, *General Hospital*, which has aired continuously for over thirty years. Thirty years! they said. What a country, where a film can last thirty years!

In the United States viewers understand the difference between daytime soaps and films and often don't mind when actors and actresses are replaced. With a chuckle they accept premises about plane crashes and drastic cosmetic surgery that mysteriously adds an inch to a character's height. When American viewers love soap operas, it is often apologetically, half-ashamed, because the genre's pleasures are cheap, predictable, constant, and sentimental.

Exactly those qualities made the show irresistible for Ukrainian viewers. Cheapness, predictability, and constancy are rare indeed in the former Soviet Union, since life has turned expensive and frighteningly unpredictable. In a society of undependable institutions and debunked conventional wisdom, *Santa Barbara*'s steadiness (not to mention its daily parade of glitz) provided a perfect escape. As for sentimentality, Russians and Ukrainians are known for their fondness of emotional extravagance verging on the maudlin. More than once I have seen intelligent, reasonable people reduced to tears by the sappy schlock of *Santa Barbara* or the Brazilian and Mexican serials like *Simply Maria*, *Wild Rose*, and (my favorite) *The Rich Cry, Too*. The emotional peaks and valleys of these shows overshadowed *Santa Barbara's*, and I learned that steamy Latin American soaps permit much more slapping and lovemaking than do ours. Some people told me they didn't like the oversentimentality of the Latin soaps, but even they placed *Santa Barbara* in a category of its own, describing it as a "good film."

A joke circulating that year described a Jewish man who receives the chance to emigrate—either to Israel or to Santa Barbara, California. When he chooses Santa Barbara, his friends ask him why. "Who do I know in Israel?" he answers. "In Santa Barbara I know everybody."

Furthermore, the show was skillfully dubbed into Russian, and each character had his or her own voice. In most Western movies, one translator droned out all the roles. Worse, the single voice was always a hideous, nasal monotone. This tradition, I was told, began when those who (illegally) dubbed movies into Russian actually wore clothespins on their noses to disguise their voices. On *Santa Barbara*, however, different actors and actresses dubbed the dialogue for each part! They emoted expressively in Russian, even exaggerating the tone of each impassioned speech. They used genuine idioms instead of literal translations: they spoke like real Russians. In 1994 when the stars of this lost soap took a publicity tour through the former USSR they were universally recognized and mobbed. They traveled with their counterpart "voices," who became celebrities as well.

Obviously, I know far too much about *Santa Barbara*. On those evenings when I was invited to Svetlana Adamovna's I sat through more episodes than I care to admit. When the trumpets of the familiar theme song blasted from the TV, I tended to wince involuntarily. Svetlana Adamovna's 25-year-old daughter Larisa noticed, and once said, "You don't like *Santa Barbara*."

"Sorry," I shrugged. "It doesn't interest me."

Her eyes widened. "And no," I added, "that's not because I know how it ends."

Larisa smiled, sighed, and with a wave dismissed my lack of appreciation for deeply felt emotion, the poignancy of repressed lust and betrayal. To prevent boredom I settled for the small pleasure of listening to the faint English in the background.

Those evenings in Svetlana Adamovna's apartment all blend together in my mind, much like family visits resemble themselves so much that memories eventually converge. Her family became my family. Whenever I attended an evening meal—every Sunday at first—I was greeted like a beloved son home from a long journey.

Four of them—Svetlana Adamovna; her husband, Victor Ivanovich; her daughter, Larisa; and her son-in-law, Sergey—all lived within a cramped two-room apartment on Shelushkova Street. From my dormitory six blocks away, I walked down tree-lined Shelushkova Street, past the picturesque cottages and goats grazing along the sidewalk. I crossed the tram tracks at Vulitsa Borisa Tema (formerly "Street of the 27th Congress of the Communist Party of the Soviet Union," now named after a Ukrainian poet). I passed the little square with the bust of Shelushkov (a partisan in the war) and arrived at the Mesyatz's five-story apartment building, a narrow concrete block a quarter of a mile long and two apartments wide. They lived not very far down, in the second entryway in back of the building. Up the unlit stairwell, I climbed four floors of steps, feeling my way along the rough plaster wall because it was so dark. The fourth floor landing was lit (Sergey installed a wire cage over the bulb so it could not be stolen again) where there were three doors. Theirs, the new light wood door on the left, stood out from the sloppily painted dark stairwell like new tires on an old car, proclaiming cheerfully that all gloominess must end at the threshold. Although the door was always left open for me, I rang the buzzer and entered.

Victor Ivanovich greeted me first. In track suit and slippers (his after-work clothes for relaxing) he welcomed me from the far end of the narrow corridor. "Good evening!" he said, with a rising-and-falling intonation that tilted up merrily and then dropped, as if to say, "At last! You're here!" We shook hands, and I bent down to remove my shoes. "Slippers!" Victor Ivanovich urged cheerfully. "Take your slippers." I took from amongst the scattered boots and shoes "my" slippers, a pair of hard plastic flip-flops with the design of a bare foot etched on the insole. Wearing an apron, Svetlana Adamovna leaned into the corridor, too—she from the kitchen, her husband still standing in the room with the TV. In that three-by-six-foot space, the three of us exchanged greetings—remarking on the weather, if I was cold, whether I was hungry, to which I said, "Well, yes. A little." Usually Larisa, carrying a dish, headed for the living room table, squeezed by, and said "Hi" in English, then ordered her parents not to keep me in the hall but to let me sit down. "Come in! Come in!" Victor Ivanovich urged. "Sit down!" In the living room Sergey watched television. "*Privyet*, John," he greeted me, shaking hands without getting up. He urged me to sit next to him on the couch and catch whatever was on at that moment. Victor Ivanovich disappeared into the main bedroom, off to the right.

The Russian word for their apartment was *uyootniy*, which means cozy, but incorporates the sense of "making a little, poor space comfortable." The sixteen-by-twelve-foot living room had a fold-out table, and thus became the dining room when guests were invited. The room also contained the television, telephone, and a gargantuan piece of furniture called a *shafa*, the combination bookshelf-china-cabinet-linen-closet-entertainment-center in every Ukrainian apartment. The room was well-trafficked; it connected the parents' bedroom to the bathroom and kitchen, and also had the only access to the balcony that served as storage area, herb garden, toolshed, and zone where the women permitted smoking. That living room used a lot of living. In addition to the massive *shafa*, the room had an armchair, two dining table chairs, an endtable, and a sofa that folded out into a bed. Though it is incredible to me now, for many months of visiting the Mesyatz family, I did not figure out that here was where Sergey and Larisa slept. They had no other room or space of their own; they had privacy only when their parents left the house. Their climb up the ten-year-long waiting list for state-provided apartments had been thrown into uncertain jeopardy by the collapse of the state, and a privatized apartment usually had to be bought, not rented. At that time a one-bedroom apartment in Zhitomir could be purchased outright for two or three thousand U.S. dollars, depending on its proximity to downtown—and no *kupons* were accepted for the sale. That seemingly low price was far beyond what a Ukrainian couple whose combined income was around thirty dollars a month could afford, so Larisa and Sergey had no way to move out. They had married in a more optimistic time, and though Sergey still cherished the hope of getting their own place, that possibility had dimmed.

Victor Ivanovich emerged, firmly holding the family's precious golden Persian cat, Betty. He cooed pet names—"Betushka, Krasavitsa" (beautiful girl)—while stroking her so roughly I was sure she would scratch him. A low whiny growl emanated from her throat. Her eyes became slits when he pinned her tightly in his lap, nuzzling his nose in her face. She scowled a long-suffering grimace but held completely still, which made him laugh. When

Betty finally leaped away to sulk and lick her long fur proudly, he turned to me.

Victor Ivanovich was in many ways a typical Ukrainian man. Now in his late fifties, he had risen through the ranks of police officers to lieutenant colonel and, near retirement, was likely to be made a full colonel. Born and raised in Zhitomir, he was genuinely Ukrainian (and spoke the language meticulously). Having spent his career in the pseudo-military police, he was conservative, proletarian, and pro-law and order if not outrightly pro-Soviet. He vehemently believed that though the communists had made mistakes, the system of social unity and fairness they promoted was the crowning intellectual achievement in human evolution. He was kind, gentle, and staunchly unshakable in his opinions. He spoke slowly to me and only in Ukrainian, which I appreciated a great deal then because I still couldn't understand a word of Russian. In a loud voice, he intoned melodiously, patriarchally, as if lecturing from a great height. He liked to corner me as he did Betty, firmly pressing upon me his assertions and beliefs, unaware of my squirming in his obstinacy. Usually he wanted to teach me something, and I intently listened to his speeches on all subjects—partly to be polite, partly to catch his meaning among unfamiliar words. Whirling his wiry arms, he liked to show me how he karate-chopped young police recruits who thought they knew judo and sambo (Soviet jujitsu) better than he. A spring about to uncoil, he was all twisting elbows and stiffly set hands.

The evenings I visited their home for dinner, we ate a miniature feast, even when the occasion was no more than a rented Guns 'N Roses video. Mother and daughter were expert cooks who spent several hours preparing food for my visit as if that were expected and necessary. We ate cabbage rolls—*holubtsi*, or "little blue doves"—a Ukrainian specialty: boiled buckwheat and meat wrapped in boiled cabbage leaves. Sometimes we ate *plov*, an Uzbek dish, close cousin to rice pilaf. Svetlana Adamovna and Larisa once in a while made *zharkoye*, a delicious beef and potato stew, each serving baked in its own ceramic pot. There were fried cutlets, potato pancakes, or crepes—the Russian *blini* called *mlintsi* in Ukrainian. Always Larisa made salads: green onion and deviled egg, garlic and shredded carrot, cabbage marinated in vinegar and sugar, or boiled beets and mayonnaise over a dish of herring. A plate of open-faced sandwiches on toasted bread or a bowl of fresh tomatoes or berries or apple slices could always be squeezed onto the table until, in typically Ukrainian fashion, dishes were set upon dishes. Hospitality customs required that if enough space remained on the table in which to place a goblet, the host has been stingy. But that was for holidays! Sergey grumbled that they only ate well when John was coming over. Even as I praised the food until they began to think me insincere, it was months before I fully appreciated the trouble they went to for me.

Svetlana Adamovna took her responsibility as my counterpart very seriously. The first remark she made in July to our principal—that she would be my Ukrainian mother—she meant literally. I was the age of her daughter and son-in-law, so it was understandable that she felt it her business to ensure that I ate well and felt happy.

On one of the first of these evenings, I made the mistake of calling her *Pani Svetlana,* as we were taught in training. Her sideways glance at Victor Ivanovich told me it was a faux pas. Now that "comrade" was politically incorrect, no one knew how to address one another. We were taught that in Ukrainian *Pan* for men and *Pani* for women were the equivalent of Mr. or Ms., but we were not told that the words had definite political connotations.

Victor Ivanovich snorted. "I am not *Pan,*" he said haughtily. "*Pan* is a Polish word, and not Ukrainian." In Polish, "*Pan*" and "*Pani*" are frequently used grammatical constructions, but they are genuine literary Ukrainian too, albeit words with an economic history. "To be *Pan* I must own land," he continued. "I must be a rich gentleman farmer." He waved at the ceiling of the snug apartment. "You see that I am not rich. Where are my riches? How can I be *Pan?*"

In later travels to western Ukraine, I heard the expression commonly used, but in the more Russified parts of the country—the other three-fourths of Ukraine—on anyone but a fervent nationalist's lips *Pan* and *Pani* smacked of mockery or obsequiousness to the new officialdom that worshipped all things western Ukrainian. Speaking pure literary Ukrainian alienated me from those with whom I wanted to get acquainted, so I dropped *Pan* and *Pani* that night for good.

The family pampered and coddled me like a baby throughout the sumptuous meal, all of us speaking Ukrainian instead of English so Sergey and Victor Ivanovich would understand. "It will give you a good practice" Svetlana Adamovna said. I didn't resist, nor did I speak up as Larisa heaped mashed potatoes on my plate without asking. I felt obligated to finish them, but when I did so she piled on more, which probably made me look as ravenous as the stray mutts that yapped outside my window at night.

"Are you doing all right?" Svetlana Adamovna inquired of me in Ukrainian. "How are things at your hostel?" Between mouthfuls I said everything was fine. After only a few weeks, I would admit to no struggles.

"I wish I had hot water in the dormitory," I told her. "That's all." Though the fall weather had not yet become too cool, I wasn't enjoying taking cold showers or scrubbing greasy dishes under an icy tap.

"What?" she exclaimed in shock. "You still have no hot water?!"

"We don't either," Sergey confided to me.

"Why do you need hot water?" protested Victor Ivanovich. "It's still summer! The weather is beautiful. You have cold water, right?"

"It usually comes on in the evening about five," I said. Not to sound whiny, I added, "But everything is all right, of course. I'm fine."

"Do you do your own laundry?" Larisa asked. She sat next to me at the dinner table; perhaps she was suggesting I needed to do it more often? "Because it's terrible without hot water. I boil water on the stove and use the washing machine." This contraption looked like a garbage can with a motor on top and was louder than a vacuum cleaner. In soapy water it agitated a tubful of clothes which still had to be rinsed, wrung out by hand, and dried on a clothesline on the balcony or in the courtyard. Larisa suddenly had an idea and told her mother, "Maybe he should bring his clothes here to be washed."

"No, no, no!" I said, sorry I had allowed myself to complain at all. "No need, no need. I can do it myself." I should have known they would offer to help me. "In fact," I added, "I like doing laundry. I put on my Walkman and listen to music while I wash clothes. It's my only chance to listen to my cassettes." That was mostly true. My shower stall held three inches of water, and (unable to find stoppers anywhere) when I plugged the drain with a washcloth I could scrub my sweaty socks and underwear until my knuckles turned pink. Doing laundry was tiresome, sure, but I didn't want to appear wimpy.

"Well, you can bring your clothes here to wash if you want," Larisa said. Happily for me, the subject was dropped.

Svetlana Adamovna was reminded of a proverb. "All things are difficult before they are easy," she said in perfectly proper English. When she added the proverb's Russian equivalent, Victor Ivanovich nodded enthusiastically and waved his fork.

A thought occurred to him. "John," he said, pronouncing it *Dzhone*. "I have one small favor to ask of you. I don't need anything special from America. We have everything here in our country, I have everything I need." He paused awkwardly. "The thing is, I don't like our flyswatters. They're flimsy—" he mimicked, waving his arms wildly, "—and they break. You can't kill the flies with them because they bend so much. So you see the problem. Also I can't find any in the stores." He concluded by shrugging his shoulders, palms up, and saying "*Ne ma!*" which meant, "there isn't any here" or "it's not there" or "it doesn't exist." He said "*ne ma*" the way all Ukrainians always did: with stoic exasperation, their voices almost cheerfully implying "that's the way the ball bounces."

"I can have my folks send us some," I promised. "No problem."

"Please, John, if you could. That's all I'd ask, you know, because at the dacha there are so many flies. Everything else a man could require I have. Just this one little thing."

Sergey looked skeptical, even disgusted. He put two fingers to his lips to indicate to me it was time for a smoke. When he stood up, I followed him—despite the glare of disapproval his mother-in-law gave me. She was long accustomed to his bad habits, but still hoped to alter mine.

"You smoke too much," Svetlana Adamovna said. "I know what this means. It means maybe you miss your friends from home." It was my turn to smile and shrug. *Ne ma*, I thought.

Sergey and I went out onto the balcony and found some space between the hoes and rakes that leaned against the windows. Straddling two fifty-pound burlap bags, he opened one to show me what was inside: gorgeous, ripe red tomatoes. "Not bad, eh?" he said, lighting my cigarette before his. He told me it was nearly time to preserve them in jars so they would have pickled tomatoes to eat all winter. The pickling process was hard labor, he said, a whole day of huddling over steaming pots and then sealing the lids on dozens of three-liter jars. "But I love tomatoes. Smell," he said, holding a small firm one under my nose. "Paradise," he said. He deeply inhaled on his cigarette and put it out in a window box full of marigolds.

Across from the balcony was a tall brick smokestack, a pipe pointing into the sky that rose from an automobile junkyard (no— a repair shop). In every direction, as far I could see, were dilapidated highrises just like this one. The sun was just setting, and the sky turned a warm orange. Down in the courtyard below I heard children scrambling around, playing until the last moment before they had to go inside. Their voices floating up on the light breeze sounded so like late summer in my neighborhood at home that a clutch of nostalgia caught me by surprise, until the alien sound of their broad vowels broke the illusion.

The next week, an older teacher I didn't know well saw me in the hall after class and asked in Ukrainian, "John! Are you going to the *pokhoron?*"

"Uhh, I don't know," I answered. "I don't understand."

"Maybe you did not hear," she began in slow, precise English. "Svetlana Adamovna's father died."

She took me to the office of the vice principal of English and explained something I didn't understand. "Yes," Galina Vasilievna said, facing me. "You will go with me." The other teacher chattered on, and Galina Vasilievna impatiently agreed. "*Da, da, da.*" To me again she said, "At twelve." My next class began at 11:35. "What about my 9B group?" I asked. She held up her palm to assure me not to worry and said that my group could go to another teacher that day, that everything would be all right. I hadn't seen Svetlana Adamovna in school all day. Gradually it dawned on me that I was about to attend a funeral.

When Galina Vasilievna and I walked around behind the apartment building on Shelushkova, the first thing I noticed was a dump truck parked by the stairwell entrance. A small group of mourners stood between the courtyard bushes and the building. Sergey saw me and beckoned me over. His face was red and twisted after much crying. I handed my backpack of schoolbooks to Galina Vasilievna and followed Sergey into the building.

"We need—," he said, ending the sentence with a word I didn't know.

"I don't understand," I answered.

"Just come with me," he said.

On the fourth floor landing I waited while he went in; the apartment was full of people, most of them crowded into the living room. Sergey returned with two short four-legged stools and handed me one. Svetlana Adamovna appeared in the corridor, and when she saw me in the hall she cried out, "John!" Her face was red and teary too, and she began crying again when she saw me. In English, I said, "I'm sorry for your loss."

"Thank you," she said crying. "It's very hard." Sergey said something to her and she nodded; he took me by the arm. We went back downstairs with the stools and placed them in the paved driveway outside the stairwell of the building. Sergey thanked me and went back up. I went over and stood by Galina Vasilievna and another English teacher, Tatiana Vasilievna. Everyone milled about idly, speaking in hushed tones, waiting. Most of them spoke in whispers in the way of acquaintances who hadn't seen each other in a long time; they muffled happy greetings, even laughing under their breath.

"He was old," Tatiana whispered to me in English. "Over seventy. Of course it's too bad," she admitted not very wholeheartedly. Galina Vasilievna explained in Ukrainian that Svetlana Adamovna's father had been a principal and then superintendent of a rural school district. Svetlana Adamovna's two sisters had married and moved away, one to Kiev, one to Leningrad. She was the middle sister, the one who stayed, the one who visited often and took care of him. A telegram had been sent to the sister in St. Petersburg, but she hadn't made it to the funeral.

A man appeared in the darkness of the stairwell; others were behind him. In the dim light from the street, they could be seen maneuvering a large box down the narrow stairwell and around the corner onto the first floor landing. They brought the body down from upstairs, where it had lain in the apartment, in its coffin—a plain pine box wrapped in black cloth.

When Svetlana Adamovna came out of the dark entryway, she was crying very hard; to see her face so contorted gave me a start of pain. Her usually elaborately styled beehive of blond-and-silver hair now lay in flat wisps, combed back behind her ears. Her husband, son-in-law, and other men removed the lid, and she cried harder. It frightened and fascinated me, and I imagined the serene, dignified face that lay in the coffin on a living man. Sergey looked uncomfortable and motioned me over. Three of the men nodded and, in hushed voices, agreed on something I didn't catch. Sergey motioned me to come up to the coffin and suddenly I was close to that white, wrinkled face, the thin old man in the black suit whose arms lay crossed over a bundle of flowers. My heart pounded in fear—not of him but that I would make a disastrous mistake of some kind. Sergey showed me they wanted to straighten the coffin and that we were to adjust the stools. The men lifted up the coffin, and Sergey and I realigned the stools before they set it down more sturdily. I nodded to him and stepped back.

The mourners approached the coffin, stared a few moments, and then set their bundles of flowers on the dead man's chest, by his side, at his feet in the box. Galina Vasilievna took hers and mine and put them in the casket, while I remained in the crowd by the bushes. I had bought four tulips at the flower section of the bazaar, and the babushka who sold them to me crossed herself in the Orthodox fashion before handing them over. On happy occasions Ukrainians give an odd number of flowers; even-numbered bouquets are presented only at funerals. Teachers and friends of the family came and laid their flowers. Svetlana Adamovna sobbed.

On our way from school, Tatiana Vasilievna had lamented the expense of funerals—upwards of two million kupons, she said. Few could save such a sum, and the meager services provided by the state were paid for with contributions from friends and colleagues. A City Bureau of Funerals handled transportation of the deceased to the cemetery as well as grave preparation and other necessary tasks. They made a lot of money this way—one central funeral service in a city of 300,000. Tatiana told me that some men had recently tried to open a private burial service but the powerful city bureau wouldn't permit it. This burial would occur simultaneously with four others.

No one officiated and no one made a speech or gave a eulogy. No priest, minister, or even city official attended. Maybe at the grave, I thought, someone will say a few words. Or maybe not.

It was taking a long time. Now only Larisa and her mother kept crying, while a line of people stood respectfully and waited their turn to place flowers in the casket. Most of us stood back a little ways, and the low murmur continued.

Galina Vasilievna opened her purse and pulled out a box of little yellow pills. She urged me to take one: "It will relax you." I guessed it was valium; the soft, dreamy look in her eyes suggested she had taken some already. "Tabletchka," she said. "They're yellow. Do you have in America?"

A babushka nearby overheard and offered (if we didn't mind) to take one. She thanked Galina Vasilievna and munched the dry pill, whispering, "Is he really from America?" Galina Vasilievna said yes, he was. The babushka's grandson hid behind her skirts and peeped out at me. Funerals happened every day, but Americans were a rare sight. "What's his name?" the babushka asked. Annoyed at being referred to like a dog, I interrupted, "John. My name is John."

She looked surprised that I spoke Ukrainian, then asked, "Tell me, please. There is something I want to know. Do people in America really have such names as C.C. and Santana? What about Madeleine, or Mason, or Cruz?"

Galina Vasilievna chimed in. "Yes, tell us. We've never heard of names like those."

The pallbearers lifted the coffin and began carrying it down the alley behind the apartment building where a bus waited a little ways off to transport people to the cemetery. Next to it was the dump truck—clean, at least, but the same ugly standard Soviet vehicle used to haul dirt or vegetables or, it turned out, people.

"By the way," the woman said. "About this film . . . you wouldn't happen to know. . . ."

"I think it's best if I go home now," I interrupted, turning to Galina Vasilievna.

"*Da, da, da,*" she said. Then in English, "Until tomorrow." I hurried away in the opposite direction from the slowly trudging funeral procession.

I loosened my necktie, and the air in my collar refreshed and cheered me a little. The beautiful day was dry and clear—Indian Summer, which they called "Baba Leto," the summer of the beauty of a middle-aged woman. None of what happened seemed real—the awkwardness of a stranger's funeral was all the more confusing here, where I understood so little. Funny, I thought, that in training we hadn't been taught the word for funeral. When planning to join the life of the community, I hadn't accounted for joining in its deaths as well. A melody had been playing in my head all this time: "Row, row, row your boat." Svetlana Adamovna and I had been discussing songs in English, and the words she knew went "Life's a happy dream" instead of "Life is but a dream." I thought my version much better.

Life did seem like a strange dream, one from which I might wake any minute—in a bed in the United States. Along Shelushkova Street I picked up a few chestnuts, whose milky sworls and twists reminded me of buckeyes. With my thumb I rubbed the smooth surface of one brown chestnut, then pocketed it.

At home I changed clothes and felt a pang of hunger before remembering I hadn't eaten lunch. Since I had some bread I decided to open a jar of jam I had managed to buy. Like all preserved goods, the jam jar had a metal lid and a rubber gasket that sealed it. To bend up the metal lid required a Soviet-style opener, called a *klyuch*—also the word for key—but I didn't have one. My Swiss Army knife had both a can opener and a bottle opener, but the can opener was for cutting triangular holes, not for prying up lids, and the bottle opener turned out to be too small to fit under the lip of the lid. Stupidly I took my new breadknife and tried to pry up the lid that way. With a "click" the tip of the blade chipped off and flew behind the fridge. The simplest everyday domestic task had stumped me, and my best new kitchen utensil was now ruined. I got angry and went at the jar with the Swiss Army knife again, which bent the lid up a little but the seal still held. Growing furious, I cranked harder, but instead of bending the lid I cracked the jar. Splinters of sharp glass and tiny glittery shards lay sparkling on the table. The jar of jam still wasn't open.

For a second I almost broke into tears. I was so helpless, so ignorant, so intensely incompetent. It hit me that a stupid jar of runny, poor-quality, state-factory blackberry jam was about to make me cry, and I became enraged. Unfolding the awl on my pocketknife, I punched a hole in the center of the metal lid and poured the black, sticky jam into a saucepan, then poured from the saucepan into an empty jar. I capped the new jar with a plastic lid and hurled the original broken, dark-purple-dripping jar into the wastebasket. I'll probably eat broken glass, I thought. Then *I'll* die here also.

I couldn't help feeling morbid; it was only my first month in Zhitomir. I had barely settled into my new life, and yet here I was attending funerals and straightening the placement of the casket of a man I never even knew. I thought about my grandmother at home, in her eighties but healthy. If she were to die, I had already decided not to return home for the service. Now that I had just attended a stranger's funeral, that decision seemed ridiculous and unjust.

I imagined my grandmother's face, then wondered if I would ever see her again. The image cause me to remember a recent dream in which I had seen my grandmother here in Ukraine riding a trolleybus. I was happily surprised at the impossibility of seeing her face in the window, smiling at me clearly, but shrouded in a blue light. I rushed up to the bus, and she saw me, but from her moving mouth I heard nothing. Long after I had stepped off the airplane in Ukraine, my subconscious had remained in the States, and I dreamed often of home: vivid images of my parents' house on West Street; my friends on summer evenings swinging on porchswings, laughing; the storefronts of the town's main street. Now, however, my nights were filled with weird mixtures of two countries, faces from home juxtaposed with places in Zhitomir.

I collapsed into bed, counting in my calendar the days I had left—more than seven hundred remaining. I tried to picture home, but kept seeing the casket being slid into the back of that dump truck. I knew I would dream about it, and I knew that as Ukraine became more and more familiar to me, it would fill up my dreams completely. There had been a time when I could, by going to sleep, return home, if only in my mind, to spend my nights visiting the places and people I loved. As I drifted off to sleep, seeing Svetlana Adamovna's sobbing face, I knew that those visits home were ending as well.

Chapter Five

Lost in the Classroom

The weather quickly turned chilly and rainy. On my soggy walk to school I slipped on a muddy patch and my right foot slid into a puddle. Instantly the cold water soaked through my sock and sopped down into my shoe. I thought: I'm cold. I'm wet. I feel all alone here, and in twenty minutes I had better be ready to face my first-period class.

My first month of teaching might have been hilarious had it not been so agonizing. I could barely keep the students—no, *pupils*, I kept forcing myself to say—under control. By evening I was too exhausted to think about another long day, and thus I planned inadequately for the next day's lessons, which were then even more challenging. Sometimes I woke early to sketch out plans I had made in my head, but sometimes, I hate to admit, I invented in the middle of class. "OK, children, uh, now . . . we'll play charades using past tense verbs." When I managed to fake it, staggering through class in embarrassing disorganization, I felt both ashamed and ebullient. There, you see? I thought. I may be a bad planner but I'm a fantastic improviser. Yet I was lost in the classroom, struggling to mark grades, pronounce names correctly, keep the lessons moving.

My handwriting on the board was laughably bad. In my defense, the chalkboard was a green vinyl panel whose waxy texture required heavy pressure to make the chalk stick in little flecks; once written, nothing erased. I sometimes scrawled a few Ukrainian words on the board in block letters (I couldn't write cursive yet), and when I apologized to my 9B class for this once, a girl piped up, "That's OK, Mr. John. We used to write like that too—in first grade."

After that I stuck to writing only English. Even so I had a lot to learn. Once when I wrote "School # 23" on the board, my whole class of ninth-graders giggled. I stopped to ask what was so funny. Ruslan, the blond boy with crooked teeth, held up two fingers on each hand and then crossed them to form the tic-tac-toe symbol, or the pound sign; his crossed fingers he then raised in front of one eye so he peeked out through the middle square.

"Prison," he said. In Ukrainian, the number sign was shorthand for "jail." I understood why writing it between "School" and "23" made them chuckle. Ruslan mimed for the other kids, shouting in fake pain behind the prison bars of his fingers as they howled with laughter.

Fourteen-year-olds there were like fourteen-year-olds anywhere: by turns giggly, inattentive, spastic, curious, and sullen. The girls were in some ways more mature than girls their age in the United States, probably because getting married young is normal (twenty-four is considered too late). They must have felt pressure to act poised and ladylike. Or maybe they only seemed polite and well-behaved compared to the boys.

Teenage boys anywhere are prone to bullying and roughness, but in Ukraine machismo, posturing, and dominance were much more intense. Life is hard, and so boys harden each other, often cruelly. Younger boys tolerated each other's quirks, but a viciousness sprouted up after puberty, whose inequitable effects were plainly evident in my class: one boy was over 180 pounds, another barely 80. The pecking order was clear, and unless the smaller ones got attention by clowning or being measurably cleverer than the others, they kept silent. One boy, Maxim, I could barely hear when he talked: he kept his head down, though meekness wouldn't take him far in a Ukrainian public school.

My ninth graders much preferred writing to speaking, and jumped at the chance to copy from the board or take a dictation. They wanted clear orders that were easy to follow. I refused, telling them "Parrot English" did them no good. But in their educational system, rote memory and oral performances were the chief instruments of teaching in all subjects, and they had always been taught through imitation and copying. Students who could glibly recite facts and texts and linguistic rules succeeded easily; individual, creative thinking was little rewarded in school or elsewhere. It took a long time for my students to decipher that what *I* wanted was for them to say what *they* wanted—to make up their own sentences. Instead they repeated each other's words and copied from each other's notebooks.

Traditionally, the brightest pupils in Ukrainian schools were expected to "carry" the weaker. Those who learned more slowly were "helped"—that is, told the answers by whispered prompting—and supposedly the whole group improved. An appearance of widespread competence was created, but in reality, teachers held two sets of expectations: Those who excelled at memorization and recitation were labeled intelligent; those who didn't were dismissed as thick-headed. However, to prevent disgracing the group (or the teacher, who was chastised when students couldn't perform), low-skilled pupils always passed. On a grading scale of one to five, the best pupils received fives and almost everyone else fours. The poorest students, instead of flunking, were given threes (the lowest satisfactory mark). They advanced to the next grade level and were ordered to shape up. Therefore, a student in the Soviet system who played along obediently might learn little more than basic reading skills, yet receive a three in every subject all the way to graduation. Advancement was virtually guaranteed unless a student behaved badly, for which the rare failing mark of two was reserved. But twos were only for severe discipline problems, special cases. In fact, any grade other than five or four was unusual. The result, by ninth grade, was a few exceptional students and a majority who had learned that, by following the rules, they could skate by on mediocrity with the barest minimum energy. For some pupils, nine years of English lessons amounted to a long period of attendance.

One day I decided to assign 9B, my best group, an activity called a Chain Story. According to the official curriculum, the subjunctive mood was an appropriate subject for ninth graders in a specialized school. They were to form simple sentences using "If I were—, I would—" and then pass the story to the next pupil for continuation. We had drilled this grammar structure every day for two weeks in dialogues. I had taught successfully using chain stories like this one during our practice teaching over the summer and didn't see why it wouldn't work here.

I assigned the topic, "If I were rich." The first girl, Oksana, misused the grammar point targeted, but invented original sentences:

> "When I will were very rich, I going to buy a plane. And I going to fly with my friend to the Havayi. I will put on beautiful green dress and will go to the restorant with him. In the restorant will play quiet and slowly music and we will dance."

That, for my ninth graders, was super work. The next boy went on:

> "We will eat fried chicken and cabbage salad. We will drink wine and champagne. Later we will go to the park."

Those three sentences took him ten minutes and four consultations with Oksana on words he didn't know, even though "salad," "park," "champagne," and "wine" were cognates, identical to their Ukrainian equivalents. Then it was Andrey's turn. Soft-spoken, bright, the biggest boy in the class, Andrey was clearly the king of his age group. He wrote:

> "After, we buy chocolates. Twix, Bounty, Snickers, Picnic, Fruit and Nuts, Wispa. All night we go to the city and sing song. We go to the disco and dance to the morning."

That took ten minutes, too. Except for padding his paragraph with a list of chocolate bars he knew from hanging around kiosks, he had written almost nothing. The last boy concluded the story.

> "After, we sit in Mercedes and I take her home. We will go the beach and be very happy."

What began as an imaginative story about a trip to Hawaii wound up as a Ukrainian high-school kid's dream date.

When Oksana saw what had happened to her beautiful opening, she cursed the boys for their stupidity, folded her arms across her chest, and told them they were all fools. They mocked her whining, and uproar ensued. When I got everyone quieted down, they were angry with each other and with me for such a dumb activity. The week of exercises and oral practice on this point of grammar had apparently been for nothing. They couldn't use what they had learned (or really, hadn't learned) any more than they could use what they hadn't learned since first grade. Only Andrey left pleased, after spending most of the class touching up an elaborate drawing of the rear end of an elephant.

Those were my best pupils. I could see they were intelligent—some way above average—but either I wasn't teaching in the way they expected to learn or they weren't participating in the way I expected them to. By that age they were burnt out on a school game that guaranteed no rewards upon completion. They had grown old enough to envision the dull responsibilities they would soon have, so naturally they grasped for the last freedom of childhood. Andrey, for example, apologized for missing two days of class, saying: "Mr. John, two days I dig potatoes." I was so thrilled to hear him use that much genuine, unprompted English that I beamed. He knew it would get him off the hook.

Every Thursday I had four periods of ninth grade in a row. Usually my teaching got progressively worse over the course of the morning until I struggled through the last lesson like a drowning man. But on occasion my ninth-graders did good work for me. We roleplayed everyday interactions in a grocery store, an activity they liked, even if the dialogue never got much beyond: "Bread." "One?" "Yes." "OK, thank you!" "Goodbye!" From a book they could read Shakespeare out loud beautifully, yet they could not ask each other the time of day in English.

They wanted to understand English, if only to comprehend the words to popular music. Because they loved listening to and identifying song lyrics, on Fridays I taught them Beatles songs. They identified words they recognized, and I wrote them on the board until they had pieced together the whole song, which they could then copy into their notebooks.

The school of course could supply little in the way of materials—no copier, no ditto machine, not even an English typewriter. I searched my apartment for anything to write on: index cards, the backs of outdated Peace Corps memos. I hadn't realized paper would be hard to find and buy. If I'd known what to look for, I could have bought paper at the huge central department store, but for months I overlooked stacks of packages of drawing paper, labeled with the unfamiliar Russian word. I finally bought some colored construction paper, which was actually white paper inked red, green, or purple on one side only. Sometimes I used the back sides. For other activities I cut out photos from the few magazines I'd brought, or I colored my own pictures on scrap paper.

In Kiev, the Peace Corps library had marketing textbooks and a few pamphlets on subjects like how to raise chickens or dig wells, but no English-teaching materials. We were the first group of volunteers and we were on our own. I had brought an activity book for ESL teachers with me from home; before long, its edges grew tattered from heavy use. I often loaned it out to fellow teachers for a lesson or a vocabulary list. Most of the activities were on too high a level for my little kids, anyway. School 23 had textbooks which, although somewhat inaccurate and mostly discredited, were surprisingly useful now and then. Their main flaw (in addition to the hilarious stories like "Lenin in London") was that their material was also too difficult. The ninth-grade vocabulary and grammar for specialized English school pupils was way beyond my kids.

Once in a lesson with 9G I smelled something burning and looked over to see both of Serhiy's hands under the desk, he and Igor huddled together conspiratorially. From the sulfurous tang in the air, I knew he had lit a match. That crossed beyond bad classroom management into the realm of real danger. For a split second I imagined my legacy at School 23: "Oh, that American who let the kids burn down the school? Oh, yes, he had *so much* to teach us."

I completely lost my temper at Serhiy and ordered him out of the classroom. "What?" he boomed. "What! I haven't done anything!" Igor smirked.

"Now," I yelled. Sheepishly he followed me into the hall.

The ensuing tongue-lashing was a linguistic challenge—I had to chastise him in flabbergasted elementary Ukrainian because English was incomprehensible to him. I scolded, threatened, cajoled, and then reasoned with him until he nodded and swore he was sorry and would never do it again. I made him hand over the pack of matches. "Please forgive me, Mr. John," he finally begged, acting like a big puppy again. I felt better, having detected and punished his mischief. Maybe I had even overreacted when I lost my temper. He would serve as an example to the others, who must have quaked when I singled him out.

When we returned to the room, the mumbling voices hushed, and all eyes turned to Serhiy. Maybe they expected him to have a black eye. My fury had cooled until I caught his furtive wink to

Ruslan, who grinned back—a gesture the whole class saw as well. So much for making an example, and so much for discipline.

My third and fourth grade pupils cost me even more energy, more shouting, and more exasperated pleading than my adolescents. Some days there seemed to be fifty of them, not fifteen or ten. Punching, shoving, not listening, they sometimes jumped from their seats to run to the front of the room and ask me questions. My language skills were still a big part of the problem. I often reminded them firmly, "We won't sing the next song until you are quiet," but by the time I had formulated that sentence in Ukrainian, a pupil had asked a question and I got sidetracked answering. I felt like the circus performer who keeps plates spinning on top of canes: one lapse of attention and there might come a crash from an unwatched corner. When I crossed my arms, looked angry, and waited them out, they eventually saw that I was displeased and tried to quiet each other down. But then they all shushed each other so loudly, shouting, "Guys, be quiet! Be quiet!" that the noise was even louder than before.

Once, abandoning myself to desperation, I grabbed hanks of my hair with both hands and began to pull, as if trying to lift myself off the floor. In a mad voice I shrieked, "Soon Mr. John will fly out the window!" The two-story fall had tempted me many times; it was the perfect height to break my legs but not kill me. One little girl took me seriously, and cried to the others, "You guys! Soon Mr. John will fly out the window!" They quieted down, though a few giggled at the sight of me pulling my hair. One boy said, "Yeah, come on, Mr. John! Out the window!" It got my point across, anyway. They settled down for a few minutes before the chaos began again.

I would have lost hope completely if they had not been so darling. If the ninth graders were my hellions, these were my precious babies, frustratingly charming even while they misbehaved. They loved to sound out new words, sing songs, and invent English sentences. To them, every day was new and unconnected to any other. The fact that I would teach in that room the whole school year had not sunk in: one boy asked if he could write to me in the United States. He meant right that minute.

My status extended after class, too, when other kids ran up to ask questions and then scampered away before I answered. They covered their mouths, pointed, and giggled when they saw me in the hall. My walk through the halls of School 23 was a constant barrage of "Good morning! Good morning! Good morning!" Even at three in the afternoon, on their way home, pupils ran up to wish me good morning. Then I had the pleasure of answering back with a question—"Good morning?"—looking at my watch in surprise. The little ones looked stunned, as if they'd insulted me by forgetting the time of day. They usually said, "Oh—!" and ran off. The older ones managed to respond "Good evening" or "Good day," or gave up and greeted me politely in Ukrainian or Russian. Others shouted "Hello," which to them felt deliciously irreverent since I was an elder figure of respect; in their language, formal address was required. I always answered "Hello" in return. It was weird and enjoyable to be greeted everywhere I went.

Except for John Maddox, there was no one in Zhitomir with whom to speak "normal" English. Communication was problematic. Accustomed to British pronunciation, many teachers barely understood my American accent; many of the idioms and phrases they knew had either gone out of style around World War II or had never even existed outside of Soviet textbooks. I longed to make friends, but still did not know for certain whether I would be accepted into the school's staff.

Most of the English teachers were like Svetlana Adamovna—sweet and motherly. We could be friends of sorts, but the pampering did not help. The only men teaching at School 23 were the music teacher, the burly gym teacher, the bald physics teacher who smelled of vodka and cigarettes, and a stately professorial man named Nestor Timofeyivich who taught

Ukrainian literature. I liked and even admired them, but we spoke only Ukrainian together. Hence, when socializing at school it was natural that I would turn to the "Younger Department," as the more experienced teachers jokingly referred to my friends sometimes. Unaware at first of the sideways glances the older teachers gave each other, I sought out Tanya, Marina, and Oksana. They were polite, but shy. Not only my status as a foreigner but as a young man—all three were married—made me wonder if we could ever really be friends. I was lonely; I had to try.

Students and teachers changed rooms during the breaks between classes, most of which were ten minutes long. On the "long break," a twenty-minute recess, children ran around the asphalt playground outside while teachers attended to minor duties, stopped for a cup of tea, and caught their breath. Munching homemade cookies, they always chatted in their own language—the one *I* needed a break from. I began to visit Tanya's classroom during that break, after she invited me to help her practice speaking English.

"I'm short-sighted," she told me one day, "so I must wear these spectacles if I am to see anything." When I laughed and asked if she meant near-sighted, she gasped in embarrassment. "John, you must always correct my English. I want to improve so badly; please tell me when I make a mistake." I complimented her fluency: Honestly, she communicated more fearlessly and proficiently than most of the other teachers. Then I added that the word "eyeglasses" or just "glasses" was more commonly used than "spectacles," at least in the United States.

"You see?" she said. "I am unsure of so much I've learned. Maybe this is the British variant." I agreed that perhaps it was so.

Tanya was forthright and curious, and she asked thoughtful questions: "What about Jews in your country? What about blacks? We were told that in America you have—how is it called... prejudice?" How could I summarize the history of racism in our country in such a few minutes? I started to describe the civil rights movement, but already a girl had returned from recess and was tugging on Tanya's sleeve.

"We never have enough time to talk," Tanya said.

"Maybe we could spend some time after school. You know, just chatting." Part of the Peace Corps project plan included practicing English informally with teachers, so after-school talks would be part of my "mission." My real motive was stronger: I longed for company and interesting conversation in English.

When she suggested that we go with Marina and Oksana to a cafe to drink coffee, I told her I wanted to see the Bashnya. Wandering about Zhitomir I had noticed an old brick building shaped like a tower whose sign read Cafe Jubilee. It was referred to as the Bashnya, or Tower, because it resembled a medieval keep. As one of the few pre-Revolutionary structures in Zhitomir, the building and its dramatic shape intrigued me. I had been told that it was originally a tower used to watch for forest fires in the surrounding countryside; later it had served as a water tower. Now it was a cafe overlooking the river.

"Well, there are usually a lot of bad guys there," Tanya said. Cafes were expensive and seedy, with thugs and punks their primary customers. Because a beer garden stood outside this cafe, it was particularly well-attended by belligerent drunks, and by no means a place for young women—especially schoolteachers—to be seen, although this didn't occur to me then. The building looked cool, and I wanted to go inside.

"I will arrange everything," Tanya finally agreed.

On the appointed day, she met me after school, and we walked to the Bashnya, a few blocks away. As usual, Tanya asked questions about the United States and was genuinely interested in the answers; certainly I didn't mind talking about a place I missed so much. The Peace Corps orientation had listed the volunteer's knowledge of America as important; I hadn't believed it then, but now began to see why. Her questions forced me to clarify and define what I knew of my country; it was so hard to answer without misleading.

We passed the county government building and a monument of a thick-shouldered, bald man holding a sputnik in his palm. Then we entered a little park, where the concrete slabs of sidewalk tilted erratically, and grass pushed up between them unchecked. Tanya pointed out the city's main library, on whose wall hung a huge hammer-and-sickle, its red paint chipped and fading. I wanted to ask her about it, but just then we came upon Oksana and Marina, sitting on a park bench, waiting and smoking. Oksana nervously asked Tanya in Russian, "You don't suppose the principal will see us smoking here, do you?"

Marina laughed bitterly, "And you think she doesn't know?"

Marina was one of the young teachers I had met during my initial visit in July. I hadn't imagined Ukrainian women like this: tall, long-legged, and gorgeous, with fine, angular features, severe cheekbone, taut jawline, and supple wrist. If she wore too much dark purple makeup on her eyelids, the haughty flash of her dark eyes made up for it. Her excellent English made her easy to talk to—and it turned out she lived in an apartment building on Shevchenko Street around the corner from my dormitory with her husband, Igor, and their five-year-old son.

Oksana had been in St. Petersburg when school began, so this was the first time I met her. She was twenty-three and had been a whiz at English at the Pedagogical Institute. Her pronunciation was flawless and she liked to throw in idioms and expressions she knew, like "it's the cat's meow." She almost never made mistakes, though she spoke more cautiously than Marina and Tanya. Oksana had a husband and young son as well.

In Russian, Tanya mumbled to Marina, "Did you bring.. . . ?"

"*Yeh*," she answered, a Ukrainian word which meant "I have it" or "there is" or "it's here"—the opposite of "*Ne ma*." I wondered what she had.

We went to the Tower and opened its massive, heavy door. Inside, it was too dark to see. "Up there," Tanya said, and I saw the rough, wooden spiral staircase. Light came in through a few greasy windows, and I went ahead and they followed. On the second floor a black metal gate was locked across the entrance to the cafe. But the stairs kept going, and up we went—past another locked cafe, then another. At the top floor of the tower, the metal gate was open, and we went in.

It looked like any old bar, except that the room was circular and the roof domed. The chairs looked like thrones, with six-foot high backs and arms wide enough to rest bear paws on. The heavy furniture was packed tightly in the room, but only one woman stood behind the bar smoking.

Tanya and Oksana were relieved to find it empty; it was early afternoon, after all. We sat down at a huge table and Tanya ordered snacks and one small shot of vodka for each of us. I looked out the narrow windows and was thrilled by the view. On one side I could see up to the waterfall—the small spillway of the Teterev River, and out the other I could see as far as my dormitory and beyond. The ugly high-rises weren't so horrible from above, and onion-shaped spires of a cathedral poked up on the horizon.

We toasted to long friendships and ate the small pieces of toast, each bearing one sardine and a scrap of parsley. Conversation about school predictably shifted to the topic of their miniscule salaries, and then, at Tanya's urging, was dropped for happier subjects. As the three chatted about aerobics classes, Marina peeked over her shoulder toward the bar woman. Gingerly she removed from her handbag a bottle of Russkaya vodka, a cheap state store brand. Under the table she removed the top and filled each glass one by one.

"No long toasts," she said. "To us."

"To us," we agreed, tossing back our drinks. "I hate long toasts," she added. The other two nodded agreement. Of course on special occasions, in sincere expressions of feeling, they were appropriate, Tanya said, and Oksana agreed with that as well. Tanya asked me if Americans formally toasted every drink.

"No, they don't," Marina answered for me. "In the West each person drinks when he wants and everyone takes care of himself.

Not like with us, *devuchki*." They called each other "girls," a term that came to include me.

"By the way," Marina added, "girls in the West—excuse me, John, but it's true—are not so beautiful." She described how they obviously didn't spend much time applying cosmetics or perfume, how they didn't fuss over their hair but looked like they just got out of bed and left it unkempt. Oksana, who wore makeup and had platinum-blond hair, pressed her for details.

"John," Tanya said, "Tell us about the women in your country. Do they wear makeup as a rule?" As usual, I hemmed and hawed: it depends, I said. Some women spent a lot of time before the mirror, others didn't. I said many people agreed with me that true beauty was on the inside and that surface appearances didn't always tell the truth. "You are being a diplomat," Tanya scolded. "You are too kind to say what you really think." Marina poured us another surreptitious drink and we toasted to women everywhere.

The ashtray filled with lipstick-smudged cigarette filters, and I mostly listened as they spilled forth whatever crossed their minds. Sometimes I asked a question, sometimes one of them made a joke. They became less nervous about speaking errors and I became less interested in correcting them. For once, it was wonderful not to have basic talk mutate into an English lesson.

Near dusk, we decided it was time to go home. At the bar I paid 37,000 kupons for what little food we had eaten and remembered being told that a teacher made less than that in a month. Marina departed to pick up her son at his daycare center. Tanya and Oksana didn't want to walk home unaccompanied, so we left together. As we walked, Tanya asked me if I knew any Ukrainian songs. Only one or two, I said, and sang the first few words of a folk song we learned in training. Oksana and Tanya laughed and joined in with me before I had finished singing the first line.

It was a silly song, called "You Deceived Me," and was good for learning the days of the week. It went:

> You told me that on Monday, we'd go pick periwinkles
> together...
> I showed up; you weren't there.
> You deceived me, let me down!
>
> You told me that on Tuesday, you'd kiss me forty times...
> I showed up; you weren't there.
> You deceived me, let me down!
>
> You told me that on Wednesday...

It was one song even the most Russified Ukrainian knew and also the kind of song to which people often added joke verses, sometimes slightly off-color ones.

When we finished that song, Tanya sang another, more melancholy one, and Oksana slipped into a kind of descant. They both sang beautifully, trading parts gracefully as they shifting from soprano to alto, then unison. Dusk had turned to darkness, and the streets were silent except for the rustling whirlwinds of dry leaves and Oksana and Tanya's voices. The songs sounded Slavic and sad, and I learned some of the words, as we strolled along, arm-in-arm. It felt strange and wonderful to sing song after song, while the soft lull of the vodka in my head, like a swaddling blanket, kept me warm. At one time, such a minor-key melody might have made me feel lonely. In that moment, it somehow had the opposite effect.

Eventually a very drunk man stumbled over and tried to join in. We leaned into the wind and kept moving, leaving him behind. He headed off in the other direction, singing the song Tanya and Oksana had been teaching me.

The next day in school, when the bell rang for the long recess, Svetlana Adamovna poked her head in my room to say, "You must come now." I followed her to the teacher's lounge, where several of the older teachers sat with plates of food spread before them. When I came in, one said, "John! Come here and sit down." A teacup was half-filled with wine from a decanter, and I realized they were about to have a toast.

In Russian, a teacher uttered several flowery sentences; I understood only "long life" and "years of happiness." We raised our cups and sipped sugary huckleberry wine, someone's homemade contribution to the spur-of-the-moment party. I asked the lively teacher who had made the toast what we were celebrating. "Tatyana Ivanovna has bought a new coat," she said slowly in English. Switching to Ukrainian, she explained the tradition of "christening" new purchases by wishing upon them durability and long years of use. Originally, farmers followed the custom when a pig or a new plow was added to the household, but now good luck could be wished on anyone with a new, expensive acquisition. The brief party was little more than the everyday gathering of teachers, with more to eat and an excuse for a nip to drink.

"Eat, eat," Tatyana Ivanovna said in Russian, laying a plate of four pieces of bread and *salo* in front of me. When I protested it was too much, she replied, "But you are the man, you can eat more." Also, she waved her teacup with a sly grin as if to say, Wouldn't want the children to sniff wine on your breath, would you? I gobbled up the bread and salo. It was hard to understand how we could christen a coat that Tatyana Ivanovna had left at home. But I wasn't about to ask: she was queen of the "old guard" of teachers. She and Svetlana Adamovna had each taught for thirty years at School 23; they were Honorary Methodologists who had both the principal's ear and everyone else's respect and deference.

Svetlana Adamovna sat down beside me and whispered in English, "Sooo. You've found a *snack bar*." Remembering John Maddox's comment about the fishbowl, I was startled that she already knew about my excursion to the Bashnya. But when she next said, "You don't have to go to Tatyana Georgivna's room during the break—we have tea and food right here next door to your room," I realized with relief she wasn't referring to yesterday's outing. She only meant to show that she knew I was having tea in Tanya's room, when she wanted me to stay and socialize with her group of friends. "You mustn't be late for your lessons," she added. It was true, I sometimes came back from Tanya's room right after the bell had rung. But the real source of this reminder was the mothering hand pulling me in closer to the old guard of teachers, who considered me "theirs."

This time, the controlling annoyed me. Marina, Tanya, Oksana, and I spoke only English in the breaks, but when I visited the older crowd, they ignored me and mostly complained to each other in Russian—not even Ukrainian, which I better understood. I felt angry at the thought of being steered toward the older, "respectable" clique—most of whose speech I couldn't understand—when the teachers of my own generation were practicing English, my purpose for being there in the first place.

Not everyone fit into the two cliques of the "old guard" and the "young disobedients." One teacher, Svetlana Alexandrovna, was young, but socialized mostly with the older teachers. To my great frustration, she repeatedly interrupted my lessons. She would enter my room, walk right in front of me to the bookshelves without so much as "hello" or "excuse me," and rummage through drawers and storage cabinets. I tried to ignore the intrusions, but the children suddenly sat at attention the moment she entered and then watched her remove large, dog-eared grammar tables demonstrating uses of "He, She, and It" or "Big, Bigger, Biggest." She walked out of the class without saying a word, leaving me silent but deeply irritated.

Later I learned that "my" classroom was in fact *hers*. After years of hard work, Svetlana Alexandrovna had earned the right to teach in that room, the best-equipped in the building. She had spent the summer before my arrival decorating it and hanging new wallpaper, all on her own time, with her own money. Now, my large wall map of the United States was taped over the top of one of the walls she had redone.

Unknowingly, I had even attempted to undo some of her work. On the back wall of the classroom hung a dozen or so large plywood cut-outs shaped like rabbits, elves, cuddly bears, and girls in peasant costume. They were painted with dull, drab colors in a gaudy, amateurish style that resembled the stylized, Soviet version of happy, chipper wildlife. My first day of class I decided they had to go. As soon as possible, I wanted to replace them with student work: charts, drawings, class exercises in English. I planned to set an example of positive reinforcement by displaying the work of individual students—a technique Ukrainian teachers never practiced.

But the day after I removed those cut-outs from their nails and stuffed them in a closet, my sad-faced pupils asked where they had gone. "Those?" I answered. "I don't like them." They looked glumly at the barren wall and at one another, but said nothing.

The walls stayed blank for about a week—I still had not been able to locate any paper—and for some reason I felt a little guilty, so I rehung the cut-outs, still planning to put them in storage once my classes had created their own displays. When the younger children entered the room and saw the characters and animals on the wall again, they cheered.

"Look! There's Bukvar! And Red-riding-hood! The Kozak and the Little Bear." For a few minutes, all they did was stare and point. "They're in different places," one boy marveled. I hadn't remembered which went where, and had indiscriminately hung them in no order. I began to realize they weren't merely decorations.

Svetlana Alexandrovna noted their return as well. "Yes," I said. "I still don't really like them, but the children seem to."

"Right," she answered in her proper British pronunciation. "They *like* them, *very* much. You see, they are from fairy tales, *right?* You can use them with your pupils. You tell them the *fairy* stories in *E*nglish, and they point to them, *right?* Don't they look b*yoo*tiful?"

At the beginning, my goal of being an exceptional teacher of English my very first year didn't seem unrealistic. But after a month, those arrogant hopes of proving to my school how wonderfully I could help them fizzled into a more modest desire: to get through each day without my pupils injuring each other, and without me hurting another teacher's feelings. I only hoped that some learning would occur between the many moments of chaos and bluster.

Chapter Six

Our Own Michael Jackson

A rooster crowed outside my window at 6:30 a.m., signaling me to get up and get ready for school. Some mornings, cold water came through the pipes, and I managed to stand in my shower of ice water for a few seconds, if not long enough to get clean. The promised hot water was long overdue and I became impatient. I foolishly counted electricity as one of my blessings until that quit as well. "You like camping," I reminded myself. "Now you can camp indefinitely, right here at home!" On the first night of buckling down to eat a cold dinner (my electric stove useless) and then to grade papers by candlelight, I kept up my positive attitude.

When the outage lasted for days, however, my attitude soured a bit, as did the food I had saved in my refrigerator. I fried and ate the meat people had given me before it went bad, but then I was back to crackers and bread and jam. The wind whipped around the corners outside my unlit, nine-story highrise, and some chilly air sneaked in through cracks between my windows. By a flickering candle I pored over my maps-of-the-world book, conjuring up the unwanted tropical heat in Thailand and Brazil and West Africa my fellow PCVs were wishing away. Some magical, good karma displacement ought to have allowed a cosmic transfer of heat to relieve all of us.

The few candles I had were gifts from friends, who claimed to have stockpiled them years ago, and I had no idea where to buy any more. So, with darkness inside and out, I climbed into bed with a sad shiver around seven-thirty in the evening. Dark evenings actually helped me to formulate lesson plans better: I went to sleep earlier and rose at six to write out detailed agendas for each class. The morning of the fourth day of the outage, the weather changed for the better, and the relatively warm spell bred in me fresh optimism. The sky was clear, the air cool, and the sweet, mulchy scent of walnut leaves fallen and decaying reminded me of home.

When I arrived at school one morning, a television crew was waiting for me. With no advance notice, I was to be filmed, interviewed, and put on display for the entire town. Worse, they had arrived just in time for 9G, the unruliest pupils in the school. Without my bringing up the subject, Galina Vasilievna, the vice principal for English, sent them to study in another group for the day. She asked, "What other groups do you teach?"

I suggested my eager, photogenic third graders. "*Da, da, da, da, da,*" she said, and summoned 3-D from a lesson in progress. For the program, we would need to perform visually exciting activities, lots of songs, and speaking. While the cameraman and producer fiddled with lights and equipment in the back of the classroom, I prepped the pupils to perform the entire repertoire of the words, sentences, and songs they already knew. As if by magic, they had transformed into serious, studious scholars, with deep concentration furrowed in their eight-year-old faces. The bright lights came on, and my pupils began to answer questions.

"What is your name?" I prompted, and began calling on them.

"My name is Natasha!"

"My name iz Sasha!"

"My name—Timur!"

They recited their ages, the names of colors, a few sentences about the animals they liked, and a few about their pets and family members. They delighted in performing for the camera, of course, and to my happy surprise, they mysteriously remembered far more than they did in an unobserved lesson. Each behaved like a model pupil, paying close attention, raising hands eagerly, even sitting straighter at their desks. I almost wished I could invite the TV crew to class every day.

After the cameramen left the classroom and the performance was over, we all relaxed, the kids at last releasing their energy through shouts and rowdy laughter. When Vova raised his hand again, I thought he wanted the game to continue, but he asked in Ukrainian, "What channel will we be on?" The Zhitomir Channel, I told him. Its low-power signal was broadcast from the small local station on Teatralna Street a block away. An argument began among Sasha and Vitaliy about whether that was Channel Two or Three.

Then Vova's face went bright with surprise. "Listen!" he shouted to his classmates. He had a fantastic idea. "Maybe we will be shown on CNN!"

The others burst out laughing. "What?" Sasha bellowed. "Are you stupid?" Natasha rolled her eyes, smacked her forehead, and groaned "Vovka!"

"It's possible," Vova protested, a little more quietly. "Because Mr. John is here."

After the lesson, the film crew asked me to pose with some of the other teachers and to speak English with them. It was a very self-conscious, awkward moment, far more false than my lesson, in which my pupils at least acted fairly natural, if slightly better than usual. One of the more experienced teachers made the phony conversation easier by joking with me: "You are like Michael Jackson here," she laughed. "You will be Tee Vee Star." I laughed, too, thinking that now I'd gotten my fifteen minutes of Ukrainian fame.

The story was shown on local TV in Zhitomir, although I didn't see it. My kids reported back with excitement that they'd seen themselves singing "Bingo." Later, the Kiev station, on the lookout for unusual news in the provinces, picked up the video of Mr. John's lesson and put it on the channel broadcast nationally. That meant my class was broadcast to an audience of about 50 million people. A business volunteer five hundred miles to the west on the border of Slovakia later told me she saw the whole segment. I really was a TV star, and to tease me about it Svetlana Adamovna started greeting me, "Good morning, Jackson!"

When I first arrived in Zhitomir, I had been nervous about being robbed; as one of only two Westerners living within a hundred square miles, I thought I would be seen as wealthy, and therefore a target. Now, though, my new status as a public figure virtually guaranteed my safety. When I walked home from school, for example, pupils I didn't even know would shout across the street in English, "Hello, Mr. John!" Passersby stopped to stare, while I waved meekly. People I had never met greeted me in Russian as I walked down the street or rode home on the trolleybus. Sleepy little Zhitomir, my village of three hundred thousand people. Tanya told me, "When someone sneezes at the bus station on the eastern edge of town, someone in Bogunia, the farthest region west, will say 'Bless You.'"

The television interview was followed by visits from reporters from three local newspapers. Their stories were mostly congratulatory, with my reasons for coming to Zhitomir generally vague and clouded. Perhaps I had not explained Peace Corps clearly; perhaps they simply hadn't believed me.

One reporter made me part of a series, called "The Seven Wonders of Zhitomir." I was "Wonder Number Three—a Teacher from Ohio":

> It's possible, if quite unusual, that American John Deever has become a teacher of English at Zhitomir School No. 23. His pupils absolutely "adore" him. 25-year-old John mastered Ukrainian (!) language (in 2 months' study in

Kiev), and English—even more so. Truthfully, his
Russian is not so good . . .

In the same slangy style, the story described me and the Peace
Corps, then concluded:

> It's funny: these Americans have arrived in our present-day Ukraine. To teach us how to live? Or to test how the organism of an "American Boy" adapts to extreme conditions? John could tell us a lot. For example, how he's begun learning to prepare Ukrainian borsch, or how he really likes our Ukrainian boiled sausage (!) ("Very tasty!"—remarked John). Or maybe how he discovered a ten-move checkmate combination waiting in the bread line in the central grocery store ("The line doesn't begin on this side!!!"). . . . John lives in our Soviet regimented dorm, and believes that he needs school like we all do. And he's homesick. Meanwhile, we're homesick for the time of "American abundance" during the [Brezhnev period of] stagnation when sausage was two rubles. Let's be homesick together!

Tanya and Oksana found this portrayal of me hilarious, and then teased me with the writer's slang phrases, especially the part about how the children "adored" me.

The school was soon flooded by parents begging my vice principal to grant permission for me to tutor their children privately. Strangers knocked at my dorm room door, sometimes late in the evening to ask if I would help them, or sometimes just to see my face. A dentist, whose office was in another part of the building, visited me after eleven one night to ask if I could help him send his daughter to study in the United States. Another time a man knocked, asked to borrow some salt, and then, once in my apartment, admitted, "Actually, I don't really need any salt. I'm staying in the room across the hall and wondered if you would like to come over, have a sip or two with us, and get acquainted."

Being recognized and known made me feel more like a resident, if only a temporary one. Zhitomir had become my home, more so than I realized. I didn't recognize how much I was changing until I had contact with other Americans.

It was a typical school day when I heard that the missionaries were coming. I was drinking tea in Tanya's room during the long break. Tanya, Marina, Luda, Oksana, and I were munching cookies and talking when Larisa Mikhailivna entered the room. Because she was a distinguished member of the older, "loyal" cadre of teachers, everyone's spines, including mine, instinctively stiffened. Larisa Mikhailivna asked sweetly in English, "Tanichka, will you be so kind as to do us a favor?" A delegation of Church of Christ missionaries from Virginia and Texas would soon visit School 23, she explained. Our principal, Nina Volodimirivna was happy to welcome foreign guests, and considered it a chance for pupils and teachers alike to practice their English. Larisa Mikhailivna then reached her point: Would my friends work as translators? Tanya immediately protested. It would take too much time, she didn't want to—and why us, after all? Larisa Mikhailivna made it clear that she was not actually asking a favor but assigning a school-related duty.

Thus, that same week I met Pastor Tommy, a tall, middle-aged gentlemen with a deep, slow drawl. Eight or ten church members accompanied him. In me, they found an American able to understand their frustration with packed trolleybuses, the lack of electricity and running water in their hotel, and the lack of variety of food: soup, bread, and potatoes at every meal. On my part, I suppose I enjoyed the chance to speak English, and (I admit) to show off my ability to live in a difficult place which they would only visit. I helped them make international phone calls from the local telephone office and shared what I knew about my adopted school, city, and country, trying my best not to express arrogance or disdain. I suggested that if they wanted to help people, gifts of medicine and medical supplies were a good place to start.

My welcoming attitude wore thin quickly, however, and not just out of jealousy, when my pupils spoke so excitedly about "guests from America." They asked if I had known the missionaries back in the United States. It soon became clear that, in lieu of regular English lessons, the missionaries would have the floor for a day, in which they would use our classes to preach the gospel. My own class was no exception. After describing a life committed to Jesus Christ, they praised a system that didn't forbid mixing church and state. "You are ahead of us, in this respect," they told my teacher friends and my students. I gritted my teeth, and encouraged the kids to note unusual vocabulary. My worries about the missionaries' influence on my kids subsided when I perceived how poorly their southern accents were understood. The youngest children, far from comprehending the religious message, were content to whisper in delight about a man named Albert's ten-gallon Stetson.

My patience was truly put to the test after class. In the hall outside my room, the missionaries gave a few kids chewing gum, candy, and pens. Like seagulls alerting each other with greedy cries, the schoolchildren swarmed and surrounded them. Screaming for handouts, the children pressed so close that the missionaries had to hold their gum and candy up over their heads, out of reach. It was an ugly sight. The kids, not knowing it was another way to sneak in scripture, thought it was a game; they jumped and tried to reach for the gum. Mobbed by kids, the missionaries laughed nervously and gave away everything as fast as they could. "Not shy, are they?" Albert bellowed at me, laughing. Our "guests from America" meant well, but in the crassest way I could imagine they verified every stereotype of Americans that I had hoped to counteract—and unfortunately the kids loved the whole experience.

More distasteful still, I found out that Tanya and Marina had been persuaded to be baptized. In the evenings, Pastor Tommy conducted immersion baptism ceremonies for the public in a rented hall, formerly a Komsomol club for teens to hold dances and drama performances. When I heard about the baptisms, I guessed that too few audience members had felt the call to come up and be saved. My friends, their translators, graciously volunteered. Marina thought it might help her turn over a new leaf in her life; Tanya said she wanted to recommit to a faith from which she felt separated. She figured the sacred ceremony wouldn't hurt.

Later, however, they realized what this meant. They were now "members" of a newly established church in Zhitomir. The missionaries talked of "building a church community," although in actuality they had no plans for now to begin any physical construction. For the moment, the church would meet in the tiny apartments of those who were baptized, and Pastor Tommy promised to return every six months to check on their progress in Christian growth. After Zhitomir's "church" grew and developed, the evangelical process could spread. At one point I asked Pastor Tommy why he chose Zhitomir. "Kiev is overflowing," he said. "We just looked on the map and chose the first large town to the west."

Being Ukrainian, that town showed them hospitality beyond its means. I wondered if the missionaries realized who had sacrificed more. Ukrainians had traded their time, energy, and home-grown, home-prepared food for an acquaintance with foreigners who had come to lecture.

Unlike others I met later, those particular missionaries were at least kind, gracious, and sincere—if a bit naive. They didn't proselytize excessively, they wanted to learn about the culture, and they had the potential to give something substantial to my community. I had weird, contradictory feelings. It seemed arrogant to proclaim that the development efforts of others, such as they were, were misdirected. In any case, rejecting missionaries altogether would prove futile and impossible. Evangelists of all kinds were descending on Ukraine like hyenas to a fresh kill.

That week the local newspaper *Evening Zhitomir* announced a discovery: our missionaries were "Mormons." In a hysterical tone, the article implied that Zhitomir's children were in danger.

"But why Mormons?" I asked Tanya. "People think Mormons are a cult," she said, "like the White Brotherhood." Throughout that spring and summer, a woman who called herself Maria Devi Khrystos led an apocalyptic cult in Kiev called the White Brotherhood. Cult members proclaimed her the Messiah, and predicted the end of the world on November 24 of that year when, as rumor had it, they would enact Jonestown-style mass suicide. Posters of her adorned every subway stop in Kiev, and the media spent inordinate amounts of time describing the cult members' public activities. Children were hypnotized so deeply, said Ukrainian television news, that even after returning home they remained in trances. For many Ukrainians, foreign religious fanaticism seemed like one more fearsome problem they never had in the old days.

Thus, our local paper lumped the White Brotherhood, the followers of David Koresh, the Mormon Church, and School 23's missionaries all together in the same paragraph. The story suggested that perhaps Ukrainian children were unsafe even at school and that our English lessons had been "used" as a platform for conversion.

All this I found disturbing enough, until I saw my own name in the article and became even more alarmed. At first, it struck me funny: I was quoted *in Russian*. I did not even know most of the words I read in print until Tanya translated. According to the story, "When Mr. John saw the group, he ran to the director of School 23 to say: 'Nina Volodimirivna! Beware! Send them away quickly! This is a very terrible sect!'"

Tanya assured me not to worry. "Everyone knows people buy this rag only for the TV program," she said.

"But this is no error," I protested. "The reporter invented these facts, and then added quotes from me!"

"It doesn't mean anything," she said, adding with a smile, "in fact, you will appear as a great protector of Zhitomir."

I was no rescuer, no expert on American religion shielding School 23 from fanatics. I had to set the record straight, despite my ambivalent feelings about the missionaries. Otherwise, I told Tanya, who could know what statements might be attributed to Mr. John in the future? I was determined to write a letter to the editor of *Evening Zhitomir*.

My letter began pleasantly, expressing flattery at all the positive attention I had received, but I then insisted that the Church of Christ missionaries were not Mormons. Anyway, I wrote, Mormonism (no longer promoting polygamy, as many Ukrainians thought) was not an errant, manipulative cult, but a rather mainstream religion in much of the United States. I did not resist throwing in a quick reminder about irresponsible journalism's dangerous potential. To conclude, I thanked the paper for letting me express my views. By the standards of Western press at least, I felt safe that my letter was excessively polite.

Evening Zhitomir, however, was not in the habit of printing critical letters. Had I considered more carefully the bees' nest such a letter might stir up, I would have let well enough alone. The principal, Nina Volodimirivna, strongly discouraged me from raising the issue at all, but when I insisted, she shrugged and told me I would therefore have to meet with the editorial board of the paper and the provincial minister of journalism.

After school the next week, my vice principal, Galina Vasilievna, my teacher friend Luda (who had translated my letter), and I walked the two blocks from School 23 to the newspaper office. We met two men, neither of whom—I was relieved to learn—was the provincial minister of journalism. One was the paper's editor, a balding man in his fifties in a Soviet-looking suit with a tie. The other man was the writer of the story—not the reporter who had once interviewed me, but someone I had never seen.

After some polite conversation, we submitted my letter in person, and the publisher read it.

"This is all well and good," he said quietly. "But we stand by our story. We know from other sources that these missionaries were Mormons."

For Galina Vasilievna, that settled it: Why confront another official person over such a trivial issue? Luda translated for me the short discussion, and I gathered that the editor was mainly giving Galina Vasilievna his reassurances that School 23 would not be made to look foolish for accepting the missionaries. This made her happy, and she stood up to go, with a look to me that said unequivocally, "We are done here." The reporter remained in his corner chair, smug and silent, watching us as we walked out.

A follow-up story a week or so later discussed cults and the spiritual quagmire of the country in general and disparaged citizens who unquestioningly embraced the newly arrived faiths—Jehovah's Witnesses, Baptists, and of course Mormonism. In a country unaccustomed to religious freedom, the multitude and diversity of American denominations was baffling. In the confusion of sorting out Catholic from Protestant, Presbyterian from Pentecostal, some people were unsure if these groups were under the umbrella of Christianity at all. No wonder: before long a different denomination was renting out the town theater every week. Some groups held revivals, some baptisms, some lectures, and one staged an elaborate puppet show of the Gospel of Matthew in our school auditorium. Afterwards, always Bible studies, Bible studies, Bible studies, each group handing out free Bibles by the crateload, each group unaware of the folks who had handed out Bibles the week before. Ukrainians quit accepting them eventually—even the speculators who had taken free Bibles to sell in rural areas. Except for cigarettes and vodka, Bibles were the only item never in shortage anywhere in Ukraine.

Evening Zhitomir got the last word. Without printing or quoting my letter, the reporter answered one of my complaints: that the missionaries were not Mormons. "Excuse us, Mr. John, but you are wrong," the paper wrote. "They *were* Mormons, and it's possible that you didn't possess all the facts to which we at *Evening Zhitomir* have access." Sick of the whole business, I let it slide. My brief crusade for a more responsible press ended, and I could see that my colleagues at school were very happy about that.

Watching the missionaries had taught me another, more important lesson. I got the chance to see what Ukrainians really thought of our country.

"Americans," Marina told me, "eat bread and sweet jam *with* their soup instead of after! That's disgusting!" Tanya agreed and wondered at American speech. "They talk so loudly, rather incautiously, I might say. They are always casually familiar, except when you ask a question about their salaries or the price of their clothes. Are these secrets?"

I had noticed more often that the missionaries frequently ridiculed Ukraine's economic backwardness and "lack of culture." They complained of the corruption, the poverty, and fact that their hotel had no electricity and bad food. They were glad they had brought peanut butter with them. While I might have shared some of these sentiments, to hear them make these comments made me feel defensive. I wanted to somehow express my newfound appreciation for a life less wrapped up in selfish worries than our own. I wanted to say, "Don't you see that, despite its economic troubles, this country's people deeply value camaraderie and mutual support, simple living and the power to overcome hardships—exactly the values so many Americans feel they are missing?" But I knew that Ukrainians themselves would really not understand such a formulation in the way that I meant it. They longed to indulge themselves in our type of outrage and frustration—about power outages or poor meals, for instance. For them, such minor inconveniences were the least of problems. Such difficulties were no less annoying than for us, but were too common to get angry about.

My Ukrainian friends also resented the implication that just because the United States possesses economic superiority, this implied other kinds of superiority as well. It was funny for me when they groaned "Americans!" in a tone one would use for silly, harmlessly unruly children. "Maybe," I told Tanya, "this attitude comes from being missionaries, not from being Americans."

Tanya laughed. "Don't worry. Of course we weren't speaking of you! You're different." Smiling slyly, she added, "You're *our* American."

I *felt* like I was different, too. I felt more at home with them than the missionaries, even when I struggled to comprehend the conversation after it switched from Ukrainian to Russian. My language skills were improving, though, and my comfort level increasing equally. The more I learned, the more I changed, appreciating the strengths and talents of the people I knew. Silently, gradually, the adjustment process sealed shut my first fears. I was settling in. The word "America" was transforming into an abstract concept, a word, an idea, instead of the place that had always been my home.

Chapter Seven

Secondary Project: "Where Is Pinky?"

One evening, when John Maddox was visiting me, there was a knock at the door.
"Whoever that is," John said, "I bet they have apples."
When I opened the door, I saw my neighbor from across the hall (another Tanya) and a well-dressed, dark-haired woman I didn't know. She held a plastic bag of apples.
"Good afternoon!" she beamed in smarmy Russian. "It's so pleasant to meet you!" Her perfume stifled me as she leaned towards my face and spoke loudly. My neighbor Tanya said in Ukrainian, "This is Larisa Petrovna from the Teacher Recertification Institute. She works with me there." I hadn't known that my neighbor was a teacher, too. Tanya walked back across the hall to her apartment, saying, "I'll be here if you need me."
The other woman came in and handed me the bag of apples. "This is a present for you! Something sweet!" I handed them to John. We both had piles of yellowish apples going soft and spilling out of our cupboards. Thanks to rain at the right time, a bumper crop had flooded the market and they were sold cheaply. I introduced her to John and asked how I could help her. If I sounded ungrateful, it was because the steady stream of unexpected visitors on dubious errands irritated me. I wanted to relax with John and not be bothered with guests, especially those

with pretenses to already knowing me and with presents that I guessed would be cashed in on eventually in the form of some requested favor.

"John, I won't take much of your time, I see you are busy. Oh, your apartment looks wonderful!" she said, craning her neck toward my bed. "You are sleeping all right?"

"Yes, fine, everything is very fine." I spoke Ukrainian, hoping she would switch from Russian so I could understand her better.

"And you are warm enough? I see you have sealed up your windows."

"Yes, well, the Komandant did it."

"Komandant?" she laughed, as if the word were wrong. "Well, good. And you are finding enough to eat?" John maintained his poker face; he wasn't going to help me one bit.

"Now that I have these apples," I said, "everything will be much better."

Her eyes turned quizzical, but she continued to grin, as if smiling through a slight headache. "Good, good," she said. "John, I want to ask you a favor. If you have the time—I know you are very busy—but if you could, please come to the Teacher Recertification Institute. If you could give a lecture to English teachers about your country, about its schools, your life, and so on, it would be excellent for us."

"In English?" I asked. Secondary activities like this were welcome, actually, and meeting Ukrainian teachers outside my school and practicing English with them was one of my objectives.

"Certainly in English!" she said, as if it were a silly question, so I agreed. She promised to visit me at School 23 to arrange exact dates and times. "The institute is on Mikhailivska Street, right around the corner from your school. I'll come by next week." I wondered why she hadn't done so in the first place instead of coming to my home. She thanked me abruptly, said she could let herself out, and left.

Later, to my embarrassment, I found out that Larisa Petrovna was, in some sense, my landlady because she chaired the Department of Foreign Languages at the Provincial Recertification Institute, the owner of my section of the dormitory. She had arranged for me to live there free for two years as a favor to School 23, which was unable to provide me with housing. (Both of my neighbors were education professors, but when they appeared in our common hallway wearing housecoats and slippers to chat or to hang up laundry to dry, they hadn't *looked* like professors.) Larisa Petrovna was also long-time friends with all the senior teachers at my school, kept meticulous track of my whereabouts, and even came to consider herself a member of my cadre of mothers. But the first time I met her, I thought she was just one more intruder.

Thus, before I even knew how to conduct my own lessons well, I took on extra work. With my newfound celebrity came many requests, and at first I tried to accept them all.

Sometimes I taught extra lessons at my school. When the tenth grade history class was studying the American Revolution, for example, I agreed to teach a lesson on the subject. It turned out to be for all the tenth graders in the school—over a hundred students. So we held my "special lecture" in the school auditorium. I spoke slow English, careful to avoid vocabulary they wouldn't know, and gave an overview of the causes and main events of the revolution. The pupils yawned and whispered to each other, pointing at me, but showed mild interest in the few pictures I shared. I asked if they had questions, and several hands went up. "Do you like our Ukrainian borshch?" a boy asked. "What do you eat at home?" "Are you married?"

I also met with the students and faculty of the Pedagogical Institute (or Teacher Training College), the complex of buildings near my dormitory where students from all over the Zhitomir province came to become teachers. There I taught students in the Foreign Languages Department, whose high standards and rigorous course of study made it difficult to join. Ninety percent of its future teachers of foreign languages sought degrees that would get them jobs translating German or English with Western companies, the best-paying work around.

In addition to my regular and extra lessons at School 23, I found time to meet student groups, consult faculty, give lectures, and make audio recordings in English for the colleges in my town. Staying as busy as possible, I figured, would help me preserve my sanity. One of the first jobs I did proved it was already slipping.

One day after school I was about to go home when Galina Vasilievna, the vice principal, stopped me and insisted that I eat in the cafeteria. I rarely had meals there because by noon I'd had my fill of screaming children for the day. Pupils raced between tables, bigger ones crashing into little ones and knocking them down, everywhere glasses tipping over and food spilling on the floor—the opposite of the strict discipline observed in classrooms. A few teachers and cafeteria workers wandered around, idly attending to their own business while the kids ran amuck. The older pupils on duty—that day eighth graders—were responsible for cleaning up. They followed after the little kids, wiping up puddles of tea and globs of porridge with tired resignation. I went past them to the lunch counter where the head cook smiled and set up my tray: a huge bowl of watery potato soup, four slices of bread, and a plate of boiled cabbage. She wouldn't let me pay for my meal. I explained that I wanted to pay like any other teacher, but she pushed the miniscule sum back over the counter again and again until I relented.

Ivan Wilhelmovich, the physics teacher, waved at me to come over to his table. I set down my tray and, still grumbling over not being allowed to pay for lunch, protested to him that I expected to behave like any normal Ukrainian teacher, and to be treated so. "Why shouldn't you?" he agreed. "You are a normal man." Then he crooked a beckoning finger and whispered to me, "Would you like fifty before you eat?" He pinched his fingers together to indicate a very small sip of vodka. My school day was over, and

I had nothing else to do. Ivan Wilhelmovich's sweet smile convinced me to accept.

He took me to a closet-sized room scattered with physics books and student math papers. On the wall several clocks showed different times, and beneath them hung a tangled mechanism that rang the school bell. From behind a cabinet he pulled out a bottle of clear liquid and told me to trust him that it wasn't *samagon*—homemade moonshine. He poured two very tall shots, no fifty-gram shotglass full but juice glasses of more like a hundred and fifty. We clinked glasses and tossed the liquid back; I nearly gagged getting it down although I had far too much practice in such customs already and could gulp large shots along with Ukrainians. He bummed a cigarette and told me his day wasn't over—he had duties in the afternoon: supervising boys who raked leaves around the schoolyard. As he spoke, I marveled at the mess of wires and trip-hammers of the bell mechanism, all covered in dust. No wonder that wreckage so often failed to ring. On the days Ivan Wilhelmovich was tinkering in his cabinet with the broken bell system, a boy on duty was sent through the halls ringing a handbell.

On our return to the cafeteria, Galina Vasilievna sniffed, frowned slightly, and insisted vehemently that I eat. The potato soup was tasty, and I dug in. Small children stared and whispered. They had never seen me eat; perhaps it hadn't occurred to them that I ever did. They looked like they expected me to bite them.

A well-dressed woman with thick glasses entered the cafeteria, and Galina Vasilievna rose to meet her. "This woman wants to meet with you," she told me. I stood (breathing gently, away from her) and shook hands with Ludmila, a professor of English from the Pedagogical Institute and a parent of a student at our school. She asked if I would be free to record some tapes for her. I said of course, I'd be happy to. "I'll just wait for you to finish eating," she said.

"You mean now?"

"If you're not busy—that is, if you don't have somewhere else to be?"

Galina Vasilievna chimed in with her unsubtle hint: "*Do you have somewhere else to be?*" I didn't—except maybe home in bed. I finished eating and walked with Ludmila to the institute to record a lecture for her class, wondering the whole time if that soft, fuzzy hum in my head would show up on the tape.

The jumble of machinery in the institute's Audiolinguistics Room made Ivan Wilhelmovich's study look shabby in comparison. Here were ancient-looking, reel-to-reel tape machines, a huge panel of control knobs labeled incomprehensibly. Square cardboard boxes of reels stacked on a table bore labels in English: "Dickens—Hard Times," "Dreiser—Sister Carrie," and of course, "Reed—Ten Days That Shook the World." Ludmila showed me how to start recording the tape, handed me the microphone and an open book, and sat back to watch.

"May I take a moment to skim over it?" I asked. Sight-reading would provoke many errors, especially given my newly impaired ability to speak clearly.

"Of course, of course!"

The English texts she wanted me to read were full of the same archaic British stuffiness everyone thought was proper English. I said I hoped she didn't mind if I spoke naturally, with my own pronunciation. That was fine, she said, so I clicked on the mike and began. Reading the first text made me giggle. It was about a first-time teacher named Mrs. Lucy whose students wouldn't listen. The second was a very silly dialogue about a dentist pulling out all of an old man's teeth and the man loving it. Although I enunciated brightly, reading the dialogue in a lively, humorous tone of voice, it sounded just plain goofy. A corny story became all the sillier in my tipsy lilt. But Ludmila sat nearby and appeared not to notice the words I slurred. She didn't mind if I went rather slow, she said—in fact, perhaps a bit slower?

Finally I came to a text about touring London. Told in my

blurred Midwestern accent, it must have been ridiculous. As I read it aloud, it occurred to me I was really describing a Soviet city. The text noted London's many beautiful parks and monuments. London was home to many "centres of parliamentary and economic activity." And at Speaker's Corner in Hyde Park, men gave speeches on worker rights or the importance of international peace. The lack of details made it obvious the text's author had never left the Soviet Union, notwithstanding a fact or two about red double-decker buses and tidal flooding. Like every text my ninth-graders had memorized about Zhitomir or Kiev, it incessantly praised "interesting museums."

After over an hour of speaking (and that after a full day of teaching), my voice became hoarse and we agreed it was time to quit. Ludmila wanted to know what I thought might be a fair price for recording the tapes. I laughed and told her I wasn't allowed to take money, and that it was no trouble anyway. She asked if I wanted her to sign some documents proving I had been there. Had I brought any special papers? I laughed again at the thought. Then a passing paranoid thought struck me: Could the tape be used against me somehow? I laughed again and told her no, an hour or two was a meager contribution, and I'd be happy to help anytime. Remembering Peace Corps's encouragement to develop secondary projects, I told her, "It's why I came here." In retrospect, such an implausible-sounding statement probably convinced her I was really working for the CIA. I hope her students understood my recording; I know any native speaker sitting in the class would have laughed out loud to hear it.

She walked part of the way with me back toward my dormitory. The conversation went smoothly: she understood everything I said and answered rapidly and fluently. She told me that the August 1991 coup attempt against Gorbachev happened right before she was scheduled to take a government-sanctioned trip to London with a group of professors. ("*Shed*-yooled," she said.) That visit would have been the culmination of her life's work.

Visiting a country where English was spoken had been her dream since she began studying as a child. Thanks to a political climate in flux, her trip was cancelled. "Now I will never go," she said, bleak resignation in her voice. "Though the borders are now opened, I will never make enough money." Incredibly, professors at the institute made *less* each month than public school teachers. Their salaries were paid out of the national budget, while teachers were paid from city funds. Like most people, her tiny wage often wasn't paid at all, and some workers were owed back salary for more than nine months. Others were occasionally paid off in goods. One factory worker whom I knew received six fifty-pound sacks of sugar in lieu of his month's wages. When he responded, "What am I to do with all this sugar?" his manager said, "If you want your money, go stand in the bazaar and sell it." Ludmila and her colleagues continued teaching at the Institute for literally nothing but empty reassurances.

I encouraged her to be optimistic. Many chances existed for professionals to travel: exchange programs, faculty semesters abroad, study grants. She told me, however, she did not expect it. "I will not see this country improve in my lifetime, nor in my children's lifetime," she said. "Maybe my grandchildren's lives will be better."

I kept thinking about what she said long after I returned home. It occurred to me how much she valued her command of English as a source of self-esteem, status, and prestige. Whether that reaction was justified or not, it reminded me that I wasn't merely teaching a language. Part of what I did by meeting, talking, and especially listening to people was a different kind of helping. They wanted to verify that they were now members of a world community from which they had been both sheltered and excluded in the past. English connected them with that community and demonstrated their ability to be a part of it. I promised myself to try to take my work more seriously.

The teacher training seminars, which Larisa Petrovna had asked me to give, took on greater meaning for me. Teachers from small towns and villages throughout Zhitomir province came to the city for "refresher courses," which were necessary to update their certificates. English study had become a "hot" field, so the lecture hall was always full, mostly with women, young and old, and by their less-sophisticated clothing I could see how "urbanites" of sleepy Zhitomir might see them as village people. I wore my best suit and tie, hoping to look experienced enough to actually conduct this level of course, but the teachers (many of whom had never met an American before) were more worried about having their own skills questioned. Most of them had never actually been forced to use English in a conversation. To reassure them, I smiled a lot, and spoke slowly, loudly, and carefully. In response came smiles, nods, and attentive faces at every lecture.

My talks about schools in the United States interested them, I judged, given the amount of questions they had afterwards. I always left plenty of time, even though many were shy to speak. Most expressed surprise that discipline often posed a problem in U.S. schools; perhaps they assumed that more resources would mean a tighter grip on student behavior. The idea of metal detectors at the entrance to some schools fascinated and shocked them. They wanted to know how many lessons were taught a week, the average class size, typical subjects, and, of course, an American teacher's salary.

I was also asked to teach a refresher course on songs and games. At first, I was unsure if this topic was something experienced Ukrainian teachers would even care about. They certainly knew many, many songs in English already, and the subject seemed trivial.

Before the seminar, we met in Larisa Petrovna's office, a tiny room with display cases full of teaching materials for Polish, German, Italian, and of course English lessons. She was responsible for arranging refresher courses for all the foreign language teachers in the province, even those who taught languages she didn't know. Because she knew that I had walked the short distance from school to the institute directly after my lessons, she had prepared weak but piping hot tea for me. A few tea biscuits and some imported chocolates sent from friends in Germany had been laid on a plate for me. She had asked how I was getting along, I had thanked her for the snack, and then I admitted that I felt a little uncomfortable about teaching songs.

"Larisa Petrovna, excuse me, but I am going to feel ridiculous in this seminar." Fingerplaying to "The Itsy Bitsy Spider" felt silly enough with fourth graders, but in a room of fifty or sixty adult women?

"*Dzhone*," she said, grinning that smile that looked like it disguised a headache. "Everything will be OK. I have heard that you sing quite well. Just be sure the teachers sing along with you."

When I entered the long, empty room filled with teachers, the eager expressions on their faces gave me courage. After all, I was Michael Jackson! I had done other lectures, and I could do this one. I stood beside the podium, and after a brief introduction and discussion of the uses of songs in teaching English, I announced that I would now teach them some songs. The teachers whispered to each other, waiting to see what would come next. After scribbling some words on the chalkboard behind me, I stepped away from the podium and began to sing.

My voice echoed in a lonely, lost way. It sounded out-of-place. The room had hushed, and I realized that I had spoken nothing but Ukrainian all day until now. The words floated through the room like an island of English in a sea of Ukrainian and Russian. The song I had chosen was "The Wheels on the Bus Go Round and Round," and my cheery, nervous solo caused even the dourest faces to turn to shy smiles. I finished, and they applauded.

"Now," I went on, "it is time for you to sing." The smiles dropped instantly. Hoping not to be embarrassed, the teachers obviously didn't want to speak English out loud, and they looked back and forth at one another, trying to judge who would sing and who would keep silent. A few of them looked up at me with confident faces, ready to try. So I took a deep breath and counted off, "One, Two . . . Three!" Only a voice or two came in with mine, but in a few moments I saw more smiles and heard more voices.

> Za Veels on za bus go round and round. Round and round.
> Round and round. Za Veels on za bus go round and round,
> all around the town.

This time, at the end, we all applauded each other. A faint voice from the back spoke up—in English.

"Excuse me, Mr. John. Would you be so kind to . . . repeat please?"

I laughed happily and agreed. The second time, more teachers joined in, and we practiced the other verses. The horn on the bus goes beep, beep, beep. The wipers on the bus go swish, swish, swish. The people on the bus hop on and off. The babies on the bus go waah, waah, waah. The teachers copied down every word as if I were giving a dictation, and they asked me to repeat lyrics and explain unfamiliar phrases. They repeated the new words to themselves, learning them instantly, pronouncing them with slight accents but quite clearly and correctly. When that song was done, I moved on to the next.

Every new song was lapped up more enthusiastically than the previous one, and I found myself feeling glad that Larisa Petrovna had scheduled two hours for this topic. Songs with motions (like "I'm a Little Teapot") or with gimmicks (like "Bingo") went over especially well; I gathered that many of the teachers taught younger pupils. For example, they loved "Home on the Range" and "The Bear Went Over the Mountain." Perhaps the most fascinating song for them turned out to be "Where Is Thumbkin?" Names of fingers were the kind of real-life cultural details about English that Ukrainian teachers craved. Their vast vocabulary often made my head spin, yet my ability to share the word "pinky" could make me a hero for the day. They really wanted to learn, which made the sessions enjoyable for me, too. Hearing sixty Ukrainian English teachers singing "There wahssa fayrmer hatteh dog" was a rewarding, if bizarre, experience.

    Thus, despite my worries, learning songs ended up being fun for all of us. When I demonstrated the motions to "Head, Shoulders, Knees, and Toes," while bending at the waist faster and faster as the song speeded up, my necktie flopped about madly. The teachers kept singing and by end we were all breathless with laughter.

My own pupils, who had such lessons every day, had grown accustomed to me. Not surprisingly, they were soon no more enamored of me than of any other teacher. My colleagues still treated me as if I were special, yet I felt terrible about teaching so poorly. All of the lessons I had prepared during training were used up, and I was running out of ways to cover the required material. The ninth-grade textbook was no help. Recommended vocabulary words were not only difficult but esoteric; why should my pupils even try to learn "drench," "percolate," or "stricken" when everyday words were still beyond their grasp? Furthermore, the book's questions, such as "How do working people in England demonstrate their solidarity with the working people of all other countries?" and texts like *Lenin in London* were laughably slanted. And I had to admit the Anglophilic bent of the curriculum annoyed me a little at the same time that it exposed my weaknesses: I was not competent to lecture much about Michael Faraday, for instance, or other famous British scientists.

    My pupils, however, had very clear ideas about how I should teach. They wanted to memorize and recite. "Mr. John," they pleaded, "you must to practice us the 'texts.'"

    I asked for an example of one of these texts. One Lena stood up and recited cheerfully: "We can't imagine an educated person without the knowledge of at least one foreign language. The proverb says so many languages you know, so many times you are a man. I study English from the first form. English is one of the most widespread languages in the world. It is spoken as the mother tongue of England, the USA, Australia, New Zealand, China, Japan. English is one of the official languages of the UNO."

There was a long pause. My ninth graders looked proud enough to applaud at the performance.

I turned to Lena and asked, "Do you really think English is the mother tongue of China and Japan?" She shrugged and sat back down. I doubted that she had understood my question and wondered if she even knew what she herself had said.

I eventually capitulated and assigned traditional tasks from time to time, like giving dictations, which they copied in their class notebooks. We did oral grammar drills, simple essay tests, and poetry memorization. Most of my pupils breathed a sigh of relief every time I asked them to do such meaningless, jump-though-the-hoop busywork. They publicly groaned at the stress of having to perform on a test, then glanced at each other's papers during the dictations and felt satisfied with the outcome. That, after all, was "school" as they had known it for nine years and was a game they knew well how to play. Teaching that way was easier for me, since it required less energy and planning, but not very satisfying.

A few of my ideas came off all right, though. Curious about Ukrainian recipes and wondering if my students could teach me how to prepare a few dishes, I decided to teach the ninth grade a unit on food. They were interested to learn simple, everyday kitchen words. For homework, I asked each student to choose a dish, write down the ingredients, and then to describe the process of making it.

One boy turned in: "Cut cabbage. Salad." Another, perhaps confused, wrote, "I love to eat potatoes. I help my mother about the house." Some of the explanations were incomprehensible attempts to describe *some* process, though I had no idea what. The worst outcome of all, however, was that my best student in 9B, one of the Oksanas, wrote a quite clear and thorough recipe describing how to make *kholodets*—the one Ukrainian dish I couldn't stand.

"Kholodets. You must prepare for this recipe pig's feet, pieces of meat, garlic, onion, peppers and salt. Put the meat and feets in the big saucepan, fill the water, and boil it 6-10 hours. After this you must strain it. Into the liquid put the cut garlic and carrots and the boiling piece of meat. Fill it in the little plate and stand them in the refrigerator. For side dish you can take a boiled potato, and of course salad."

Kholodets is head cheese—a pale, gelatinous, shivery loaf of cold meat parts. Every time I visited someone as a guest, they served kholodets, declaring it a Ukrainian delicacy: cold, slimy, spattered with flecks of nameless flesh, a bowl of disgusting jelly. Refusing it as diplomatically as possible, I told my host that kholodets was honestly the only dish in Ukrainian cuisine I didn't adore. Ukrainians, without exception, urged: "Then you haven't ever had *good* kholodets. Try *mine*." To be polite, I placed one wobbly forkful onto my plate, and slurped it into my mouth. Nearly gagging, I ate a bite of spicy mustard or black bread to force it down. I never met a Ukrainian who didn't love to eat kholodets; I never saw a foreigner who could bear to.

As the class got used to my methods of teaching—mostly a struggle to get them to speak in their own words—some of the work improved. Even the boys did a little better. One time, when they paired up to create dialogues, I was treated to an original, unforgettable one that made me believe they were learning to form their own sentences. Read in the squawky adolescent voices of two young men, in thickly accented English, it went:

> VITALIY: You no must victory.
> ANDRIY: I pull out your eyes.
> VITALIY: You think? I kill you.
> ANDRIY: We'll see.
> VITALIY: OK.

Though seemingly simple and juvenile, that accomplishment thrilled me. Brief and lacking some grammar, at least the dialogue was genuine. It was no "Parrot English." In their attempt to be funny, the boys translated a few of their thoughts into the words of a foreign language: the difficult skill I wanted them to learn. Most of their rote sentences, like "Friendship—it is so important to everyone," were so trite and rehearsed that I welcomed one like "I pull out your eyes." Gruesome and simplistic, yes, but inventive, honest, and most important, all their own.

Chapter Eight

Friendship and Then Some

I always imagined that dramatic historic events would seem dramatic at the time—that an earthquake, for instance, would feel . . . well, earth-shattering. But the mundane details of everyday life continue to exist—even shift to the forefront—during times of chaos. That took me by surprise.

One typical Sunday evening I was invited to visit Svetlana Adamovna's family for dinner, and for once, I planned ahead and brought something to eat. All those apples spilling out of the cupboard needed to be used, so I fried them lightly with a pat of butter, sprinkling on cinnamon sugar while they cooked, then at the end crumbling in some of my dry tea biscuits. It came out something like apple crumble, not very exciting but easy and edible, my two criteria for food preparation. I knew Svetlana Adamovna and Larisa would love it—it was sweet and full of cinnamon. Spices of all kinds were hard to find, and I wished I had brought tins of oregano, paprika, chili pepper, even plain old black pepper from the United States. Ukrainians used lots of salt, then added flavor by tossing in freshly picked parsley, dill, or sorrel, along with handfuls of chopped garlic or green onions. But powdered spices—especially anything with a kick of heat—were unknown and unavailable. Everyone knew cinnamon, but it could be hard to track down and the two-year supply I had brought from home disappeared in a month.

When I arrived, Svetlana Adamovna was the only one home. After accepting my apple crumble with an exclamation of surprise, she sat me down in front of the TV. Everyone would be home soon, she said, and no, she would not allow me to help in the kitchen, it was too messy.

I sighed, mentally flogging myself for coming over too early. Watching TV in Ukraine was boring for me, partly because I understood so little, but also because the programming was dull. On the local channel, for example, ran an hourlong show announcing citizen birthdays, while soft Muzak played and soothing nature scenes appeared—like a full hour of Lawrence Welk and Willard Scott combined. Some shows seemed paced to keep the populace calm and relaxed after a day of Ukrainian reality. Only Channel One blasted a cosmopolitan, glossy New Russia into people's homes, and Ukrainians watched that broadcast from Moscow far more than either of the two Ukrainian channels. In addition to its more comprehensive news, it had always been the central voice of the country. It also had lots of lively game shows, all of them downright weird, such as *What, Where, When*, a quiz show played by a team of contestants, shouting and arguing like *Jeopardy* gone communal. The cameras zoomed and zipped around dizzily, worse than any dad experimenting with a new Handycam. The most popular game show of all, *Field of Wonder*, was no different from "Wheel of Fortune." In this context, no wonder *Santa Barbara* looked good.

For me, the interesting moments were the commercials, such as the bank ad where the camera zoomed in on a tall stack of books, each with the word "Kapital" on the spine—an ironic post-USSR redaction of Marx. The majority of commercials advertised a handful of Western firms. It seemed the same five commercials cycled over and over: Pedigree Pal dog food (not even sold anywhere in Zhitomir); Twix candy bars; Herbalife "nutrition supplements"; and Smirnoff vodka, four times as expensive as the state brand. Every other commercial showed the same Russian soccer star enjoying a Snickers and saying "Satisfaction!" as he kicked a goal.

Happily for me, that Sunday evening at Svetlana Adamovna's, Channel One had a soccer game between Moscow Spartak and St. Petersburg. Watching sports was all right: even with the sound turned down hockey and soccer still made sense. However, this was one evening when television programming turned extraordinary. In the middle of game, the screen went blank—actually blue, as if the signal had been interrupted. Technical problems, I figured, not much alarmed. But in a few moments, when the picture returned, a frightened-looking man sat behind a news desk. With no introduction, he stuttered with hurried urgency that a mob armed with grenade launchers was shooting its way into the TV station.

"Channel One is under attack," he said, and the screen went blank again.

Up until then, the two-week standoff between Boris Yeltsin and the Russian parliament had seemed like typical, if intensified, Russian politics: gusts of harmless hot air. Yeltsin "dissolved" the parliament and called for new elections, and representatives in turn locked themselves in the White House (the Russian parliament building) and declared Yeltsin "deposed." The reactionary "acting president" had thousands of supporters, but no one expected their posturing with submachine guns in the parliament building to result in real bloodshed: Russians killing Russians on the streets of Moscow. That Sunday—October 3, 1993—might have turned into the coup that restored a totalitarian Soviet Re-Union. After taking over an office building next door to the White House, supporters of the rebel parliament then attacked the television station, blasting down the entry door with a rocket grenade launcher. Yeltsin supporters there defended the station, and more than sixty people—including civilians—were killed by both sides in the machine-gun battle that ensued.

In Svetlana Adamovna's apartment, after Victor Ivanovich arrived, we watched an announcer on a different channel read teletypes about the fighting. My hosts gave each other grim looks, but didn't discuss it. Svetlana Adamovna despised politics and preferred that we focus on the positive, so we switched over to a Ukrainian channel showing a terrible American movie. Instead of watching a revolution in Moscow live on CNN (as anyone in the United States could have done), I watched *Death Flight*, starring Robert Reed—father of the Brady Bunch—as captain of a doomed airliner. A few hundred miles away, tanks rolled into the streets of Moscow, and each side believed the army had come to support it.

Sergey and Larisa came home and, after a hushed conversation with Svetlana Adamovna, offered to show me their wedding video. Perhaps they wanted to shield me from the embarrassing banana-republic style political warfare in their former capital. Or maybe they expected the worst. Shooting in Moscow could mean anything for Ukraine. That night it was not clear who would rule Russia the next day, and the possibility of those tanks heading south to reclaim Russia's breadbasket was an impossible nightmare that had now become possible.

Obliviously, then, I watched a videotape of a typical Soviet marriage ceremony in the official wedding bureau. The building, which stood near my dorm, had been an attorney's mansion before the 1917 revolution. On video, on the steps outside the pale green building, Sergey and Larisa waited for the quick procedure to begin. They would enter the wedding bureau, sign their names in a book, hear a brief pronouncement of marriage, and then snap a few photographs before bolting for the reception. But first, they had to wait. The bureau was only open Tuesdays and Saturdays, so the video showed a long procession of young men in tight suits and young girls in white bridal gowns. Some stood inside the door under a banner of Lenin and received the identical blessings Sergey and Larisa were about to receive; behind them a row of three couples waited their turns. Even for their own weddings, Ukrainians had to stand in line.

The woman conducting the ceremony wore a robe and a gaudy, mystical amulet straight off a *Star Trek* set. I asked Larisa who she was. She answered, "That worker. She just works there." They didn't know her name and hadn't really entertained the idea of her as a person; in their minds, they were married by the state. I pondered all of this a long time, and the video soon grew dull, its greater part being the reception afterward with many long toasts and much dancing. To make the newlywed couple kiss, guests chanted "Gorka, Gorka," which means "bitter," and is repeated at weddings to ward off bitterness for the rest of the marriage. On another channel Yeltsin addressed his country and warned viewers to stay calm while "the armed fascist putsch in Moscow was crushed."

It was late for a Sunday night, and I had to be at school the next day at ten after eight. Svetlana Adamovna gave me a small plastic bag of flour and the rest of the open-faced sandwiches to take home. I was stuffed, warm, and woozy—ready to go home finally and sleep. As usual, Sergey and Larisa offered to walk me back. They liked to get out in the fresh air at night and welcomed an excuse to go for a stroll alone. Halfway up Shelushkova Street, where we usually parted, Sergey suggested we visit a friend of his. Using one of Svetlana Adamovna's favorite phrases, I told them it was "high time" for me to go home, but they persisted. "Just for thirty minutes. We have to go home, too, of course."

It was after midnight, and Sergey's friend Valery was about to go to bed when we came pounding on his door. Sergey introduced me with babbling abandon as if my nationality should be an entrance card and an excuse for a party. Valery and his wife, Tanya, didn't show even a hint of annoyance but said they were glad to see that we were obviously having such a good time and welcomed us into their apartment. Their son, Andry, a first grader at my school, came out to see what was going on, but was quietly ushered back to bed. From their refrigerator they served up the leftover meat and potatoes of their dinner, as well as another bottle of vodka. Valery got out his guitar, and we drank and sang until almost two-thirty. Their apartment was more cramped than Svetlana Adamovna's. Dozens of huge jars of preserved apples, tomatoes, and pickles were stacked under the table and along the wall. Valery and Tanya were kind, generous, and patient with our drunkenness, as if the imposition were excusably minor, as if appearing on a friend's doorstep to continue a party was common.

By the time I wobbled home it was very late and the dormitory was locked. I had to wake up the *dezhurnaya*, who stayed on guard all night, sleeping on a cot in the front office. She couldn't be roused for half an hour of pounding on the door, but finally, after peering out the window to see who was knocking, she came in her robe and slippers to unlock the door. "John!" she scolded, "You must not walk on the street so late. Very dangerous!" Muttering excuses about a friend's birthday party, I begged her pardon and asked for my room key. She fumbled in the special drawer where it was kept and finally found it, handing it across the desk.

"*Dzhone*," she called, as I headed to bed. "Don't study vodka drinking while you're here."

During Peace Corps training, our manual described drinking as part of the initiation into friendship:

> People who have become close associates—even friends—continue employing the formal *vy* form of address. This reinforces mutual respect and does not in any way signal arrogance or dislike. The transition to the more familiar *ty* occurs upon mutual agreement, and, frequently, is accompanied by a special "kinship toast," that takes place over a shot of *horilka* [vodka]. The raising of elaborate toasts accompanied by the clinking of glasses is a longstanding custom. When clinking glasses, it is good manners to look in the eyes of the other person and

most impolite not to take a sip after a glass has been raised and the glasses have been clinked. All this is part of an elaborate way of sealing friendships.

Friendships and then some. What can be said about a whole culture's longstanding, tempestuously destructive love affair with alcohol? Socially accepted (or readily excused), drinking and drunkenness remain Ukraine's cheapest source of pleasure. Imbibing occurs during work, over business deals, and at every social event—and in a culture hotly proud of its hospitality, merely the unexpected arrival of a stranger is a pretext for a social event. Drinking, eating, and long hours of conversation are the chief form of entertainment in Ukrainian life, synonymous with leisure in a place with not much else to do. After a good meal and many toasts comes the other cherished national pastime, singing. But to get to the singing, you must first go through the drinking.

Ukrainians show their guests respect and honor by filling and refilling glasses. An empty glass on a table instinctively grates upon people's sensibilities: like an unresolved chord, it nags at them until it is refilled. Sometime after midnight when the very last drops—tellingly called "tears"—have been wrung from the bottle, it is far from rare for someone to slip out and return minutes later with another. Foreigners, especially, must be treated to prosperity, demonstrated by bottle after bottle, and while an outsider may not be expected to keep up, his mettle is evaluated by how much he can hold, and with how much grace.

Twenty years ago in *The Russians*, Hedrick Smith wrote:

> Those who have not been exposed to Russian drinking do not appreciate how hard Russians drink, but travelers to Russia, astonished by it, have remarked about it for centuries.... Nor can foreigners spend much time in Russia without having their livers threatened by vodka... The guest who hesitates or sips instead of joining in the Russian "bottoms up" is sternly told that

he is insulting the host, for Russians take no little pride in drinking foreigners, especially Americans, under the table. Like corruption, vodka is one of the indispensable lubricants and escape mechanisms of Russian life. It helps people get to know each other, for many a Russian will say that he cannot trust another man until they have drunk seriously together. Vodka-drinking is invested with the symbolism of machismo. Once the bottle has been uncorked, it must be finished.

Substituting the words "Ukrainian" and *horilka* would not make this paragraph any less accurate.

Innumerable customs surround pouring vodka, toasting vodka, drinking vodka, and then repairing oneself the following morning—sometimes with a shot of vodka at breakfast. The phrase "fifty grams" or "100 grams" signify not amounts, but a whole series of shots, each kicked back neat and then chased with a bite of bread, pickle, or herring. Eating snacks of some sort after each shot occurs without exception, but in desperate straits when nothing whatsoever was at hand, a substitute was to down the shot, then grab the man's head next to you and deeply inhale from the scent of his hair. ("The army way," they explained.) Not a soul doesn't know the poem, "Between the first and the second, a short break, not too long." When offered *Choot-Choot*—roughly, "barely any" or "the tiniest sip"—I always received a full shot glass and then another. If I demurred, my host pleaded, "Just one toast—only symbolic." But after that one symbolic toast, the drinking continued. After a sly smile, another was poured, then another, until the symbolism (and eventually the room itself) was lost on me.

A universally understood gesture for "Let's drink" was a flick on the side of one's throat. According to the legend I was told, the gesture originated when a nobleman who saved a tsar's son's life was offered any reward he named. The nobleman requested a lifetime of free drinks anywhere in all the empire. To grant him his wish, the tsar had his royal emblem tattooed on the man's neck, for all to see. The nobleman, upon entering any tavern in the empire, might point—or flick, or slap, or touch in any way—his neck, and his bill was to be considered paid.

Ukrainians shared all of these traditions and, naturally, made their own local contributions. Whereas the Russian word *vodka* derives from *roda* (water) and means "little water," the Ukrainian word *horilka* literally means "a little burning," or perhaps "firewater." The traditionally famous Ukrainian variety of vodka has a red hot pepper soaked in it while it ferments.

Vodka, like bread, is both a staple and a sacred commodity. Both are surrounded by so many customs, legends, and traditions because Ukrainians—especially in the countryside—have depended on them for centuries. Without these two beloved friends, they say, how could we have survived privation and misery through a thousand harsh winters?

This intimate love affair, a sizable element of my host culture, presented challenges to my goals as a Peace Corps volunteer. To get over being seen as a guest, I first had to *be* a guest quite often. Even later, participating in life as Ukrainians really lived it meant, for me, a lot of drinking.

One volunteer never touched vodka throughout his entire two years of service; I have to admit that set an admirable example in a society where alcoholism is an epidemic. Alcohol is probably destroying people's lives more now than ever. With the disappearance of a central authority, drunkenness has increased even from its already high level in Soviet days. Gorbachev's attempt at prohibition failed, and now that the repressive political climate has disappeared, previously stigmatized behaviors of all kinds are more widely practiced. The state-controlled price of vodka was around seventy-five cents a half-liter bottle, a price too high for many, so homemade *samagon* was available everywhere as well. More than a few cynics noted that the government overlooked the social cost of widespread abuse of alcohol in part because cheap booze kept the average Ukrainian pacified. Instead of resorting to Yugoslavian-style civil war, Ukrainian men seemed to have turned their bitterness and helpless anger not on each other but mostly on themselves. To say that millions of people are intentionally poisoning themselves slowly to death may sound like exaggeration, but there is no way to describe Ukrainian drinking without hyperbole.

In that context my friend's firm course of abstinence made sense—except that he missed out on an integral part of his host culture. He once remarked that the single time he tasted cognac at a party, he noted with surprise how warm and mellow he felt and how pleasant the company was that evening. Most people shared their true selves only on occasions involving big meals and heavy drinking. An energized directness suddenly, magically, appeared in their faces after they felt willing to open up. Maybe the average Ukrainian is too inhibited to speak freely without alcohol, or maybe I was. I reasoned that I had to meet people where they were—which, in Ukraine, is often sitting around a table—to cross into the culture and gain perspective on their lives.

Of course the *opposite* of abstinence (what I prefer to think of as "too much socializing") presents its own dangers and, admittedly, I erred on that side. It was hard not to. Gracious refusals were taken as unfriendliness or lack of appreciation for the hospitality. Drinking only a sip of your shot was considered deceptive and sly. On picnics I tried tossing it over my shoulder into the bushes, but to no avail; I had to drink a "penalty" for insincerity. After all, my presence was often the reason for the occasion, and my drinking its focus. The fact that I drank too much, too often, can be blamed on nobody but myself, of course, but it made communication easier and briefly relieved my loneliness. The company of fellow intoxicants provides unmatchable comfort and solace in a sad, heavy sort of way.

So I could say that on the night of the October 1993 coup attempt I stayed up late drinking in order to escape the sense of disaster we all felt, as gunfire and rioting overtook the streets of

Moscow. I could say that our desperate expectation of new, repressive leadership provoked me to join with Ukrainians in their mourning the setback to stability. But that would not be true. For me the night of the coup was another run-of-the-mill evening of socializing in traditional Ukrainian fashion. If the goal was to turn away from problems by celebrating, then I was acculturated enough to go along.

Like TV viewers throughout the former Soviet Union, over the next few days I watched on the newly reopened Channel One as the October 1993 coup attempt unfolded. Mostly the station broadcast live CNN footage of the "constitutional crisis," resolved when T-72 and T-80 tanks loyal to Yeltsin shelled the Russian White House. A CNN camera was perched on a hotel roof across the street, and Channel One showed its footage while a Russian interpreter translated CNN's every word. When CNN went to commercial break, Channel One stayed with live feed and kept translating. So in both English and Russian I overheard American takeout orders for pizza and cigarettes and a blasé discussion of hairstyles. The translator conveyed the CNN reporter's outbursts of "Jesus Christ!" as best he could, and even rendered a clearly audible background telephone conversation: "Hi, this is Clair. Who is doing the five o'clock show? . . . Why is he doing it? . . . Do they not want me to do it? . . . Should I update my kit? I did it in a real rush. [Sound of foil unwrapping] Want some chocolate?" In the confusion, CNN later carried reports from Russian television, which were based on what the Russian reporters watched on CNN. As so often occurs in Russian affairs, the world had little information; sitting only a few hundred miles away, I had even less.

Had I had access to the *New York Times*, I might have read its October 4 banner headline proclaiming "Yeltsin Sends Troops to Oust Armed Forces from Parliament; Fierce Battle Rages in Capital." A telling sidebar beneath it noted "Despite the Violence, Muscovites Go Shopping On This Rare Sunny Day." The story read, "A mile away, Muscovites generally carried on as if it were just another day when Russia's future might be decided. The usual line for ruble-paying customers snaked outside the Pizza Hut." And hundreds of miles away in Ukraine, where even the capital, Kiev, had no Pizza Hut, people spent the day as they would any during that time of the year—harvesting potatoes from their gardens.

In the final analysis, the Moscow coup attempt affected Ukraine little and me none. No one on either side expected such drastic, and ultimately conclusive, action. Yeltsin's strong-arm tactics caused some Russians to gain new respect; others expressed dismay that the leader credited with bringing democracy to Russia so readily used authoritarian force on those who disagreed with him. Ukrainians, for their part, were pleased that tanks never rolled south in their direction.

During the shelling, flames leaping from the Russian White House windows left the building charred. One ninth-grader told me the parliament building could now be called the "Black-and-White House." His grim wordplay—"black-and-white" was "Chorno-bily"—referred to Ukraine's own large-scale, politically mismanaged disaster.

From my perspective at the time, one possible outcome could have been evacuation of Peace Corps and the end of my time in Ukraine—a prospect about which I held mixed feelings. Americans had other reasons to be horrified that week: the day shooting began in Moscow, a dead Marine was dragged through the streets of Mogadishu, Somalia, the image of which I saw only years later. Isolated and unaware, my life in the United States faded into distant irrelevance, and sometimes seemed like a faint dream.

I wrote letters home full of upbeat, cheerful half-truths: "It's hard to believe I've lived in Ukraine for only six months, because I already feel at home in this city. I undertook this adventure thinking of it as a little bit of a sacrifice—of time, material comfort, and so on—but I have so many privileges, freedoms and interesting experiences, it's more like a fantastic opportunity. You can be assured I'm fine." That was the best explanation I could give for being treated as a celebrity and for all the "socializing" that was changing my view of the place. The missionaries had showed me how I had lost some of my Americanness, and this didn't seem like a bad thing.

One Friday after my regular classes I met a group of English students at the Ped Institute, and we stayed out talking until late in the evening. I finally arrived at my dorm around ten p.m., an hour before the building would close for the night. When I entered the lobby, the *dezhurnaya* cried, "John! Where have you been? You must go to room 54." She pointed toward the student-only wing of our building and handed me a note. "Your friend has been waiting!"

I misunderstood, assuming she meant John Maddox. "It's OK," I said, "I saw him today."

She scowled and mumbled something to a student who sat nearby. The girl ran off. "Dzhonik," the woman said through pursed lips, "read what's written on that note." I unfolded the paper and read:

> John—
> Suddenly I find myself in Zhitomir. I went back to the post office, be back about 5:00. Will you be here?
> —Love, Liza

I slowly registered happy surprise. Liza, the volunteer fluent in Russian whom I'd gotten to know during training, had been assigned to a school in Vinnitsa, a city similar to Zhitomir about seventy-five miles away. I hadn't expected her to visit, or I would have met her at the bus station. How had she found my dorm? What had she been doing since five o'clock? No—earlier! She had written the note before five. So where could she have gone now?

I stood there so long that the student sent upstairs had already returned. With her was a young man I didn't know. He wore a T-shirt, tracksuit pants, and slippers, comfortable at-home clothes that told me he was a student living in the dorm. His black, shiny hair was very long by Ukrainian standards—several inches over his shirt collar. He moved toward me with gawky energy and shook my hand, greeting me with "Hi, John" as if we were old friends. With a nod of his head toward the student wing, he said, "Come with me."

"Thanks, Misha," the *dezhurnaya* said. At that time I had no idea that Misha and I were going to become close friends.

I followed him into the other wing, which was completely dark (the lights in the halls had no bulbs), and then up the stairs. As we climbed six flights in the dark, Misha apologized in Ukrainian that the elevator didn't work, but then said he remembered that the one on my side of the building didn't either. Apparently, he knew where I lived as well.

On the sixth floor we zigzagged through another maze of dark hallways to a nearly empty room with a bare concrete floor, where a bucket overflowing with potato peelings stood next to a blackened stove in the corner. Four plain-looking doors opened into the room, and Misha went straight for one of them. I followed him into a tiny room crowded with four girls—one of whom was Liza.

"Hi, John," she said calmly. "I was just getting ready for bed."

Crossing the lobby again, this time with Liza beside me, I smiled at the *dezhurnaya* to show that I finally understood. "Now you are happy," the old woman said with a note of finality, and then added sternly, "Good night."

Inside the protected walls of my apartment, I could relax at last and savor the joy of a visit from Liza. I apologized for leaving her stranded all day. "That's okay," she told me. "You didn't know I was coming."

She had the whole weekend free and had originally planned to travel to Ivano-Frankivsk and visit Adam, but when there were no tickets, she jumped on the bus to Zhitomir at the last second. "I had your address and figured I could find you." Upon locating my dormitory (her excellent Russian allowed her to ask directions easily), the *dezhurnaya* told her I usually arrived home about five—true enough on normal days. She wrote the note and ran an errand to the post office, returning to the dorm to find me still not there.

That was when a freshman girl named Vita saw her. Liza was sitting on a bench outside the dorm wondering what to do when Vita approached her and asked if she needed anything. Vita was seventeen but looked younger, a freshman with large, sleepy eyes and a gorgeously sweet voice. She ended up talking with Liza for hours—they had liked each other immediately. When Liza had asked if Vita knew me, she replied, "Of course. Everybody knows John."

So when, by ten p.m., I hadn't arrived, Vita invited Liza to spend the night, in a ten-by-ten room already shared by three girls. I apologized again, but Liza said once more, "It was fine. I can take care of myself." She stretched out on one of my single beds and went to sleep.

The next day was Saturday, so Liza and I walked around town, talking about the strange country of Ukraine and how difficult the first month had been. She had survived four months of winter in Leningrad, but this was far different, she told me. Her city, Vinnitsa, had no business volunteers, so she was the only native English speaker in a city of 300,000. Although she liked her school, the past few empty weekends were making her stir-crazy. She craved travel.

I showed her around sleepy Zhitomir, listening to her horror stories and telling mine. Liza adapted well to Ukraine, withstood stress much better than I, and handled any mishap without breaking stride. With winter coming on, few chances remained for her favorite activities of hiking and being outdoors, so when I asked if she wanted to walk out into the country, she agreed.

A mile from my house was "The Park of Culture and Rest

Named after Yuri Gagarin, First Human in Space." More like a tree-lined promenade or boulevard, the park stretched from a statue of Pushkin at one end past pre-Revolutionary stately houses (now law schools, police academies, agricultural colleges) all the way to the cliffs above the river Teteriv. There, the park ended at an enormous three-hundred-meter-long suspension bridge. John Maddox had told me it was the longest bridge of its kind in the world; when I frowned skeptically, he added, "It took the longest to build." Although wide enough for one car, the bridge was restricted to horse carts, bicycles, and pedestrians. It stood nearly two hundred feet over the water level, so to cross its span was like walking through air to the cliffs on the southern bank. Up high, suspended above the river, the view was magnificent.

At first sight, Zhitomir's strange, Soviet-looking apartment buildings had struck me as grimly urban, their concrete flaking off, their strings of laundry dancing in the wind. But here in the park (only four blocks from downtown), high cliffs overlooked a narrow, slow green river far below. Birches, pines, poplars, maples, and chestnuts crowded thickly together on either side of the red granite banks. A few cottages peeked down into the river's canyon, where fishermen in rowboats drifted along trying their luck. Women in kerchiefs carried water from the well, and a man far down the river dug slowly and steadily in his kitchen garden. Smoke curling from the cottages' chimneys created a pastoral, even fairytale-like scene. All of Zhitomir was as still as a night in the country—quiet but for the barking of a dog chasing geese or the shouts of children running along the water's edge, catching crayfish in the shallows with bare hands. Only the intrusion of a high smokestack poking up far down the river hinted at the presence of the textile factory and near it, an enormous chemical plant. From up here, though, with the park's fantastic view, those ugly truths faded into the background. For the first time, I could imagine how someone in the days before perestroika would have believed what was written in the Soviet newspapers *Pravda* or *Izvestia*. Walking across that beautiful bridge, I too might have thought, "Thank the stars that I live in the safest, most beautiful, prosperous country on earth."

On the other side of the bridge, Liza and I followed a worn path through dense woods to find ourselves in an apple orchard. The trail cut deep into the soil, winding crazily between trees until it entered an immense field pocked with stubble. From there, our path cut through up to the horizon, toward the long straight line dividing yellow field from grayish-blue sky.

We took the path further on, catty-cornered across the field, past a giant haystack—bigger than a building—that looked like the hump of a whale surfacing from out of the field. In the distance black and white cows grazed on even, neat grass. Then, perhaps startled by our speech, ahead of us a flock of hundreds of black starlings lifted into the air at once, swarming like bees, first swirling together, then landing haphazardly in a jumble. They continued taking off, caroming, sweeping, settling. The stillness felt eerie, with the chilly air of autumn creeping in but not yet arrived, its grayness held at bay these final moments.

At the end of a field we saw a fenced-in cemetery, dark monuments spearing upwards, an orthodox cross atop each. Our path met a dirt road, where a wooden shed housed a well and marked the crossing. Thirsty from walking, Liza and I lowered the bucket and cranked it up. The water tasted cold and sweet. Then an old woman, who appeared from nowhere, moved up to me to ask the time. When I mumbled it out, grammar askew, she answered, *"Molodyets"*—good boy—before taking a drink and shuffling away.

In the village we saw more cottages like those along the riverbank, where horses pulled plows through family gardens. Liza suggested we look in the cemetery, where clumps of mistletoe hung in trees squeezed between graves so close together as to be touching. Beautiful, sad poetry adorned the black marble headstones, some in Russian, most in Ukrainian, some in the ancient-looking letters of Old Church Slavonic. On many gravestones we found faces etched in realistic detail, portraits of the deceased as young, healthy fathers, daughters, sons. The grins, so stylized as to be gruesome, suggested that the departed spirits perhaps hovered nearby, gazing at their own once-lively faces.

The light was dimming and we had a long way to get back home, so we started back across the field, this time noticing the onion-shaped spires of one of Zhitomir's orthodox churches in the trees on the city side of the river. Halfway across the field we met an old man. Like a weird, hobbling gnome, he stood on the path with a crooked stick, watching the cows. He was dressed in rags, mumbling to the cows in a whispery, gravelly voice. When he saw us coming down the path, he croaked a question to me I didn't understand; then I saw he wanted a cigarette, which I gave him. In the whole scene there was nothing that wouldn't have fit into a nineteenth-century Russian painting, and for a moment I imagined peasants herding cows in this same field a hundred, two hundred, a thousand years ago.

That evening—if I had, for some reason, been reminded of it—America would have seemed like another planet, and a shabby, superficial one at that. The world I lived in before Zhitomir had drifted away into dreams, though it had been only a few months. When I tried to recreate what it felt like to be there—its daily minutiae, the smell of its air, the color of its skies—it receded into darkness, and my senses could not resurrect it.

Back in the dorm Liza and I opened a can of sardines in tomato sauce and spread it over our vermicelli; garlic bulbs and butter rubbed on roasted bread completed the meal. Afterwards we made chocolate-chip cookies with some imported chocolate bars I bought in the bazaar. Though produced in Poland, they bore labels printed in hapless English. The wrapper showed a sunset over an orange desert, but read "Dessert Chocolate Like With Peanuts." We broke the chocolate into chunks, sprinkled the pieces into our dough, and soon dropped rounded balls onto a big frying pan that served as our cookie sheet. The Cookies Like With Chocolate Chips were delicious.

The next day at the bus station, Liza pushed and shoved her way through a throng of people and managed to catch the 1:40 bus back to Vinnitsa. Her surprise visit left me sadder than I had expected. The first, most difficult months had ended, and I now lived in another country—sometimes absurd, sometimes frustrating, but ancient, strange, and exotically beautiful in its own, solemn way.

By the end of October, I still had no hot water. I gave up hoping for it, which brought relief of its own kind. One day, when I turned the left faucet for the first time in weeks, *something* came out—a thin stream of what looked like hot chocolate.

"Who knows?" I thought. "Maybe it's a sign. Maybe tomorrow . . ."

Chapter Nine

Here to Stay

My sixth month in Ukraine, all the trees shed their leaves at once in a bitter frost, and suddenly it was winter. The trees, now black sticks jammed in the ground, clawed upwards toward a perpetually overcast sky. When the temperature dropped below zero Celsius and stayed there, Ukrainians noted happily: "Today it's ten degrees of frost." No one mentioned minus this or minus that; the "minus" was a given. "Today it's fifteen." "Already it's twenty!" "Can you believe it's twenty-five?" they marveled. "And only November!" Converting to Fahrenheit only made me colder, and I got no comfort from the thought that at forty below the scales correspond. My friends answered my complaints with the Russian aphorism: "There's no such thing as bad weather; there is only bad clothing."

Ukrainians seemed to love the cold: they bundled up in boots and scarves and marched, ruddy-cheeked, about the city on their business. Victor Ivanovich told me what others would repeat often: "It's only too bad we don't have snow like we used to. Voh!!" He raised his arm to chest level. "So deep we had to dig our way out of the building! Earlier—before Chernobyl—we had real winter. Now it only rains and sleets. Awful! Ugly!" Many people seemed to believe that the reactor explosion had mutated the weather or that in the "golden days" of communism even winter had been more satisfactory.

In any case, it was cold enough for me. My apartment had two radiators—one in the kitchen, one in the bedroom, both of which stood barely higher than baseboard moulding. I moved my bed against one and tucked the covers over it at night, hoping to contain a little heat. But when my bare foot touched the radiator's cold metal, I started from the chill. Sleeping in long underwear, a sweatshirt, and wool socks became automatic.

There might not be hot water all winter, I was told. I made do with an occasional sponge bath from water heated in a bucket on the electric stove; once every two weeks—or when I felt unbearably scummy—I withstood the torture of showering in ice water. First, I turned on my portable electric heater to warm up the room, then started the kettle boiling. I wouldn't be in long, and hot tea afterwards helped. Then, I steeled myself for the ice-cold bite that sent me jumping and gasping for breath. The water was bracingly, stingingly cold, but I managed to get all the way under. To warm up I whooped and belted out, in my best Puerto Rican accent, "I like to be in America. . . ." Suddenly, the cold water started to feel warm, and I wondered if my nerves were shot.

No, it was getting warmer! After three or four minutes, the cold gradually dissipated, and as hot water whined through the pipes I sang a Ukrainian folksong I remembered a few words to. With manic glee, I babbled nonsense words for verses I didn't know, marveling at how the small comfort of hot water could so alter my mood. Naked and soaking wet, I ran to gather my lunch from the kitchen; giggling with glee I danced back to my shower carrying pretzels, a bottle of beer, and an apple. I sat in my shower, and soaked, as if enjoying a private picnic in a summer thunderstorm.

I spent all afternoon luxuriating in the hot water. I hauled all my greasy dishes into the shower, where I squatted and scrubbed them clean. I piled heaps of dirty—oh, how dirty!—laundry into the shower, and scrubbed and twisted until the water I wrung out turned from black to clear. Yellow sweat stains left my white dress shirts; underwear and socks took on a forgotten spring smell. My walkman, stuffed in the back pocket of rolled-up jeans, blared while I wrung and rinsed, wrung and rinsed, wrung and rinsed. The clothesline strung from closet to bookcase to wall hook to front door formed a web around my room. Almost all the clothes I owned hung there, dripping little puddles of clean water on the carpet and hall floors. The whole apartment turned warm and damp as a locker room, perfumed by the clean, bluish scent of my laundry detergent, a thin liquid called "Hello!"

My colleagues, though, had more serious worries than hot water: they weren't being paid. An assistant to the principal, a man they called Grisha, went to the City Executive Committee at month's end to collect salaries for the hundred-some teachers of School 23, all in cash. He frequently returned empty-handed and listened while the staff complained furiously. "Grisha, can't you do something?" they pleaded. Grisha smiled sadly—patient and sympathetic, but stoically silent.

One day Grisha arrived with a briefcase stuffed full of kupons. Word swirled around school, and even the students whispered to each other, "*Zerplata priyshla.*" The salary has come. A line of teachers formed on the second floor, waiting glumly. Grisha sat in an office and counted out 5,000s, 10,000s, 20,000s, and the teachers emerged one at time with their month's earnings, a few nearly worthless bills amounting to ten or twelve dollars for weeks of hard work. Because pay was based on seniority and the number of lessons taught, younger teachers often accepted heavier courseloads—up to thirty-five lessons a week. Bonuses for serving as classmistress (homeroom teacher), for assuming extra duties, or for possessing a title like Honorary Methodologist (as Svetlana Adamovna did) added something like sixty cents. All day teachers murmured a drone of laments and helpless protests.

"And we thought 80 rubles in Gorbachev's time was low pay."

"For this salary," an English teacher said, "There's no reason

I should teach more than A, B, and C. If they want me to teach the rest of the alphabet I should receive a few kopecks more."

"If I sold my cookies in the bazaar, I'd make this much in two hours."

Teachers did head from school straight to the bazaar—to buy, not to sell—and the tiny sum went for eggs, butter, or sunflower oil. Often, they spent it all within a week.

When Svetlana Adamovna received her pay, she left Grisha's office clucking with grim laughter. "We must laugh at this," she told me, "because if we do not, we will cry." Tears in the corners of her eyes told me this was no figure of speech.

As the end of the first quarter neared, so did the time for assigning grades. I had logged marks—fives, fours, threes, and twos—in an accounting ledger I bought at the local department store, a good facsimile of a gradebook. This procedure astounded students and teachers alike. "Mr. John," my fourth graders asked, "why don't you ever use the journal?"

"I have my *own* system," I said. The proper procedure, as they and I both knew, was to enter grades in one huge book called the *Zhurnal*. Each class had its own journal, with several pages for each subject—from physical education to Ukrainian history to English language—and teachers officially recorded marks for other teachers and the director to peruse. Slots in a cabinet in the teacher's lounge held each class's journal—yet those slots were always empty. "Besides," I told my pupils, "I can never find the journal."

Half the boys suddenly raised their hands, shouting, "Mr. John, I'll go get the journal right now! I can find it!" Teachers took the journal to class and wrote in it while their students worked: oral performances could be assessed on the spot and an official, irrevocable number recorded immediately. The journals were thus perpetually in use when I wanted to write in them.

Nikolai said, "It's third period. Maybe Valentina Ananivna has it."

"What, are you stupid?" Zhenya replied. "Right now is English. Marina Mikhailivna has it." Normally, a Ukrainian teacher sent a student racing around the school to hunt down the journal. In the teacher's lounge I regularly saw students throw open the door, dive for the shelves of journals, grab one, and race out with a slam of the door.

As my pupils began to argue over the location of the journal, I interrupted them. "No thank you," I announced. "We're in the middle of a lesson. You will sit right where you are. I don't need the journal right this moment. Now let's take our test."

Their faces returned to confusion. If I was giving a test, didn't I need the journal to enter grades? At that point, one of my smartest girls confidently addressed the class. "Guys, Mr. John doesn't use the journal. He has his *own* system." They nodded, as if I hadn't used those same words myself moments ago.

"Yes," Nikolai answered. "He's American. They have their *own* system."

My system was to record absences and grades for homework and tests and then average those numbers to assign term grades—a logical plan, I thought. But it wasn't the way it was done at School 23. In other teachers' classrooms, the journal sat on the desk, a threatening reminder that talking out of turn or misbehaving could instantly earn a pupil an irremediable two—a *droika*—a symbol of shame and severe consequences. A senior who had all fives the whole year could receive a two in a single class period and be denied the Gold Medal of Achievement, the highest high school honor. Students who received twos were called *Dryechki*, a name bearing the stigma of stupidity; the odious two hung like a black sword over every pupil's head. I never heard of anyone ever receiving a one—it was unthinkable.

One time when Sasha, one of my bright third graders, acted up in class, Vitaliy cried "Mr. John, give him a two!" Sasha held up two fingers in the peace sign and then made a scissoring motion. "Go ahead! Give me a sweet pair!" All the kids broke out laughing—a recent Twix candy bar television commercial showed kids scissoring two fingers this way, saying "sweet pair" in reference to the two Twix bars. From that day on, a two in my class was always called a sweet pair. "How did I do on the test, Mr. John?" they asked. "I didn't get a sweet pair, did I?"

My students received twos not for oral flubs or loud talking but for missed homework, poor results on tests and dictations, and shabby work on dialogues. In my class, a hard-working student who made a few failing grades could always redeem himself with fours and fives later. To my pupils (who were accustomed to showing up and doing as they were told), my evaluation of participation and investment of effort were foreign concepts. By the end of the term, they had no idea what grades they would receive.

In the next to last week of the term, my friend Marina entered my classroom at the end of a lesson. "Oy!" she said. "Your room is so warm."

"I know. Isn't it nice?"

"You are lucky. The director loves you," she said, insinuating that such a fact was not true about herself. I smiled and shrugged. "But John," she went on, no longer kidding around, "they say you haven't been writing in the journal."

"I know about the journal," I said. "I'll copy in all my grades next week."

"No, you must do it today. They are preparing report cards." She explained that the director had sent her to help me register final grades for 4G. Marina taught another third of the same group, and so we knew each other's pupils. When one of us was absent, the other taught a double-sized class of the two groups combined.

"What about next week's grades?" I asked, thinking of the term exam I'd planned.

"You can mark something then if you must," she said, "but to write marks for the whole term will take a long time, so you must do it now." I didn't see why—it was no arduous chore to copy down a few grades. Then I saw a section of the journal I'd never noticed before.

"That section?" Marina said. "That's where you write the lesson plans."

"For the whole term?" I had sketchy agendas for each day, but I'd backtracked, restrategized, and reevaluated. The record of what I'd taught would have to be reconstructed from scraps of paper littered about my apartment. A sick sensation crept into my stomach.

"Don't worry," Marina smiled. By now she knew me well enough to guess which rules and procedures were beyond me. "I will help you with the Ukrainian."

I gasped. "In Ukrainian? Everything I taught, in Ukrainian?"

"No, no," she said. "You don't understand. Not everything you taught, but the *official* lesson plans for the term." I was baffled. "For example," she explained, "your ninth graders were reading Shakespeare in September, right?"

I mumbled sheepishly. "Uhh . . . well, that's not really what I've been teaching."

"It's not?"

"No, well, the difficulty of the—"

"All right," she sighed heavily. "I will write this section for you. You just enter the marks."

"You're going to write in the journal that I taught the official subjects? But I graded my pupils on my own material."

"Don't worry about it. Just make sure that you write a mark for those days on which you were supposed to give dictations. You should have a mark for each day, but you can leave some days blank." Ukrainian teachers who made a mark every day for every student were considered superior teachers. Visiting officials from the Education Ministry liked to see neat, even rows of numbers, and the more fives a teacher wrote, the better the teacher appeared to be teaching.

It was my turn to sigh heavily. "Do I really have to finish the journal right this second?"

"Yes," she said. "I'll write your lesson plans in later."

I took my pen and started copying my grades into the journal.

Marina studied my map of the United States taped to the wall, and after a while came over to see how I was doing. When she saw what I had written, she screamed and grabbed the pen from my hand.

"What are you doing!" Her eyes were wide with fright. "This is a black pen!"

I stared at her again, feeling like a stupid *Dryechik* myself. I looked at my hand as if it had wronged me. Innocently, I said, "I should have used red?"

"Red! Red?" She looked more shocked than before. In a lower tone of voice, she said gravely, "John, you must use only an indigo fountain pen. Black is very, very bad." Wondering if I had overlooked something blatantly obvious, I meekly asked why.

"Well . . ." she paused, looking upwards, "it makes it seem that you don't approve of your pupils." Changing tactics, she added, "John, 'why' is not important. Just write in blue." She reached in her purse and handed me a pen. "It's okay," she reassured me. "You didn't know. You can leave the black as it is. Or maybe you will write over it in blue?"

Sighing again, I traced over the black numbers with her blue pen. They still looked black. When I finished, I showed Marina my work.

"Okay," she said. "Now write the marks for the final dictation, for the pupils' notebooks, and for the term."

"I haven't given any final dictation," I said meekly, fearing she might scream again. "And I was going to collect notebooks next week."

She looked exasperated, and used her favorite English exclamation: "Wow. John, listen. You *know* your pupils by now. If he is a good one, put fives. If he is not so good, put fours."

"What about averaging all the grades for the quarter?" She didn't follow me, and I could tell she was tired of explaining and justifying bureaucratic procedures with which she herself didn't like to comply.

"Just write in what you think they should receive. If you

gave mostly fives, then five. If you gave some fours, then put four." She scanned the numbers I had written. "What are these twos?"

"If a pupil didn't turn in his homework, that's a two."

"No, that's *not* a two," she said. "Whatever you do, you mustn't write any twos for the term. You'll have to have a meeting with the director and the pupil's parents to explain why he isn't studying." She looked over the names on my 4G roster. "Yes, I know this boy is terrible. This one too—an idiot. If he is a *tormos*, just put a three." (*Tormos* meant "handbrake," and was teacher slang for those who held up the rest of the group.) "You can give the bad ones threes."

Even my worst pupils had enough threes that I could slide them through in fairly good conscience, passing them along, competence or no. Some pupils with many twos had a few fives here and there, which Marina explained wasn't possible. A five pupil never gets a two, and a two never gets a five. Obviously I had evaluated the class wrong the whole term, she said.

"Just make up final grades you think are fair and don't put any twos."

With a deep breath I stared at the pages of the journal, once more reading the names of each of my pupils. With each name, I pictured the face of an eight-year-old boy or girl straining to spit out words and sentences in English. Feelings of sympathy for my kids welled up in me. They were trying, I was trying; what more could be said? Thus, with a shrug of abandon, my American "system" evaporated into nothingness, and I rapidly scribbled indigo fours and fives in every blank box on the page, merrily capping the fives with an authoritative flourish. I invented final grades—fives, fours, and a couple of threes—and handed the journal back to Marina with relief.

She looked it over quickly and nodded. Then with a mischievous smile, she turned towards the door. "Now all you must do is find the journals for your other three groups," she said, breezing out into the hallway.

I continued to visit other schools whenever possible. Most of Ukraine's English language students did not attend a specialized, or "English magnet," school like mine. Their teachers valued me as a prestigious resource, and wanted their pupils to have the opportunity to speak with the famous Mr. John. They usually asked my vice principal or principal for permission to invite me, as if I were private property of one school; this put me off at first, until I realized that I could never say no to all the offers myself. The system of permission helped me manage my time.

Students always asked the same questions: "Do you like Ukrainian borsch?" "Do you like Zhitomir?" "Are you married?" Their teachers winced, but I happily answered each as well as I could; they all seemed so eager and excited to have the chance to try out their English with a real, live foreigner. At such visits, I was treated as if I were Yuri Gagarin, first man in space, the hero returning with news from otherworldly places. After every session with students, a small "tea" was held in my honor, always accompanied by a series of toasts.

But after a while, the novelty wore off. I trotted out my same old photographs, performed the show-and-tell routine I had done so many times, and always got the same laughs and knowing smiles at the same points. ("Do you miss America?" "Only when I am taking showers and there is only cold water.") Always I answered the same barrage of questions. I smiled and answered, but could no longer enjoy those sessions the way I had on the Day of Knowledge, the first day of school in Svetlana Adamovna's class. Being a circus performer grew tiresome.

The students themselves usually performed for me, too. Unfortunately, this was often the worst part of the experience. Usually an adolescent boy recited his favorite poem in English, inevitably Byron or Shelley, the heavy-breathing romantics. Sometimes they read "humorous" passages from O. Henry or Jack London, American authors who were officially approved for their critical stance toward capitalism and thus accessible during Soviet times. After these readings, sometimes a student would perform an interpretive dance. It was as if they understood that I had come to share my culture, and they wanted to share theirs in return. But after so many of these clumsy, tedious events, my patience wore thin.

One performance in particular never failed to annoy me. At every event where English was spoken, always—*always*—somebody had to sing the Beatles' "Yesterday." Even today, hearing the song makes me cringe. The melancholy, simple lyrics of "Yesterday" must strike chords in Ukrainian souls, because everybody loved it. Policemen, train conductors, shop clerks, all knew some of the words and burst into the song at any opportunity. Maybe also the line "All my troubles seemed so far away, now it looks as though they're here to stay" spoke to people's feelings of nostalgia for better economic times.

At school events I winced to hear it introduced and thought, "Now *I* need a place to hide away." I heard countless renditions, all of them screeched out by a nervous teenage girl. Eventually I couldn't even admire the singer's English, and had to take secret solace in a bad pun. I perked up at the line, "Viiiiy . . . Sheeee . . . Haddoo Go, Eyedoe Know, Sheewooden Say . . ." Next came my moment of silent laughter, when the poor girl, in her heavy Ukrainian accent, sang: "Iiii . . . Said . . . Some Sing Wrong, now I long for Yesterday-ay-ay-ay . . ."

At the song's end, I joined the applause with as convincing a smile as I could muster, thankful only for its merciful conclusion.

After such events, I especially enjoyed visiting Tanya and her husband, Max, with whom I could communicate honestly and genuinely in a way I found harder to do with others. Around them I felt free and relaxed; no role was expected of me. Furthermore, they helped me see Ukraine differently, more clearly. From them I learned how to beat the cold by eating and talking away the long, dark evenings.

The night before the last school day of fall term, I headed for Max and Tanya's. Coming straight from one of those school visits on the edge of town, I still wore a tie and my threadbare brown suit, my uniform for such tasks. My hands stuffed in the pockets of my cheap wool coat, I got off the bus and shuffled the few blocks to their "Krushchovka," a building hastily constructed during the postwar Khrushchev era. At their apartment on the top floor, the door opened and a rush of warm air poured out. Max welcomed me in, saying, "Take off your tie. You're out of the noose for today."

It was just like him to know an English word like "noose." Like Tanya, he had studied English at the Pedagogical Institute where they had met. Max was an enormous man, rather fat, but with the air of a king; his black mustache, black hair, and not-so-fair complexion betrayed his partial Turkish ancestry, he told me. Intelligent, wry, and gentle, he smiled often, usually right before adding an ironic turn or joke to the conversation. His wit counteracted Tanya's earnestness, and the couple seemed to represent complementary polarities: her seriousness and his sardonic wit; her hair light and her features Ukrainian, his dark and Oriental. Two other qualities joined like puzzle pieces to make their marriage work: Tanya loved to talk, and Max loved to eat.

In their apartment we did a lot of both together. At the coffee table in the living room where we ate, Tanya made me sit in an easy chair while she took a stool nearer the kitchen, from which she could shuttle back and forth with food. Unlike most of my friends, Tanya sometimes allowed me to help her prepare food, partly because we were close friends and partly because there was so much to do. That night we ate plov, sliced sausage, a huge piece of well-boiled chicken, coleslaw, and my favorite salad of shredded carrots and garlic. Other times we had roasted pork, little sandwiches with sardines and cucumbers, and boiled potatoes slathered in butter and sour cream. Tanya always fixed great quantities of delicious food. "No matter how much I fix, for Max it won't be enough," she'd say. He praised her and her cooking often, and their relationship seemed happier than most.

Max obscured his chair, which he occupied as if it were a throne from which he laughed, told jokes, ate voraciously, and repeatedly filled our tiny glasses with vodka.

Both of them loved to speak English, and our conversations lasted hours and hours. They talked and talked, practicing their speaking skills by discussing, clarifying, and correcting each other. From Max's amazing memory emerged arcane vocabulary which aptly fit the moment. "You see," Tanya frequently said. "Max has no good practice, yet he remembers perfectly."

When I first met Max, we had liked each other right away. He was able to be funny in a foreign language, and more than his imposing figure commanded respect. "I don't know if this will make much sense in English," he said once, "but in Russian there is a saying that goes something like this: 'You and I will drink beer and stomp in the flowerbeds like gorillas.' I took him to mean that he envisioned our future together as playful, uninhibited, and even a bit reckless. Imagining Max—as big as a gorilla himself—stomping flowerbeds made me laugh in agreement.

Unlike other people, they never plied me with simplistic questions, but instead spilled forth with hundreds of things they seemed to need to tell me, while I ate, listened, and once in a while prodded them to elaborate. Tanya like to propose convoluted extended toasts, which Max punctuated with one short ironic remark; this sent Tanya off happily on another subject.

Eventually, after heavy helpings of vodka, Max opened up and reluctantly talked more about his business. I had been curious about it for a long time—he was the only person I knew who had built a private enterprise from scratch and made money. He employed several seamstresses who made winter jackets from material he purchased from the local linen factory. He cleared about $1000 a month, huge money in that place and time. But it meant running here and there to secure permission or documents or inspection certificates. He spent long hours in meetings with petty officials, at which he supplied champagne and caviar or treated them to evenings at the steam bath. "The greatest curse you can put on a man," he told me, "is this: I wish you to live in a time of change."

After the big meal, he and I went out onto the balcony. From the top story I could look down into a huge pit across the street, where the concrete pilings of an unfinished high-rise rose from a black sheet of ice at the bottom of the hole. Trolleybuses clacked through the night, crossing Lenin Square at the town center. We had been discussing the mafia, the difficulty of making money in the present climate, and the people who now owned the factories once controlled by the state. I wondered aloud to Max about how that new class of the very rich affected the psyche of average people.

"Maybe in the West, where you are used to capitalism, you don't mind so much to see others far, far ahead of yourself," he said, turning to me. "Let me tell you a story. Do you know about the Ukrainian peasant who is given a wish? A peasant was fishing and caught a strange, marvelously colored fish. This fish could speak. It told the peasant, 'If you release me, I will give you anything you wish.' The peasant was overjoyed, and dreamed of mansions, riches, great feasts. . . . But the fish added, "There is one condition. Whatever you are granted, your neighbor will receive the same twofold."'

Max paused for effect, but I couldn't guess what was coming. "What do you think he chooses?" he smiled, his eye agleam.

"The peasant asks the fish to put out one of his eyes."

At the end of the first term, school was dismissed for a week to celebrate Revolution Day. Because of calendar changes, the Great October Revolution of 1917 was commemorated in the first week of November. Even more absurd, the birth of Soviet communism was still celebrated even though the Soviet Union no longer existed. That year the holiday was renamed something like World Revolutions Everywhere Day, to vaguely recall the struggles of all oppressed people, but it was the Bolshevik revolution that was honored—primarily out of ingrained habit. For me it meant a chance to return to Kiev, where several volunteers including Liza had arranged to meet. But returning to the capital proved more difficult than leaving it.

When I went to the bus station on Saturday morning to buy a ticket, I found the large, dusty room full of people who crowded toward the eight ticket windows like refugees. The noise and the smell were overwhelming. Instead of a line, a mass of people pressed forward in no discernible order. I joined the unhappy mob and tried to work my way forward, scooting my heavy bag along the floor between my legs. Some people stood and waited within the crush of bodies, apparently resigned to going nowhere. An old drunk breathed in my ear and grumbled loudly, his breath reeking of vodka and sausage. With each inch I got closer, but it took half an hour of shoulder-to-shoulder, nose-to-back-of-neck shoving before I finally reached a cashier and mumbled my request, hoping to avoid revealing my status as a foreigner.

The cashier had run out of patience. "What do you want?" she screamed in Russian. "Speak normal!"

"I can't speak normal!" was the only phrase I could put together.

"Then I have nothing for you."

"Kiev!" I shouted. "Kiev!"

"No tickets to Kiev," she growled.

Other people pushed in front of me, shouting out the names of other cities, and I was swept backward again. I needed to breathe, so I gave up and went outside to the buses. Maybe I could board without a ticket.

The bus on Platform One displayed a placard reading "Zhitomir-Kiev," but the driver wasn't accepting favors from anyone. Many people tried to sneak on board; once firmly planted in the aisle, they could refuse to budge. But the driver, a stocky, thick-shouldered man, stood in the doorway and let no one pass without a ticket.

A babushka nearby began to howl, begging the driver for

mercy. "I have to be at a funeral," she wailed. "If I don't take this bus, I'll be too late!"

"Do you have a ticket?" he said indifferently. "No? Then stand back. You're not going."

She sobbed, repeating, "It's my sister. My sister!" until the door squeezed shut and the bus pulled away.

At that point I was ready to give up, nearly resigned to spend the week at home alone. But other buses were going to Kiev that day, so I steeled myself for another attempt. I fought my way to the cashier again, this time less squeamish about jostling people along the way. The woman ahead of me reached the window and asked for a ticket to Kiev, and when the cashier turned to her computer, my heart surged. Silently I repeated the Russian phrase the woman had used, inflecting her intonation precisely and getting the case endings right: "One to Kiev, please. One to Kiev, please."

Just then a babushka behind me started poking my shoulder. "Ask if there are tickets to Fastiv," she urged. "Ask about Fastiv." We were so close she could have whispered in my ear, but I ignored her completely. I knew I couldn't correctly form the sentence she wanted me to say; I could barely remember my own. She persisted. "Hey, young man. Why won't you ask about Fastiv?" So near the goal, I couldn't swerve from my mission.

Finally, up close, I saw the cashier struggling with her computer, pounding the keyboard in irritation. She kept accidentally printing out the wrong tickets and adding to a pile of paper scraps no one had ordered: three tickets to Berdichiv, two to Lutsk. Finally, the woman in front of me got her ticket to Kiev, but another man squeezed in from the side, then a second, and a third. After the third man, I pushed hard and leaned in to plead under the smeared window. "One to Kiev, please," I begged. The cashier, without looking up, shouted back the number "1135." I slid 2000 kupons under the window. Raggedy small bills in change appeared in their place, and then—a ticket! I checked the destination and time, reeling with joy to find them correct, and was again swept backwards by the crowd. I held onto my bag and let the tide carry me out.

Back on the platform I was triumphant: my dogged persistence had paid off. A ticket for a 120-mile bus ride cost me two wretched hours of jostling—and the equivalent of only fifty cents. The woman going to Fastiv came up to me, holding a ticket too, but scowling. "What's wrong, young man?" she said. "In such a hurry you wouldn't even ask about Fastiv for me!"

My ticket safely in my hands, I could admit my secret. "I'm sorry," I apologized, in halting Russian. "I didn't know how to ask for you. I'm an American."

"Oh!" she said, registering surprise. But perhaps she read truthfulness in my eyes, because she added sadly, "You see how we live?"

Yes, I thought. It's how I live now too.

Arriving in Kiev, that exchange ran through my head again and again. Had I been assigned to the capital, I could have spent time with expatriates, embassy personnel, business volunteers, and other Americans. Without standing in lines, I could have bought fresh fruit, packaged hamburger, or Oreo cookies; I could have taken taxis from a huge, warm apartment downtown to a school full of children of well-placed officials and taught them British and American literature. But I was sustained by the belief that in Zhitomir I was doing something rare and special. Not a westernized outpost in the heart of Kiev, my home was real Ukraine, with average Ukrainians for my friends. The capital was nice, but it was not the life for which I joined Peace Corps.

For a few days escape, however, Kiev was a treasure, and with several other volunteers one night, I rode the subway out to a place called Playoffs, in a huge hotel in Victory Square. Allegedly run by mafia, the newly installed sports bar and casino catered to tourists or anyone who could afford to act like an American. For the first time I had the chance to experience reverse culture shock, for Playoffs resembled a sports bar exactly like any in America: long pool tables, neon American beer signs, a dozen televisions hanging from the ceiling, and a small parquet dance floor where jeans-wearing Westerners danced to the Black Crowes. The wall-to-wall carpet startled me with both its familiarity and its foreignness. Even the bathroom had tile floors, electric hand dryers, and imported urinals.

On television was American football, which, when described to Ukrainians, was dismissed as slow and boring: "We know about your American football." Some added, "Very violent." Here in this bar, no explaining was necessary. Although never a big fan at home, I fell instantly into the trance of a Lions-Vikings game on TNT and bought a Budweiser in an aluminum can for three dollars.

Immediately I felt guilty at my indulgence, remembering the salaries so recently distributed at School 23. There went a third of my colleagues' monthly wages, wasted on twelve ounces of watery fizz. The American bartender, a big fratboy-type with close-cropped hair brought out the beer, and later the pizza we ordered, which unlike the Ukrainian kind was topped with absolutely no fish whatsoever. I resolved to forget all about Zhitomir, just for a little while.

The bartender noticed my Ohio State sweatshirt. "Wanna see last Saturday's OSU game against Penn State?"

My mind whirled back to earlier months—was it only months? it seemed years—when this big game had been arranged. From some muddy corner of my brain I'd forgotten, the hype surrounding this matchup reappeared to me, and I stuttered out an eager "Yes!"

In minutes, there on the screen in a Soviet-style hotel in Kiev, were week-old moving pictures of Columbus, Ohio. Like a mirage, through a spatter of the wet snow of November, appeared a hundred thousand scarlet-and-gray-clad fans, packed tightly into Ohio Stadium. They cheered and waved, right in the same room with me. At home I would hardly have cared about the game, but now it mattered deeply. It served as visible, tangible reassurance that life there went on as usual. That was how I wanted to think of home:

frozen in time in the patterns in which it always took shape, nothing changing, nothing happening without me.

Homesickness for me meant wishing not to lose a life I had left behind. My faraway familiar world hadn't disappeared—I had only exited from it. There it stood, bright and intact. Such an obvious revelation—that is, that home was still there—made me realize how much my mind had been altered, my assumptions transformed, my self twisted into another shape. It seemed impossible that the two vastly different worlds of my two different selves existed simultaneously.

Hypnotically, that evening, I watched not a football game, but an image of myself that I had lost. It was like looking in the mirror and seeing a young, dimly remembered face and knowing that, even though I could return to that place, I would never be that person any more.

A phrase from a song popped into my head, and I almost started laughing. "Yesterday . . . all my troubles seemed so far away. Now it looks as though they're here to stay."

"Nice tackle," said the Peace Corps volunteer next to me. I hadn't noticed. I sipped my can of beer, which was weak and tasteless in comparison to good Ukrainian beer. The thought of this reminded me of all the beer bottles, soda bottles, and milk bottles that were cluttering up my dorm room kitchen in Zhitomir. At one time, even purchasing milk or beer in a bottle had been a challenge, but now I had bottles stashed in corners, shoved under the table, and lined along the wall against the ice-cold metal radiator. My kitchen had so many bottle that I could hardly move around it without making clinking noises. When I got back, I reminded myself, I needed to go return some of those.

At these thoughts, the fake American sports bar where I sat looked tacky and despicable. Seeing my home on television meant something important, but I could not help but think about Zhitomir. It had become my new home. It was where I belonged.

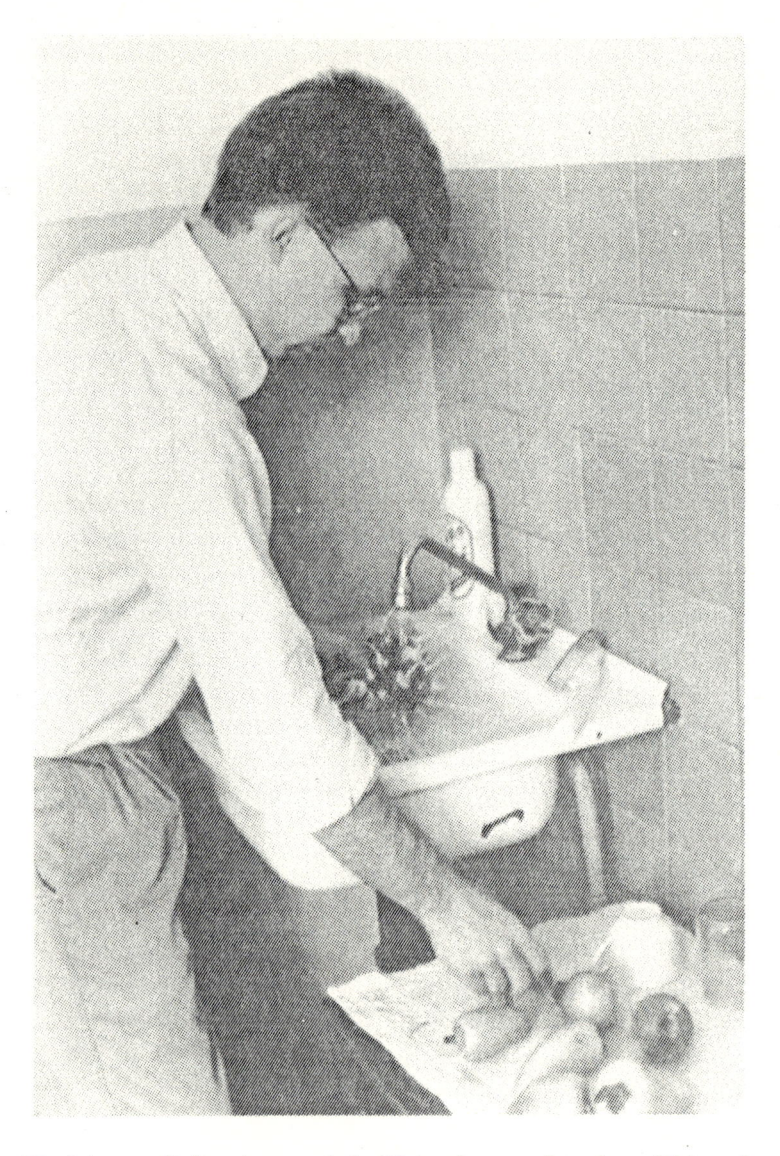

Washing radishes in my sink. This photo, taken by a Zhitomir newspaper photographer in my dormitory kitchen not long after I arrived, ran alongside his story titled "One of Zhitomir's Seven Wonders: An American Teacher."

Singing on the Heavy Side of the World | 167

Celebrations on the Holiday of the First Lesson, the First of September, in the playground behind School No. 23.

On the First of September, first graders through high school seniors present flowers to their teachers.

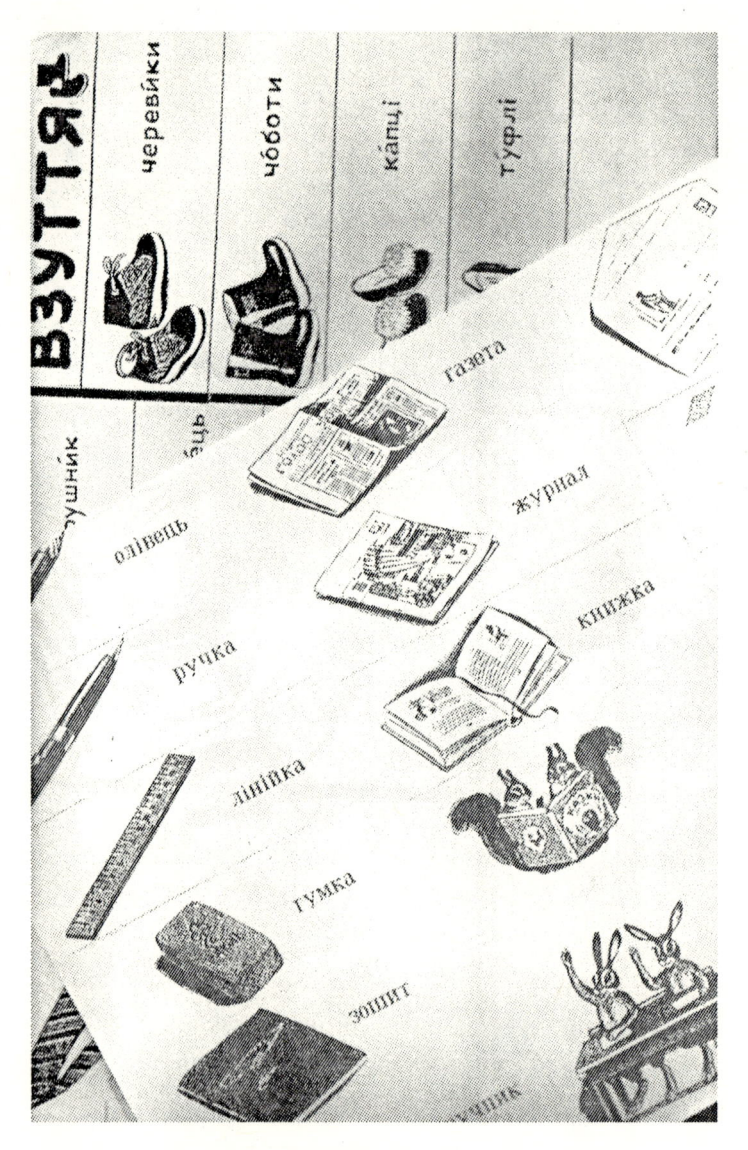

Meanwhile, I worked on my Ukrainian, trying to master enough simple vocabulary to communicate.

Singing on the Heavy Side of the World | 169

Cafes sell inexpensive if occasionally mysterious treats from kiosks and little booths on the street.

Misha in Baranivka.

Chapter Ten

Baranivka—In the Village

I began to see my new friend Misha almost every night. Not out of choice—home from school I became exhausted and even antisocial—but because he was so persistent in cultivating my friendship. After meeting me through Liza, he felt included enough to show up at my apartment door at any hour, knocking as briskly and repeatedly as a cat scratches to get in from the rain. He lived in my building, studied half-heartedly, and on every study break came to see if I was doing anything entertaining. Usually I was sleeping—which was entertaining for me, in that it gave me much-needed relief. But if Misha saw any light coming from the gap beneath my door (sometimes even if he didn't) he stood patiently in the hall, knocking and murmuring, "Joooo-ohn. Open up! It's Misha!" Sometimes he pounded for twenty minutes. There was little I could do but get up and let him in.

He always barged in, cheerful and energetic, to ask a small favor or to invite himself to sit down for coffee. If I told him I had been sleeping, he said, "Okay, I'll only stay a minute." Since Misha spoke almost no English, his visits tried my already frazzled Ukrainian, and though I liked him, I wanted desperately to be left alone in the evenings. It was rarely to be. Once I put the kettle on, he started to talk.

In his department at the Ped Institute, he was the only man except one; preparation for elementary grade teaching was primarily a field for females. Perhaps that's why he chose it. Misha was constantly in trouble with the dean for skipping lectures, wearing his hair too long, and posting a John Lennon poster on his dorm room door until the Komandant—strictly enforcing the dorm's rules—ripped it down. Without a malicious bone in his body, Misha simply craved rebellion in the same harmless way any college freshman takes pain to carve out an independent identity. In a small, conservative town in an institute not known for liberality, Misha's lackadaisical attitude meant he always skated on the edge of flunking out.

"The dean asked me into his office this week," he told me once. "He told me if I miss sixty sessions during this term, I'm out for good."

"How many have you missed so far?"

He looked at the ceiling and counted on his fingers, mouthing numbers silently. Then he grinned with pride and said, "Over two hundred."

"Misha! What are you going to do?"

His grin widened, and he flipped his long hair out of his eyes. "I promised to behave, and the dean crossed out some absences in my record."

"He must like you," I murmured, wondering if he'd somehow paid a bribe.

"It's not what you're thinking," he said, turning serious. Misha was in no position to bribe anybody. His stipend from the institute was the equivalent of two dollars a month—an incredibly paltry sum with which he was somehow supposed to feed himself. "The dean understands me and wants me to stay," he said knowingly. He thought a second, then smiled again. "So I'll have to work hard for a few weeks before I can start skipping again."

It was a shame he didn't try a little harder since he was clever, likable, and at heart a responsible person. He was also a good teacher: patient with my limited vocabulary, careful to slow his rapid-fire speech when he sensed I couldn't follow him. Because I learned a great deal of everyday Ukrainian language from Misha, I never needed a tutor. Unfortunately, and to everyone's amusement but mine, my speech became peppered with college slang that embarrassed me when I used it elsewhere. But thanks to Misha, eventually I even thought in his language. At night in my dreams, I spoke Ukrainian to my friends in Ohio; it saddened me to discover they could not understand me.

At first it annoyed me when Misha borrowed or outright asked for gifts of items like pens, cinnamon, cigarettes, or Ziploc bags—like an aborigine who'd never seen trinkets of modernity, he carted away stuff sent to me from home or that I had searched town to buy. I begrudged him such trivial impositions, but later felt greedy and ungrateful. So I stocked up on the instant coffee he loved, and together we ran through can after can of "Bon" or "Pele" (cheap powdery brands made in Brazil or India) and, when I could find it, higher quality Nescafe. A two-dollar tin of coffee was unthinkable luxury for Ukrainian college kids, who survived on pots of black or green tea, brewed strong and sweetened with heaps of sugar. College students traveled home to their villages on weekends to collect potatoes, salt, preserved vegetables, rice, and macaroni from their parents; with little money to pay for meals, they ate what their mothers and their gardens could provide. Misha often brought some of this food to my apartment, suggesting we cook it together. Without hesitation, he shared everything. When I realized what a sacrifice such commodities meant, my coffee, time, and attention seemed paltry offerings in return.

Often Misha brought his girlfriend Natasha, a chirpy, sweet freshman of seventeen, and also Oleg, Misha's roommate. "Hey, Johnik," Misha would say, "show Natasha your magazines." The Peace Corps office in Kiev sent us *Newsweek* and, of all things, *Forbes*, which I suppose the business volunteers enjoyed. Both offered good material for teaching, and I shredded them with scissors almost as soon as they arrived. Still, Misha found a few intact pages—advertisements for Corvettes, Brooks Brothers suits, Obsession cologne, or laptop computers.

"Oho!" he marveled. "Natasha. Check out this car." She cooed and then giggled, while Misha tossed his head back proudly to flip his long hair out of his face. "Looks like mine, huh?" Natasha laughed, but Oleg said, "Only one difference: that car's 200 horsepower, versus your one horse—with no power."

Misha spat out a filthy name; Oleg answered with an even more profane one. Natasha cringed, then slapped Misha on the arm for swearing in front of her, but then they all laughed. Even funnier for them, I repeated the terrible words and made them explain what they meant.

When they weren't admiring the glossy parade of clothes, they sometimes admired my tattered Betty Crocker cookbook, an old-fashioned, plaid-covered tome from the fifties that displayed photos of fatty pork roasts and Jello desserts. The high-quality color photography intrigued them, and they were amazed by delicious-looking dishes they had never heard of: overflowing fruit salads, or coconut cream pies, or even broccoli and cheese.

Most of all, though, when Misha, Natasha, and Oleg came over for coffee, they looked at my own photographs of home, in the small album I took on school visits that helped me answer questions about my life in America. Always curious about food, Misha studied not my friend's faces so much as what was in the background, the tables stacked with party trays of cheese and crackers we'd simply picked up at a supermarket deli. When they saw my parents' house, they asked me how many rooms it had—I couldn't count them instantly, and they shook their heads enviously. College apartments, cars, dogs, and cats—everything fascinated them. Sometimes I joked that I was going to start a museum in my house and charge entrance fees, but Misha didn't think that was funny. Despite their thirst for the everyday luxuries of American life, they stopped short of worshipfulness. If they sensed me being patronizing, they would turn silent.

One day Misha and Oleg showed up with towels and bars of

soap. "No water on our side," Misha explained, charging past me into my apartment. "Can we use your shower just this once? You have hot water, right?" The student side of the building (with somewhat less clout than the teacher side) had cold water only or no water at all. Misha took the first turn. Then while Oleg took his, Misha made himself comfortable in the kitchen with me.

"Did a woman spend the night here with you John?" he asked coyly.

"What makes you ask that?"

"I saw the shampoo," he said plainly. "You have shampoo in your shower."

"Are you a fool?" I responded, using slang he'd taught me. "It's mine, of course." The bottle, labeled "Lux Shampoo—for Women," was the only kind I'd found in the department store. Though watery and sickly sweet, it lathered up all right and got my hair clean.

"You use shampoo?" he said.

"And what! You don't?"

We stared at each other, both in slight surprise. Quicker than I, Misha concluded that we'd hit upon an awkward cultural difference.

"No, well . . . I've always just used soap," he said meekly. I worried I had hurt his feelings by implying he was poor or unclean, but he changed the subject and showed no embarrassment.

"Look, I have a proposal," he began, already cheered up by a new idea. "Come visit me this weekend in Baranivka." Baranivka (roughly translatable as "Ramville") was his small provincial hometown, where his mother and brother lived. "You must come with me! It will be *Klassno*." Cool. I told him I'd think about it.

"You have to see my nephew Maxim. He is so cute. Like a big doll."

Oleg emerged, clean and well dressed, and I wondered how he had managed to change clothes in that cramped closet of a shower. "Come on," Misha told him, getting up to go. He turned to me and stage-whispered: "We've got dates tonight."

* * *

Misha was more relaxed than I had ever seen him as we stood at the bus station waiting for the bus to Baranivka, but I felt nervous and uncertain about how to behave as a guest in a strange family when I hardly even knew Misha. "You'll see," he told me happily. "We don't live in a bad way." I reassured him I was eager to visit.

We were on platform fourteen far down the row from where I had caught the bus to Kiev. The bus that pulled up was much smaller and dingier than those that drove "important" routes. White and blue, flaking with rust, its curtains in the windows looked raggedy and yellowed. As usual, a crowd of people pushed and shoved toward the doors before they opened. With his student passport, Misha had secured us two discount tickets that guaranteed us seats, and we crowded on between old women and students heading home for the weekend. He crammed me into a seat by the window, right over the wheel well, and I rested my bag at my feet, my legs bent tightly until my knees jammed almost up to my chest. Misha took the seat by the aisle, where twenty or thirty passengers would stand for the hour-and-a half ride. Misha spotted his friend Sasha in the aisle and offered him a place with us. Sasha gratefully accepted, and sat down in Misha's lap. After backing away from the platform, the bus pulled away, as the passengers in the aisle held the overhead bar to keep from swaying.

When Misha introduced me to Sasha as the American who lived in his dorm, the nearby passengers turned to look. Sasha was unfazed, but asked me a few typical questions about how I liked Ukraine, and I noticed when the other passengers chuckled to themselves at my answers. Sasha talked casually about his "small business," supplying kiosks in villages with Snickers he bought in Zhitomir. He hired boys younger than himself to sell them and was making a lot of money. "I do all right," he explained. "But it's 'monkey business'—just for kids. I want to move on to bigger things."

Fields rushed by—or rather glided by, the bus barely topping 35 miles an hour—and soon we were in forest. "*Polissya*," Misha explained "Our kind of region is *Polissya*: half meadow, half forest." Between a dense mix of pines and birches, there appeared an occasional field, its treasured black earth, the *Chornozem*, famous to Ukraine.

Sasha said, "Did you hear the rumor? The Germans are digging up Chornozem and taking it away by the truckload." This sounded unlikely, but an old woman standing in the aisle said, "It's true, it's true. Soon you'll have nothing, boys, not even the ground you stand on." Such wild ideas went beyond any economic pessimism I'd ever heard. "I don't really think it's possible," Misha said. Sasha nodded. "No one—not even the worst corrupt goats—would allow it."

The late November sky dimmed, even though the middle of afternoon had not yet passed. We cruised along for forty-five minutes, occasionally stopping along the roadside to let off people. Hauling heavy bags, they walked off into the woods on paths that seemed to go nowhere; no towns or villages could be seen from the road. Then, at a stop where a dirt road crossed our bumpy highway, the bus stalled.

The driver cranked the starter, but the electric whine fizzled out. A few people standing in the aisle groaned quietly. Still on Misha's lap, Sasha deepened his voice to imitate the driver and quipped, "That's all, guys! We've arrived." The whole bus broke into grim laughter.

The driver turned around. "All right, boys, let's go. Off the bus."

"Let's go," Misha repeated. I followed him and Sasha out the door, my legs aching and grateful for the stretch. I wondered how long it would take for a replacement bus to arrive. The gray sky was already dusky; if the wait was long, we'd never make it to

Baranivka by dark. Looking around I saw only dark, eerie forest, and uneasiness about sitting in the middle of nowhere settled at the bottom of my stomach.

But I was sorely mistaken. I hadn't noticed that the only passengers exiting were about twenty-five young to middle-aged men, who gathered at the back of the bus with hardly a word between them. Maybe, I speculated momentarily, they're mechanics. But then, in a group, they crouched down low by the bumper, careful to avoid getting soot or grease on their clothes. Misha waved me over, "Come on, John. Help us push."

Grunting and straining, we all leaned into the bus and it began to roll. In a few seconds it was coasting rather quickly; we dug in and kept pushing. With a lurch, as the driver popped the clutch, the engine turned over with a roar. The men cheered, a bit wearily. Together, we had bump-started our bus as easily as if it had been a run-down Volkswagen beetle.

The men dusted off their hands, and as they climbed back on the bus, one of them turned to me to say, "Probably, you've never seen this in America, have you?"

Volodya, Misha's older brother (and my age) met us when we arrived at the small, quiet bus depot. With a slight accent he said, "I . . . am . . . very-glad-to-see-you," as if planning the brisk end of the sentence while laboring over the beginning. He shook my hand vigorously.

"Look how well your brother speaks English," I teased Misha, who glowered. Misha had told me Volodya was an art and history teacher in Baranivka, and from his confident, capable manner I could see how he might make Misha both proud and envious.

Volodya promised to show me around, but first we were to go home and eat. We passed a monument of Lenin shaking hands with somebody, but otherwise, the streets were empty of both cars and people, though it was just after five. We entered a wide street, walked by a small bazaar and bread store, and then an ornately decorated wooden orthodox church. Intending admiration, I told Misha it appeared the best-kept building in the village. Misha chided me: "It's a Regional Center, not a village." I apologized, but could not help wondering how there could really be 30,000 residents in this tiny hamlet. The few people we met on the street all greeted Misha and Volodya by their first names, while eyeballing me cautiously. If Baranivka wasn't a village, it would take a better eye than mine to distinguish why not.

We turned the corner into a road rutted with ankle-deep trenches, all frozen and packed hard since the first cold snap. I could imagine it in spring—a sloshy mess. Passing a few houses with brightly painted metal fences, we came upon a well-kept red house surrounded by a large yard, most of its soil broken open like emptied eggshells, now crumpled up in dark clumps and clods. There were bare fruit trees, a grape arbor, and some chickens pecking the dirt, their dirty white feathers ruffled by wind. There were also rose bushes and flowerbeds, empty and barren-looking at this time of year. The apparent barrenness, though, suggested not poverty or waste; the house had a homey, well-tended look.

As we came up on the porch I felt more out of my element than ever before until Misha's mother met us, giving him a hug, and greeting me, "*Duzhe priemno*," pleased to meet you. She was breezy and talkative, and she made little of my being American—something I'd feared—and treated me as if I were any friend Misha had brought home from college, instead of someone experiencing the rural life of her country for the first time. His family spoke Ukrainian at home, and this made me feel better equipped to communicate. The enclosed front porch was covered with old boots and *tufli*, the slippers or flip-flops Ukrainians wear indoors. I took off my shoes, and Misha pointed to a guest pair for me to put on.

Once inside I saw three very large rooms at once and a lace curtain hanging in a doorway, veiling a bedroom. Misha took me into the bedroom and showed me two single beds, one of which (he pointed out) would be mine. I had half-wondered if perhaps we would share a place atop the *pech*, the brick stove built into the wall and traditionally the warmest and best place in homes in rural Ukraine. But this home was no nineteenth century hut by a long shot, and I felt ashamed to have expected thatched roofs and a dirty hearth. In some ways it surpassed other homes I had visited, even in Kiev. Wonderfully warm and spacious, it had windows on four sides with views of the garden, the similar neighboring houses, and the alleylike street.

I dropped my bag and went into the largest room to meet Misha's grandfather. He sat on a long couch, a huge man bulging at the waist and with neckrolls of fat. His eyes glowed a dull yellow-red, and his tiny, squarish teeth mesmerized me as we shook hands, so that when he mumbled something I could barely understand him. But then I saw he was pointing to a playpen on the floor, showing me his great-grandson, Maxim.

Maxim lay in the playpen, his round face staring up. His plastic toys were spread about the playpen and all over the room. One was a set of brightly colored plastic donuts that stacked on a column in order of size; it looked exactly like one I had played with as a baby. Grandfather picked Maxim up and jiggled him lightly, for the first time smiling.

"Maximka!" he cooed. "You're my big strong boy!" Maxim, less than a year old, was plump and cute as a floppy puppy. His mother—Volodya's wife, Luda—was finishing medical school a hundred miles away and saw her husband and baby only on weekends. Still, Maxim got the lion's share of attention; like most Ukrainian babies (whose parents are alternately stern and hypercritical, then pampering and indulgent), Maxim would not grow up feeling alone. He drooled a little, then smiled at his uncle Misha, who cooed and lavished praise on him as his great-grandfather had. I shook Maxim's tiny hand in greeting and said, "Good day, Maxim," and Misha laughed.

On the television sat a VCR, its brand name in Cyrillic letters. Videos were common even in rural areas—perhaps even more so, given the scarcity of leisure activities there; still, the VCR struck me as an out-of-place oddity, especially because the house had no running water.

"Misha," his mother said. "Put on the kettle and we'll have tea. Luda will be back soon. She went down the road to her mother's."

We went back outside into the chilly wind to the well in the front yard, and cranked the bucket down. "*Klassno*," I said. "Not when you have to do it five times a day in the winter. Here. Taste." Icy cold, it made my teeth ache, but it was clear and sweet. Misha poured the water into another bucket, and instead of going back inside, went into a kind of shed five steps from the front door. The shed, I discovered, was actually a separate outbuilding for cooking. Volodya, who was already there, asked me to excuse the clutter. Glass jars were scattered on the floor, table, and sill of the single tiny window. A dented aluminum saucepan held a spray of cooking utensils; china bowls piled on black iron,pots were piled on cauldrons, stacked like those wooden souvenir nesting dolls. On the uneven floor sat a pail half-full of table scraps, mostly rock-hard stale bread. A rope of garlic bulbs hung on the wall, next to a gas stove. With a match, Volodya lit a burner and then a filterless cigarette from his pocket; Misha and I did likewise, and I listened to the two of them catch up on news since their last meeting. Together they spoke blisteringly fast Ukrainian.

Volodya kicked the pail of scraps with his foot, then started, as if he had just remembered something. He asked me in his jerky English, "Do . . . you . . . want . . . to-see-pigs?"

I laughed yes, and he picked up the enormous bucket full of eggshells, stale bread, potato peels, and other garbage. Outside the "kitchen" door was another door in the same wooden-plank outbuilding, as well as a patch of deep mud surrounded by high wooden fence. Volodya dumped the slop in a trough, entered the pigshed, where he threw a latch and then leapt backwards; if he hadn't, the two voracious pigs who charged past him would have run him over. One was gargantuan. The other one, which was smaller, pushed and squeezed against the sow, trying to force its head under the great gobbling snout and get a little dinner. Volodya poked at the big pig with a stick to make it leave room.

"When one gets fat," he told me, "we slaughter it and buy another." He said matter-of-factly. "It's almost time to cut this one."

"Oh, you should be here for that," Misha added. "You can come back in two weeks or so. It'll be a big party." I asked Misha if he would "cut" the pig. He scrunched up his face, and answered, "Volodya will. I don't like to. *Meni zhalko.*" His phrase—literally, "It's too bad for me" or "It's a pity"—sounded funny, though I understood why he preferred not to do the butchering.

"Then you'll hold it while I cut it," Volodya said. He drew a finger across his throat and gurgled a scratchy sound. "It's a pity for me, too, but we have to eat."

Volodya explained. "Look John, everything you see, everything here, is ours. It's all ours. We can vegetables and fruits, we preserve meat from the pigs we fatten, we eat potatoes and cabbage from our garden plot over the hill. Want to see our root cellar?" The pigs had finished their food, but Volodya let them stay out in the pen while he walked over to a door set into the ground. When he opened it, I saw a ladder extending into a cavernous hole. Lying on the ground, Volodya reached into the darkness, found the light bulb, and tightened it in its socket. A sulfurous yellow shone down onto a dirt floor nearly ten feet below. We climbed into the musty cellar, where it was surprisingly warm. Back in the shadows shelves were stocked with hundreds of jars of preserved coleslaw, pickled apples, tomatoes, and peppers. The floor was heaped with piles of grubby potatoes, beets, onions, carrots. "Last year's," he said. "That's why there's not so much."

With a tone of slight disgust, Misha added, "Everything you see we planted with our own hands, weeded with our own hands, plucked, cleaned, and canned with our hands. A hell of a lot of work," he said bitterly. But then he smiled too. "But it's all ours."

I remembered my own garden in Ohio, which I'd always tended for fun—as a hobby. If something didn't grow or was eaten by rabbits, I shook my head sadly and bought inferior (but omnipresent) vegetables in the supermarket. Compared to Misha's, my life in the American economy seemed sheltered in store-bought luxuries. The prospect of having to grow a winter's worth of food for a family of six gave me a momentary fright.

"We hardly even need money," Volodya bragged. "This kupon, this inflation—forget it. At the store I stand in line only for butter, flour, sugar—that's all. We can't wait for somebody else to take care of us. Everything here is ours."

Misha spotted a jar of tomatoes and squealed with pleasure. Tucking it under his arm, he remembered aloud, "Teakettle." We scrambled up the ladder and into the kitchen, where it burbled away. Volodya went to poke the sullen pigs and coax them back into the shed.

I whispered to Misha several of the impolite words he'd taught me, and he said, "Oh! See the outhouse back there in the corner of the backyard? It's all ours too."

I went back to investigate the weatherbeaten wooden privy, in which I found, held down by a rock, a stack of pages of a Russian book I couldn't read. My own water closet in the dorm really wasn't much warmer on cold mornings, I ruminated. The impression of Misha I had in the dorm had changed. In Baranivka, no more the long-haired rebel, he was the youngest son in a country home, with a difficult and perhaps rather dull life ahead of him. He would return there to take care of the household and teach in the local school as his brother did. Volodya was talented and got along well with everyone; how did that make Misha feel? Their father left home when they were very young, a fact Misha didn't want to talk about.

By the time I had returned, Misha had wrapped a towel around the long handle under which swung the steaming kettle.

He carried it up the front steps, making happy, hungry noises. I could see how difficult life would be in winter: cooking outside in the shed, carrying food through the front yard, over snow or ice. Or drawing water, the well's stiff ropes hard with ice, the bucket cold enough to rip skin if touched bare-handed. Misha couldn't see his home as I did, but took for granted their way of life. Balancing the kettle carefully so as not to spill, he bounded up, two stairs at a time, with the easy certainty of someone who has taken those steps innumerable times in the dark of night and knows the way.

We spent the next day, Saturday, walking around town. Misha was happy to be home, but wanted avoid the chores his mother had saved for him. So he, Volodya, and I did some sightseeing.

It was strange to enter a store and find nothing on the shelves but three-liter jars of apple juice. But we bought sweet rolls and strolled over the whole town. Misha pointed out the "House of Culture"—a monolithic Socialist Realist monstrosity. "Disco tonight," Volodya said casually. "That's great!" said Misha, leaping for joy. "John, you'll have a great time there." Just then, some soldiers approached us in their long, heavy wool coats. Three were walking, one rode a bicycle slow enough for the others to keep up. One shouted at us.

"Hey boys!" Volodya said. We went over, and I was introduced to Volodya's friends, the members of the local army volleyball team. Hard-faced, middle-aged men in good shape, they were crossing town on some errand and invited us along. Volodya told them he and Misha were showing an American around town.

"Vova," one said, "take your American to the porcelain factory." To me, he added, "World-famous." Built before the revolution, Misha said, the factory was so prestigious that Lenin himself was known to have ordered a tea set made there. The volleyball team waved goodbye, and we made our way across town, through a soccer field, and across an empty roadway. There stood the ancient factory, its paint chipped and scratched like an old teacup. We sneaked past a few men milling around the entrance gate and walked straight on the length of the long, dusty building. Although it was Saturday, some people—mostly women—were at work. From the roaring, decrepit machines, they removed punched-out bowl shapes of soft clay. Quickly wielding long knives, they trimmed the edges and placed the bowls on a conveyor belt that ran through the kiln. Other women busily applied glaze. At the end, a few workers hand-painted the finished bowls, saucers, and teacups. There were some truly gorgeous-looking tea sets, quite elegantly designed. "Our region has some of the best kaolin in the world," Volodya said. Like every person I met in the former Soviet Union, he knew myriad details about the raw minerals, agricultural products, or specialized industries in his local area. People were proud of industry and what it had contributed to the national economic machine—if only because the propaganda of earlier days would not let them forget.

Tempted to buy a blue-and-gold hand-painted tea set, I told Volodya such beautiful work on a set of four cups and saucers might be worth eighty, a hundred dollars, or more, in the United States. "Then you and I should go into business," he said, "Because this one's yours for twenty dollars worth of kupons." The idea of taking a tea set home on the bus deterred me; getting it to the States even less feasible. Anyway, I wouldn't be back for almost two years. "Maybe the next time I visit Baranivka," I said. That pleased them both, and we left.

When we got back to Misha's house, he suggested that we take some photos of Maxim with my camera. At that time, color film for consumers had been introduced into the country only a year or two before. In the USSR, shutterbugs had to buy all the low-quality developing chemicals and paper they could get their hands on and develop black-and-white snapshots in their bathrooms. Now Kiev had Kodak and Fuji overnight color print developing services, and anyone who could afford a fifty-dollar camera, a five-dollar roll of film, and thirteen dollars for developing could have glossy, brilliant colors. Because Misha's family couldn't spend that much on photos, I said I would be happy to take some pictures of Maxim.

It turned into an all-afternoon affair. For starters, Luda and Volodya got dressed up, and Luda caked on a great deal of makeup. Color photographs were taken only in studios, and so for now the house would be a studio. It was clear that natural shots were out of the question. With his parents in their Sunday finest, Maxim (also in his best outfit) posed in the living room. They stood rigid and dour as pall bearers. "Smile!" I said in English. Maxim alone smiled—hugely. I shot the photo although Volodya and Luda still looked serious and grim. After the shot Misha tried to convince his family that smiles would make better pictures. They asked me to take another. This time Maxim looked away, Volodya smiled, and Luda turned her chin up a degree, perhaps trying to look prouder. We kept shooting, trying different poses and expressions, all the while explaining to Grandfather how the automatic flash worked.

Luda wanted a few shots of Maxim alone, so she posed him on the couch. He could sit up if he was propped, and she fussed over him, smoothing down his few strands of flyaway hair and straightening his clothes. She finally got him to sit still on the couch, but he started to cry. We waved toys in his face until he quit, and got a few more nice pictures.

Several times Maxim looked away a split second *after* the flash had gone. The shutter snapped, the flash lingered in the dark room, and the family thought I'd missed the shot. "Oh," Volodya said. "No, didn't get it. He looked away."

Having seen through the viewfinder, I knew the shot was fine. "No, I got it. It's okay."

"No, well, he looked away at the very last moment."

Rather than attempt to explain the shutter/flash mechanism in Ukrainian, I just kept shooting. I was thankful I'd brought three rolls with me, then wondered if I would shoot them all up on Maxim and what it would cost to develop them. But when I remembered how generous Misha was and how welcoming his family had been, it seemed greedy to suggest stopping. So I took some more.

Some with Maxim and Grandpa. Some with Maxim and Grandpa and Misha. Then Maxim and Misha and Volodya. Then Mother alone. Then everybody. After every permutation they could think of, Luda finally said, "Well, good. That's probably enough inside. I'll go change him into a new outfit and then we can take a few in the sun in the backyard. All right?"

The photos we took out in the backyard came out great. So did the ones we took in the front yard, the side yard, Maxim in the stroller, Maxim on Grandpa's knee. My personal favorites were the ones of Maxim getting his bath on the kitchen table in a big metal basin full of warm water from the kettle. Yet after all that, I don't have one photograph to show for it. The next time I went to Kiev, I developed all three rolls and gave the prints and negatives to Misha.

When the afternoon light grew too dim and a sudden chill brought evening, we sat down to dinner. Before the visit, I had asked Misha what I should bring as a gift. He advised me to buy the skinny one-liter bottles of orange pop sold everywhere in Zhitomir, and I was glad I had, for an unexpected reason. When the table was laid out, Grandpa arrived carrying a clear, unlabeled bottle with a bent bottle-cap pressed on the top. I guessed rightly that it was *samahon*—moonshine. "Be careful," Misha whispered. "It's *Buryachik*." He raised his shoulders to his ears and shuddered violently. I wondered what that was, and thought perhaps I should pass.

"Nonsense," Misha's grandfather said gruffly. "Totally normal. Just have a little." He toasted my visit, and I thanked them in return for their hospitality. Holding up my half-full shot glass, I exhaled strongly, then tossed it back. The acrid smell startled me before I even tasted it, and the moment it went down, like sharply astringent mouthwash, I comprehended. The acid, caustic burning in the back of my throat had a very distinct flavor, and I knew beyond a doubt I was drinking alcohol made from distilled beets—*buryak*, in Ukrainian.

I munched on bread, and within seconds my whole body felt hot and flushed. With a puckery grin and a thumbs-up to grandpa, I kept eating—pickles, more bread, and homemade sausage from the big pig's predecessor. Then all at once, I felt better! Calmed, soothed, I basked in a balmy cradle of dark-purplish light. "Beets," I thought. "Whaddya know. Beets." My skin had turned warm all over. I had, at least, gained an theoretical appreciation for the awful-tasting poison.

Misha's grandpa drank some orange pop and declared it satisfactory—though disappointingly unlike real oranges. "Did you bring this from America?" he asked.

"No, grandpa," Misha said. "We bought it in Zhitomir. A lot of things like that are there now. This stuff is made in Poland."

"Poland?" his grandfather answered. "Can't be."

"Look at the label," Misha said. "It's in Polish. See? 'Produced in Poland,'" he read. Although written in Latin letters, the words resembled Ukrainian so much even I understood them.

"This can't be from Poland," Grandpa repeated, squinting at the label. "I've been to Poland. They don't grow oranges there."

Misha lightly made fun of his grandfather, but Grandpa wouldn't let me think for a minute that he was provincial and ignorant. "You know," he told me, "I fought in the Red Army in the Great Patriotic War. I remember very well what the Fascists did to my country. I was captured by German troops and imprisoned in Norway. Hard labor. I worked in a quarry for over a year, breaking up rocks.

"So I know about the West," he concluded. "I was there. I saw it."

After the long meal, Misha and I headed back out into the empty streets, now cold and dark. The disco, in a huge room in the House of Culture, was like most Ukrainian discos: blasting Europop, which they call "techno": bass pounding, industrial clanking, and drilling sounds shrieking to the beat. I could barely see anyone, except when the strobe illuminated a teenage body frozen in motion. Misha took off into the crowd and took up the crazy bobbing and bouncing of some acquaintances he hadn't seen for a while. Bracing myself for an unhappy evening, I stood against the wall feeling out of place. Everyone was more dressed up than I, and besides, I had no urge to thrash around on the stuffy, sweaty dance floor. I walked back out into the hall to look around.

A young-looking policeman saw me. "What's the matter? Why aren't you dancing?"

"Oh, I don't know. Don't really want to." As far as I knew, there was no law requiring me to dance, but I didn't say so.

"Hey . . . where are you from?"

With a sigh I told him I was American, here visiting with my friend Misha.

"Yeah, I saw you come in with him." With a funny, simple curiosity, he asked, "How would our Misha get to know an American?"

At that point, I told him my name, then about my school, about Peace Corps, about living in the Misha's dorm. The policeman listened intently, nodding and wrinkling his brow to process what I said. When Misha came out a moment later, they shook hands. "School friends," the cop said to me. "I'll tell you what. I want to give you a present." He removed his policeman's hat and handed it to me. Red and gray, the color and style of militiamen's hats all across the former USSR, it had a shiny black bill that looked very authoritarian. In my hands, though, it looked very silly. "Try it on," he urged.

I knew I would look foolish, but I put it on my head. It sat up much too high, stiffly at attention. Both of them laughed, and a few other people gathered to look. "You keep it," the policeman said. "It's yours."

I laughed at the thought—surely he was just being friendly. It was probably illegal in Ukraine for me to wear a police uniform, and anyway it wasn't exactly the kind of thing I would wear to parties. I handed him back his hat. "It's very nice of you. But of course I can't."

"No, I'm serious. I want you to have it." He pushed my hands away from him and would not take it back.

"But it's your uniform!"

"Don't worry," he added. "I have another, the new Ukrainian-style. This old one's Soviet." He pointed to the hammer-and-sickle emblem. "Keep it as a souvenir."

"If you don't want it," Misha said, "I'll take it." He put it on and the people around us laughed even harder. The policeman grabbed it and gave it back to me. "It's not for you. Only for John."

The policeman looked strange with no hat, but nobody cared. It was awkward to hold, but I couldn't think where to put it. So I put it back on my head. Misha took me by the elbow and led me back into the sweaty, dark gymnasium. In the meantime, someone had told the deejay about me. I was startled half to death when a voice over the loudspeaker boomed: "This next song is dedicated to our very special guest, here tonight from America—his name is Dzhone! Let's show Dzhone that we Ukrainians know how to have a good time, too—American-style!" Everyone screamed wildly. Merely my presence added coolness to the event; also, probably, they were cheering for what they thought America represented, in this case wanton abandon on the dance floor. Mostly they were just young people having a good time on Saturday night, happy to let loose a yell for any reason. For me, though, it was completely weird. A stranger in town for the weekend, I was once again an instant celebrity. When a spotlight found me on the dance floor, I waved my new police hat and cheered too.

On Sunday afternoon it was time to go back. Volodya suggested we take one last walk around town. He liked having Misha home and wanted to go back with us—or maybe I could visit the weekend after? Misha reminded his brother to come to Zhitomir every now and then, where he could always stop by my dorm room. "Just drop in," I laughed. "That's where you'll find Misha."

We hadn't walked far before Volodya suggested we stop for a beer. "Baranivka has very good beer," Misha added. "You'll see." If it was anything like its *Buryachik*, I said, I'd do better without. They laughed, and Volodya said "One for the road" or, in Ukrainian, "Onto the horses."

The only bar in town was a dingy cinder-block building with a sign that read "Bar." Inside, an old woman stared deadpan at us as we ordered. "We want our American friend to try beer made in Baranivka," Misha told her cheerfully. She didn't answer, but put three bottles on the counter.

The dimly lit bar had the air of a 1970s dive, with luridly painted dark red walls and huge circular vinyl-seated booths. From a corner in the back, a voice called out to Misha. It was Sasha, sitting in a booth with the four teenage boys in his candy bar business.

"Well, how do you like it here so far?" Sasha asked me as we sat down. The boys watched carefully, silent but with great interest.

"I like it," I said. "It's not quite what I expected."

Sasha laughed, and repeated my Ukrainian word "expected." He said to the boys in Russian, "John speaks only Ukrainian—pure Ukrainian. How about that?"

Just then a bellowing shout came from the end of the bar. I looked back towards the bright light of the doorway and saw the tall silhouette of a man haranguing the old woman tending bar.

"Oh, great," Misha said. "Drunk as a pig."

"Do you know him?" I asked Misha, who shook his head stiffly, and said, "Shh." The drunk staggered towards our table, hollering belligerently.

"Hey boys! What's going on? Having a little party?" His black hair was wild and stringy, his teeth askew, and his black leather jacket looked dusty, as if he had fallen down quite often this morning. He scooted into the booth, edging Volodya over closer to me. Misha, on my left, glared at the drunk with curdling suspicion.

"I heard you've got an American here," he said loudly, before hiccuping violently. "I'm going to buy him a drink." His ugly leer terrified me. "Hey woman! Bring us a bottle, and quick." At the far end of the bar, the old woman polished glasses quietly and pretended not to hear.

In a genuine-sounding voice Volodya welcomed the drunk. "Hey brother! Looks like you're the one having a little party. You heard wrong, though. Look around. There's no American here."

The drunk looked at the faces of Sasha's boys, at Sasha, then at Misha, then me. His eyes were literally almost crossed, he was so intoxicated. My skin prickled; he was erratic and maybe on the edge of violence—not by a long shot anyone I was interested in getting acquainted with.

"You," he grunted. "You're an American. I can tell by looking at you." I didn't move. "All that long hair." I turned to look at Misha, whom the drunk had addressed.

"That's right," Misha said half-smiling, his Ukrainian spotless. "You figured me out. I'm an American student at the Ped Institute in Zhitomir. Nice to meet you." The boys stifled a giggle; Misha's "Nice to meet you," imitated my accent and intonation perfectly.

"What's so funny?" the drunk said ominously. "You think I'm not as good as an American? I can kick ten American asses any day of the week! Even after a drink or two." His eyes lost focus, and he swayed in his seat a second. "You, the hippie," he blurted at Misha (who hated to be called a hippie). "You don't fool me for a second."

"You're right," Volodya reassured him. "We can't fool you, can we." I sat still, trying to look nonchalant.

"Just a bunch of boys," the drunk said, mostly to himself. He stood up to leave and nearly fell over. He grabbed the table to steady himself, and then his eyes widened to bleary, yellow ovals. I shouldn't have stared so closely.

"Hey, professor!" he growled through his teeth, this time glaring directly at me. "What are you looking at?"

I was chewing the earpiece of my glasses, an unconscious habit and a gesture unusual enough to grab his attention.

"Nothing," I mumbled, looking down and hoping my accent would be inaudible.

His eyes turned towards the door, and he smiled idiotically. "Well, then boys! See ya later! His tone had flip-flopped to general well-wishing, as if the past few moments hadn't occurred. "Have a good time with your little party!" The drunk stumbled out the door, and I drank a deep swig of the beer. It really was good. Sasha and the boys started laughing.

"Hey, Misha," Sasha said. "Tell us about America! Ever been to Disneyland?"

Misha smiled, but ignored them, instead turning to me in curiosity. "I think it's your nose. Or your blond hair. But you look more Ukrainian than I do."

In spite of our side excursion to the bar, we made our bus in time. On the way back, we did not have to get out and push even once.

Chapter Eleven

Bread, the Soul of Our Motherland

Misha and I were eating in my kitchen on a dark November evening. With our coffee we ate buttered bread, soft slices of which I cut from a brown, circular loaf shaped like a dome: flat on the bottom, rounded on top. After cutting enough bread I replaced the loaf in the breadbox, carelessly tossing it in upside down.

"Hey!" Misha said, "What are you doing?" He looked alarmed. Gently he removed the bread, turned it right side up, and replaced it. "You don't stand bread on its head. It isn't nice."

Apologizing, I asked him why. He paused, frowning, as if trying to come up with an explanation. He couldn't, and instead answered, "Well, how would you like to be left standing upside down on your head? You wouldn't like it, would you?"

Normally I might have teased Misha about hurting the feelings of a loaf of bread. But he turned so serious that I knew better than to insult him. Bread was a sacred treasure. To treat it lightly was irreverent, like a form of blasphemy.

When I looked around, I noticed that message everywhere. The blank notebooks my students bought (all from the same store, of course) differed only in the varieties of instructional messages printed on the backs. Curious, I frequently paused in my grading to read the new propaganda. Liberated from Marxism, the notebooks now admonished children just to be well-behaved. Like Biblical commandments, the short, simple paragraphs encouraged protection of nature, performing kind deeds, or not speaking loudly and rudely. Out of all these rather inane messages, however, one moved me deeply. It concerned a child's proper attitude to bread.

> Bread! Don't we care for it with such respect! Always people speak about it with deep honor, and take it in trembling hands with great solemnity.
> From childhood, learn to see within the life of bread the soul of our motherland, our nation's sun and sky. Learn to see in it the work of all, the people who give their lives to it.
> Old people are able to honor bread—respect them for this, and learn from them. Remember: your presentation of bread educates others.
> If a person asks you for bread, break your own piece into two, even if it's your last.
> Remember: so that you'll have a piece of bread, toil for humanity. The portion of bread depends on every one of us.

Children were indoctrinated from birth to believe in the holiness of bread; as soon as they could read, it was imprinted on their brains. Afterward, cultural traditions reinforced the message. For instance, bread was a traditional wedding gift presented by a mother to her daughter and new son-in-law, symbolizing prosperity and a happy home. The bride and groom each attempted to take the biggest possible bite from the loaf, for whoever did so would dominate in the marriage. Bread was so much more than a diet staple that to waste it was worse than insensitive—it was an assault on good morals.

Misha chastised me for throwing out crusts gone completely

blue with mold. "What am I supposed to do?" I asked him. "You don't see a pig around here, do you?"

"Give it to the *dezhurnaya*, like I do," he said, and told me to which dorm mother he gave his scraps. She took the dried-up, hardened pieces home for her dogs, after softening them in water or a little milk. The tiniest crumbs went to chickens. Never a scrap was wasted.

Maybe that was why standing in a long bread line every day was tolerable. Bread was worth waiting for. Most of those queued up for bread were old men and children, because other family members were busy with more difficult chores (or stood in other lines). Seven-year-olds stood alone in a store for half an hour until it was their turn. The old people around them—strangers—asked them questions and chatted. Standing in line for bread was tedious, but when everyone suffered equally, like a family sharing a common burden, it didn't feel so frustrating. I still wished the cashiers would hurry up a bit, but when I complained about the long lines once, Svetlana Adamovna told me she actually *liked* standing in the bread line. "It's where I learn the whole town's gossip," she said. "I find out secrets, like where cheap lipstick is being sold, or that the minister of defense will visit next week, or about good fishing in a lake on the road to Novograd-Vilinsky. Sometimes I hear news about someone across town I haven't heard from recently."

Bread was like a pillar of society: an adequate supply meant no panic, no riots. Failing to honor bread was like feeling immune from fate, from an apocalyptic skeleton always lurking around the corner.

"Probably, there won't be a famine next year," Max had told me with utter earnestness. His tone was optimistic, as if that were good news. Tanya shook her head sadly—so little to hope for.

"Probably?" I asked, hoping to hear the familiar ironic tone in his voice.

"Probably there won't be," he said, deadpan as could be. "Rumor has it."

Rumor was awfully pessimistic—for good reason. With salaries long unpaid, even good weather was no reassurance. With no paid workers to reap them, collective farm crops sometimes rotted in the fields. The farm workers that year lost over half the year's sugar beets when no one harvested them. And sugar beets were primarily for export; the grain harvest, most essential of all, gave most concern.

As I shopped in my local market, the Ukrainian word for famine kept ringing in my ears: "Holod." It sounded almost exactly like the word for cold: "Kholod." I knew the latter—chilly November promised a winter of shivering, wishing for hot water and heat. But hunger . . . I had never known hunger or anything like it. Eating skimpy meals in my dorm and walking everywhere, I had lost fifteen pounds since I left the United States. But even when I went to bed after suppers of nothing but bread and jam, it was more because I was too tired to cook than because of scarcity of food. In the market I saw bucketsful of cabbages and potatoes; outspread cloths cradling eggs; wire crates overflowing with dirty beets. I haggled for pork chops and bacon in the meat market. The big grocery store had barrels of buckwheat, rice, flour. . . .

Famine?

Despite its thousands of square miles of fertile soil, Ukraine suffered famine so horrific it defies reason—most of all because starvation resulted not from Soviet inefficiency, disorganization, or bad weather, but from a clearly structured, carefully executed policy of one powerful, evil man.

In the 1930s, Stalin purposefully forced the starvation of four to twelve million peasants, most of them in Ukraine. Robert Conquest's *The Harvest of Sorrow* recounts in excruciating detail the attempt to exterminate the Ukrainian nation. Soviet communism had to be forced on Ukraine, especially on its rural people. First, in the 1920s the government convinced peasants that they were threatened by the "rich, exploitive peasant"—a *kulak* in Russian or *kurkul* in Ukrainian. Kulaks, morally corrupt wreckers of society, had to be punished, and not surprisingly they were found everywhere. Not only a peasant who employed a farmhand but any person who owned as little as one cow could be labeled a kulak. Perhaps ten million people were killed or arrested and sent north to prison camps.

Next Stalin forced collectivization on rural Russia, Ukraine, and other republics. Resistance was fiercest in Ukraine. Peasants were forced onto farms, their livestock and land taken; those who resisted were killed or exiled. Out of spite, some peasants slit the throats of their own horses and cattle to prevent the collective farm from appropriating them. Especially in Ukraine, villagers resisted what they saw as a return to serfdom. Forced collectivization went ahead anyway.

Khrushchev admitted in 1956 that during the 1930s, Ukrainians posed a problem for Stalin, who was sending entire minority groups into the camps. The problem was that there were 50 million of them. "Only because there were too many [Ukrainians] and there was no place to which to deport them," he said. "Otherwise [Stalin] would have deported them also."

Instead of moving all of Ukraine to Siberia, Stalin turned Ukraine—an area the size of France—into one gigantic gulag. The resulting struggle by rural people resulted in what is perhaps the least-publicized genocide of the twentieth century: the terror-famine of 1933. Stalin's sly methods helped him escape historical blame. In the fall of 1932, officials first set wildly unreachable grain quotas. Then they requisitioned more grain than was produced; everything, down to the last kernel of wheat, was put on trains and shipped out of the rebellious oblasts in Ukraine. Some of it was only shipped as far as the border of Russia, where it was dumped and left to rot. Finally, by the winter of 1933, there was nothing left to eat in the Ukrainian countryside. Now that property and land had been declared state-owned, peasants who were caught digging up potatoes, or gleaning wheat from a field, or even hiding a sack of wheat in the house were shot. Even children.

By March 1933, death began on a mass scale. No cats were heard meowing or dogs barking in the villages, because they had all been eaten. The villagers then ate mice, sparrows, ants, dandelions, and nettles. Document-checking prevented villagers from reaching towns like Zhitomir or Vinnitsa or Kiev; those few who did were sent back to the starving region or deported, or died in streets that filled with swollen bodies. Deprived of food and unable to leave, people starved in their homes. People dug up dead horses. Children starved when their starving parents were shot. Hunger makes people insane before it kills them, and reportedly even cannibalism occurred after people went mad. When the villages were empty, Russian peasants were moved in to repopulate the empty towns—even the very same houses—which stank of death.

Unlike in the 1921 famine, no relief effort was allowed to enter Ukraine. No official body count was made, and the Soviet census quietly stopped recording figures for Ukraine until after World War II had taken more lives and obscured the numbers killed in the 1930s. Some provinces lost 20 percent of their people to the famine. Some, like Zhitomir province, lost perhaps "only" 15 percent of the villagers in an 1100-square-mile region. The death rate was lower than in the regions consisting of nothing but sweeping fields because the forests, streams, and lakes north of Zhitomir (the same ones now eternally ruined by Chornobyl) sustained villagers who found wild plants and surreptitiously caught fish (which was also punishable by death). Other starving people in the Zhitomir region survived in slightly higher numbers by resorting to the more desperate of measures.

One day Luda, her ten-year-old daughter, Julia, and I took the number nine trolleybus out Schorsa street toward Bogunia, the eastern edge of town. Luda nodded when our stop approached, and we squeezed through the crowd to get off the bus, Julia tightly grasping her mother's hand. "That way," Luda said, pointing downhill. We walked down a quiet street toward a bridge over the Kamenka, a creek that ran into the Teteriv. At the river's edge, we stopped at the Polish cemetery.

National distinctions mattered even in death, and so the Polish cemetery was distinct from both the Eastern Orthodox cemeteries and the Jewish cemetery. Zhitomir had once been within the territory of Poland; it also was in the heart of "the Pale of Settlement," the region of the Russian empire to which the Jews had been banished. Remnants of the competing cultures remained: the Catholic church in the center of town was full on Sundays and holidays like Easter and Christmas, and a small synagogue served the few remaining people who religiously practiced their Judaism. Otherwise, these cultures, as a result of the catastrophes of the twentieth century, were nearly invisible—especially Jews, who had once formed ninety percent of the population of some towns and villages in the Zhitomir region.

Luda and Julia and I visited the Polish cemetery even though Luda knew no relatives interred there. She liked to feel connected to her Polish ancestry, which she considered something like a noble background. Inside the stone walls surrounding the cemetery, the hillside was draped with trees, and it seemed like a serene grove except for the tipped-over, cracked, mossy stones, nearly all in disarray. Julia studied Polish as well as English and practiced reading the Polish names and the eighteenth- and nineteenth-century dates. "Look! Ma," she cried, jumping from one broken stone to the next. "Mother and daughter, Edwiga and Katya Krajewski." The trees had slithered their gnarly roots around rocks and stones and seemed to be tiptoeing around in the cemetery. Set into the side of the hill and sealed up with more recent-looking concrete were the crypts of those who had been wealthier. Many of the crypt walls had holes where bricks were missing. "Ooh," Luda shuddered. "I don't like this place."

"It's nice to walk here, though," I suggested. "It's interesting."

"Too bad so many graves are disturbed," she noted, pointing

to a hole dug underneath a horizontal slab. "Hooligans. I'd never come here at night."

"I see bones down there," Julia announced with glee. I saw where she pointed. A thick legbone with knobby ends lay on top of a pile of rocks and mud. Raiding graves probably could be blamed on "hooliganism," but in the 1930s, during the famine more desperate motives had been at work. Then, Ukrainian peasants had broke open the graves of wealthy Polish Catholics who had lived in the Zhitomir region during pre-Revolutionary times. The starving people stripped rings from bony fingers, peeled necklaces from human carcasses, and removed the gold or jewelry they found.

After all, the Soviets were ransacking their own, living treasures by burning icons and destroying churches. Many peasants took down the ancient icons from the sacred corners of their huts and folded up their holiday clothing, meticulously embroidered in patterns unique to each village. Then the peasants gathered these valuables—which by tradition held special prominence in Ukrainian homes for almost a thousand years— and hauled them to bazaars in bigger cities like Kiev, where they stood and waited for the richer, well-fed cityfolk. All of these valuables they exchanged for loaves of bread.

"Let's go," Luda said, turning back down the windy hill. "I'd forgotten how much I don't like cemeteries."

With such a history, it was remarkable that Ukrainians were so generous with food.

No matter whom I visited, a table was spread for me, often with food that had been saved for a special occasion. I felt guilty for eating up half of my town's food reserves; anyone I visited broke out their best garlic pickles or deliciously juicy preserved tomatoes. When they knew I was coming, they bought meat to grind up for cutlets or spent extra on the better kind of sausage, even though they might not have spared money for meat the whole month up till then. My hosts shopped in extra stores to find cheese or cheaper eggs or a favorite kind of expensive canned fish. They harnessed all their resources—their friend whose grandmother had fresh milk, or another friend who owed a favor and hoarded Estonian pickled herring, or the relative who had tucked away a special bottle of Moldovan wine. Ukrainians were ingenious at scrounging up one or two special items to make a meal turn fantastic. Any single thing on the table might have cost half a month's salary, had it been purchased. The Russian saying goes, "Better a hundred friends than a hundred rubles." Of course, at that time a hundred rubles was worth one-fortieth of a box of matches, so people joked, "Well then, better a hundred friends than a hundred *million* rubles."

Food not obtained by cashing in on favors might have been bought with someone's last scraps of money. Out of Soviet habit, or to beat inflation, people spent money as fast as they got it—which sounds irresponsible only to someone with an insured bank account. Unable to save for the future, Ukrainians often used up their earnings immediately on something cheerful and diverting—often a good meal, an indulgence they could not afford every day.

I knew for a fact what people ate for normal meals, and it was not the chicken or beef stew or even rabbit I was served when I came as a guest. I knew because I shopped in the same stores they did, like the one down the street from my dormitory, where every day the old women protested, "No, no, only the very cheapest macaroni, and not too much. No, scoop some back, that's too much. There. How much will that cost?" For old people, a lifetime's work rewarded with that kind of life is a raw deal. It was an ugly prospect for the young people of today looking ahead to a future that looked no brighter.

Such poverty had to be hidden for visitors, however, even if great sacrifices were required. According to ancient tradition, "God enters the household with every guest." So they prepared dishes that took hours to make: *rareniki*, ravioli-like dumplings; *holubtsi*, cabbage rolls filled with buckwheat groats; or *shuba* (which means fur-coat), a layered salad made of herring, potatoes, mayonnaise, and beets. Meals lasted hours; conversation was vivacious, loud; boisterous, and opinionated; and we talked until the vodka was gone. No Ukrainian wanted to be accused of spreading a meager table or of being inhospitable. To refuse a helping of something was merely standard politeness the first three times. By the fourth time I had protested, "No, really, thanks—nothing more for me," more food had already been put on my plate. How odd that in a country of famine I grew accustomed to eating until I thought I would burst.

When the 1933 terror-famine was happening, the West mostly looked the other way. Walter Duranty of the *New York Times* described "fat calves" in Ukraine and declared all reports of famine to be fabrications; this was after being shown Potemkin villages and being escorted on carefully conducted tours displaying only well-fed workers. He benefited from good treatment by Soviet authorities and won a Pulitzer Prize for "dispassionate, interpretive reporting of the news from Russia." His selective vision allowed the United States to diplomatically recognize the Soviet Union in 1933 and aided later historians who claimed the famine was a result of other factors and not of a consciously planned policy of terror.

World War II—which devastated the territory and people of Ukraine worse than either Russia or Germany—obscured the tragic famine. Unfortunately, the 1930s had driven some Ukrainians in western Ukraine to view Hitler as a savior from Stalin. After 1945, many Ukrainian nationalists were suppressed, killed, or exiled, as sympathizers to the Fascists. The terror-famine that killed six to ten million people and perhaps many more was covered up and disputed. Another Holocaust had come to the forefront, the one that left western Ukraine with only 2 percent of its Jews. This event entered western consciousness and history in a way that Stalin's 1933 terror-famine in Ukraine never will.

After all, for us today it takes some imagination to feel

connected with the life of an early-century Ukrainian peasant, who, much like his medieval ancestors, plowed his farmland behind a horse, lived in a mud-and-brick hut, perhaps could read but most likely could not, and had never been more than a few miles from his village. Even Ukrainians told me, "Yes, well, that was a long time ago." But not that long—plenty of Ukrainians over seventy are still alive. The children and grandchildren of famine survivors heard whispered stories. Even those who do not personally recall the ghosts of Stalin's victims inhabit the cities, towns, and villages that are haunted by them. For Ukrainians the desire to remember may be dwarfed by the desire to gain distance from a past that is awful in any number of ways.

Suffering to death by starvation must have been horrific; it was unprecedented in scale. However, the genocide of Ukraine in 1933, now called the *Holodomor*, was not only an assault on its people. As part of the terrors of the 1930s, it was meant to crush the drive for Ukrainian statehood. Like in Russia, the intelligentsia were jailed and killed, and theater, literature, and language abolished if it was not pro-Soviet enough. In Ukraine, however, the rural folk culture that formed Ukraine's identity was attacked as well. For example, blind musicians traditionally wandered Ukraine from village to village, playing their banduras, stringed instruments resembling (and descended from) the medieval lute. These bards, or *kobzars* as they were called, sang ancient folk songs that celebrated Ukraine's past and handed down its oral traditions. In 1934, these *kobzars* were invited to Kharkiv for a "conference" on folk music. There, they were shot. Since then, even certain Ukrainian songs were forbidden—right up until 1991.

Whenever I wanted to curse Ukrainians for lying down in front of their fate (or for inventing sly ways around it), I tried to focus on the lessons their history had taught them, in contrast to those I could take from mine. Their ancestors had been deliberately starved to death, all voices of outrage were stopped, independent thought was squelched, and, in a kind of unnatural selection, the sneaky side of human nature was rewarded. Such thoughts made me wonder how people kept from going insane and why the country was not even more chaotic than it was.

The famine's wounding of Ukraine has hardly begun to heal, perhaps because the injury itself is so little discussed. The sixtieth anniversary of the genocidal famine in 1993 was also Ukraine's first national recognition of it. As the guilty die out, it is safer for the rest to remember. Or perhaps memory has always been expressed, if silently: as caution about the future.

If someone as clear-headed and practical as my friend Max could say, "probably there won't be a famine this year," then the fear of undernourishment has not disappeared. Until it does, every loaf of bread in Ukraine will stand for more than an essential component of every meal. "Bread! The soul of our motherland, our nation's sun and sky!"

Chapter Twelve

If You're Happy and You Know It

By January, nothing about Ukraine was new or fun anymore. After weeks at −10 degrees the weather became slightly warmer, but this only meant that the streets and sidewalks ran with gray slush that refroze at night. Walking became treacherous. Puddles froze into patches of black, and as soon as my feet touched them I hit the ground. On the days I didn't take a hard fall, I picked my way along, slipping and skidding, wobbling and flailing my arms clumsily to regain balance, all the time cursing: at Zhitomir, at Ukraine, at the weather, at people who didn't shovel sidewalks—finally at myself for moving to such a dark, gloomy place.

The holidays of Christmas (Catholic or "Polish" Christmas, some called it), then New Year's, and then Orthodox Christmas had all come and gone. On January 13 we had even celebrated the paradoxically named "Old New Year," a holiday commemorating the day that *used* to be New Year's in the Old Style calendar—the Russian empire had been almost two weeks behind the West and at the end of 1917, leapt ahead to match the West. Even two Christmases and two New Year's Eves were not enough to cheer me up. Icy winds whirled between the apartment buildings, and people went indoors to wait out a traditional time of inactivity.

Economic conditions had worsened, and cutbacks to survive winter were introduced. Rumors had it that school might be canceled for several weeks if fuel for the heating system did not appear. My dormitory's daytime running water had been turned off, so for the few hours in the evening I had water, I would fill metal buckets in my shower with water for my morning cooking, washing, and a single flush of the toilet. To emphasize how serious the energy shortage was, the television signal from Moscow was cut off. Then, all the stores in the country closed for a day to update the state-controlled prices: everything from bread to trolleybus fares tripled in cost. It felt like the newly independent, newly impoverished Ukraine was spiraling downward out of control. My own daily life had lost its rustic charm, and my sustaining sense of mission and pride to be working in a difficult place had faded like an unrecallable dream.

As for school, January was considered a loss to be written off. My pupils were absent for long periods, partly because Ukrainian parents tended to believe that even the slightest cold was reason enough to stay home. Without inexpensive, widely available medicine—even aspirin could be difficult to acquire—it was best never to take chances with one's health. The pupils who did reluctantly come to class were tired after the holidays. Languidly staring out the window, chin in hand, the ninth graders answered questions half-heartedly, hypnotized by the falling snow. The only lesson in which a brief moment of excitement occurred was when Oksana jumped out of her seat one time to exclaim, "Look! The soldiers are playing hockey!" Everyone ran to the window to peer over the schoolyard fence into the military compound next door, where a parking lot stood half-full of olive drab army trucks. Soldiers were zooming around, pushing sticks ahead of them—but they were pushbrooms, not hockey sticks. The soldiers sweeping the parking lot dashed back and forth, in the distance looking like toys. Their Soviet-style uniforms—big fur hats and long trench coats—evoked for me an image of official, stern intimidation. Hilariously, though, they skidded playfully around the ice in their cheap, slippery boots, looking like bored kids sliding to idle away the time. My pupils and I stared quietly at the intriguing scene while the young men swept up the snow even as it fell. After a quiet moment or two, they sat back down and we continued the lesson.

I had to admire those soldiers, who kept at their task even as the snow fell faster than they could keep up. They could even feel playful in the face of such an impossible-seeming task. I had come to feel that School 23 did not really need me whatsoever. My idea of "helping" them had been vainglorious, if well-intentioned. I vowed to work harder, but with less urgency. Performing so many outside extra lessons led me to neglect my own classes, and after I dedicated myself to more thorough planning, my lessons went better. In the school library I dug up a few copies of *The Great Gatsby* in both English and Russian. My 9B class surprised me by handling the difficult material well. I focused not on correct translations (since they had the text in both languages) but on understanding vocabulary, analyzing the story, and talking about characters. Perhaps my own language skills had improved, or perhaps they were merely used to me by then. In any case, their work improved.

The 9G class was still another story. Someone from that class, I was certain, had stolen from my classroom, which was also the language lab. They left apple cores, sunflower seed husks, and wads of paper in the drawers where the big rubber-padded headphones were stored. Most of these drawers didn't lock. Behind my back someone had apparently dropped a pair of headphones into his bookbag. I would have solved the problem by simply buying a new pair myself, but not a store in hundreds of miles had them. They were basically irreplaceable. I couldn't help thinking that a native teacher would never have let this happen.

When I told the vice principal for English, Galina Vasilievna, her face turned red, but she kept silent. The next day she stormed into my first period class to confront the 9G pupils. Her piercing voice made all of us wince, as she berated them at high volume for several minutes. If the headphones were not returned, they would all have to pay. Ruslan, the small boy with crooked teeth, boldly (or foolishly) retorted, "It wasn't one of us. Why should we have to pay?" He had a point, I thought. Anyone could have slipped in between lessons while the room was left unlocked and sometimes unattended. If only Ruslan weren't so well known as a liar. At this, Galina Vasilievna screamed even louder. She threatened to switch them to another teacher if they didn't shape up. Part of me wished she would; I was so tired of fighting the class to no purpose. But part of me felt protective of these pupils, who, because they were not the school's best and brightest, were being accused on suspicion alone. The girls especially felt it unfair and hated to be shouted at, but they simply waited until it ended. After that, I locked the classroom between class periods.

Despite the missing headphones, ignited matches, and indifference to my style of discipline, I was determined not to let the antagonistic subtext conquer me. I insisted that all the pupils speak, even the weakest ones. I reported misbehaviors to Galina Vasilievna, and the offending students returned to my class apologizing—sincerely, this time—and promising to do better. And they did. A few of these students—kids who had been basically parked in my class—showed real interest in English and spoke a few, cautious, original sentences, a feat I considered progress.

Half the time I feared they were picking up English they shouldn't. When I scratched on the waxy blackboard with a thick block of chalk, it flaked off and fluttered to the floor. Not being able to write on the board frustrated me so much I occasionally cursed at it. Since I was facing away from the class, I thought they wouldn't catch my muttered obscenities. But Ruslan, the crooked-toothed boy, had very sharp ears concerning anything he shouldn't know. "What did you say, Mr. John?" he asked politely, grinning like a cat in a creamery. "Say it again!" he added, and then turned a Soviet Pioneer phrase to new use. "I'm always ready to learn!"

As if my accidental cursing wasn't irresponsible enough, I found out that some sounds in English can be highly suggestive in Russian. The expression "blah, blah, blah," for example, does not stand as a substitute for irrelevant talking as in the United States. (Ukrainians said "lya, lya, lya" to mean the same.) I learned this the hard way by telling my ninth-graders, "There is too much talking! All I hear is blah blah blah!" They went from startled horror to nearly hysterical laughter. No wonder: The word sounds very much like Russian slang for "whore."

They already knew well enough the rough edges of life in the Soviet Union. One day I asked the 9G class about a famous surgeon and the only person except for Lenin in the USSR to be mummified and preserved. One student shouted out the man's name: "Pirogov!" The voice was Igor's—the worst troublemaker in the school and the last I expected to hear from. The only other time he had volunteered information up until then had been to ask me whether I knew what "cosa nostra" meant. So when I answered, "Yes, that's right. Very good, Igor," I must not have hidden my surprise very well. Igor's friend Serhiy guessed what I was thinking, and in his deep voice boomed out: "No, Mr. John, he doesn't dream of becoming a surgeon. He just likes to cut people with knives."

Most, however, just wanted to get through the school day as smoothly and as comfortably as possible. I struggled to control what they thought of as "helping" and what I called "cheating." On written assignments, "wandering eyes" were the norm, and even when in oral drills, those who knew the answer whispered the answers to those who didn't.

Cheating developed into a kind of ridiculous charade, in which, if the act were not acknowledged, denial could seemingly be endless. I would tell Luda to stop whispering answers to Ruslan. Ruslan would then look back in startled amazement, on his face the most unconvincing "Who, me?!" expression I'd ever seen. Luda would nod knowingly, suggesting that she and I were the only ones with secret knowledge of Ruslan's mischief, and her eyes, somehow expressing both agreement and remorse, said, "We both know I was helping Ruslan, but you can trust me not to do it any more." Even when I would catch a boy red-handed with a cheat sheet in his lap, he still maintained a pose of denial, or, at best, dismissed my accusation with a shrug. Outwitting those sly ones never worked. My only vindication lay in the knowledge that Luda's "answers" were most likely wrong as often as they were right.

One time I spied Ruslan busy writing, with not a glance to anyone around him. Proud of his independent efforts, I went over to check on his progress. I should have guessed: He was writing a note, which I immediately took away. When several girls demanded I read it out loud, I sensed that something was going on. Ruslan's note read (in English) "Natasha, I love you—Sasha." Ruslan liked to set up Sasha, who would protest to no avail that he didn't write the note. Then Ruslan, Natasha, and her girlfriends could share a laugh at Sasha's expense (and thereby verify a secret flirtation between themselves).

It was important to remind myself that, after all, they were fourteen-year-olds, and were spending their adolescence in what was mostly a dark, often hopeless time. With no economic security in sight, they foresaw dangerous, unhealthy daily lives without real promises that conditions would improve. The brightest students (and those with newly rich parents) now had great opportunities compared with the generation before; the rest of the kids had it much tougher.

After the last lesson of the day, two pupils would always appear and begin to clean the classroom. Skirting the rules about peeking at someone else's paper might be acceptable, but failing to show up for "duty" was not. Often the students were girls, because the boys always managed to take fewer turns. Still, the boys performed their after-school duties, too. Even Serhiy and Ruslan did their jobs well and without any instructions. Unsupervised, they each took on a task, one wiping the chalkboards, one sweeping, and worked steadily. They mopped every day, using a long T-shaped pole, at the end of the which was wrapped a burlap rag. A bucket of water sometimes had to be fetched from downstairs when our floor had no water. The young men or women dragged and pushed those damp rags across the floor until it had wetted the surface and picked up some dust. They did this with an air not of enthusiasm but of boredom, of course; yet they would not have thought of complaining. Ukrainian kids accepted mundane chores as normal components of school life.

When I would stay behind and help them place all the chairs onto the desks upside down, I could see that it made them uncomfortable. They always said, "No, Mr. John, you don't need to! We can do it." Perhaps they worried that another teacher might think they had tricked me into doing their work. More likely, they preferred me to remain in my respected position of respect. Teachers might be tricked, but they were not to be disrespected, and duties like cleaning the classroom—which fulfilled teachers' expectations and demands—were never taken lightly.

With my third and fourth graders, in contrast, school was still interesting enough that they felt no need for tricks. I followed the Soviet-era textbook, and their skills in very basic English improved, if slowly. In January, we had worked up in the textbook to lessons that practiced "will" and "won't." These phrases were challenging even for the quickest kids. How enviably easy the construction is in Ukrainian: "will" and "no will." (As in "Mr. John, I no will do this home task.") We also learned the articles of clothing, and each pupil delighted when it was his or her turn to recite the textbook's tongue-twister of a poem: "Shoes and boots, boots and shoes. Which to choose? Which to choose? Shoes and boots, boots and shoes."

My only disciplining of the younger pupils came when they brought toys to class. Ukrainian kids—no different from Ukrainian adults—loved the colorful, novel gimcrackery flooding in from the West. The cornucopia of good toys strewn about a typical house in the United States was not only beyond the means but outside the imagination of Soviet kids. Naturally, kids anywhere play happily with whatever they have at hand; they only feel slighted when someone else has a great toy they don't. Now that they know, they've got to have Western toys. Barbie dolls, for example, were deeply coveted, but at ten to fifteen dollars apiece they cost half or all of a typical Ukrainian monthly salary at that time. Most kids had to settle for Crackerjack-style prizes and the variety of other newly introduced cheap bits of plastic: superballs, tiny cars, noisemaking keychains, Mercedes and BMW trading cards—all of which ended up in my classroom. It probably seemed the best place for informal show and tell.

My room must have seemed a kind of "no-teacher" zone to the younger kids, and they liked to spend the whole five—or ten-minute break before the lesson playing in my classroom. The third graders raced through the halls, dodging and weaving between slower-moving pupils, rushing to see who could get to class first, and finally bursting into the room as if the building were burning and Mr. John had to be told. Often I was treated to the funny sight of them crashing into sluggish ninth graders who were just leaving and in no hurry to go anywhere. For the little ones, school was still a good game, and getting to class first was a daily contest. A boy, usually overly competitive Vitaliy, charged in shouting, "I'm first!" As the only one there to hear him, I dryly responded, "Good boy." Sasha and Vova followed, crying "Second!" and "Third!" before chubbier Timur tumbled in and sadly huffed out, "I'm fourth." Masha and Annya skipped in next, then froze in the doorway to count how many early birds had beaten them. With a sigh, Masha said, "Well, it means I'm fifth." Sniffly little Annya Koaleko would add proudly, "And I'm sixth!" *A ya shosti.* But Annya came to class rarely that winter because of illness, so I didn't see her often. Natasha, my genius girl, was too mature for racing around, and usually strolled in last. She calmly rolled her eyes with genuine unconcern when Vitaliy joyously shouted, "Natashka, you're last! I'm the very first!" Tilting her head slightly, she retorted, "You're the very stupidest."

Before the lesson began, I confiscated all the toys I could

see. If I didn't round up the play equipment, it appeared on laps and under notebooks throughout the period. Most children stuffed their Barbies and racecars in their backpacks and satchels as soon as they saw me coming. Other kids couldn't resist playing after the bell had rung, and according to my rule, I collected toys by the pocketful. I hid the toys out of sight when I realized that a little motorcycle or doll left on my desk at the front class would be stared at by its owner with a fondness nearing total distraction. At first, whenever I took away Vova's toys, he attempted to persuade me not to by using English: "Please, Mr. John!" he said, "I—play—*no* will!" Later, in an effort to show me his maturity differently, he voluntarily handed over his toys even before the lesson started, this time telling me (in Ukrainian) with a serious frown: "Mr. John, you had better take these now. Because I know myself and I can't help playing with them."

Another issue was bubble gum, the word for which literally meant "Chewing Rubber." But everyone called it *Zhuvachka*—the word for a cow's cud. Hardly a misnomer, it described the way these children chomped wide-mouthed on the same piece all day. During class, they tried to hide their *Zhuvachka* between cheek and gum, but the moment they spoke it was obvious. "You can't have gum in class," I reminded them. "Oh!" they sometimes shouted guiltily, before parking the gum behind their ear. Chewing gum, they believed, was very American and therefore very cool. Without exception, in every skit or play I saw in Ukraine, the way to portray an American was to walk bow-legged and gnash a piece of gum.

Even more than the gum itself, the kids coveted Bazooka-Joe-style comics from bubble gum packs. Everyone had at least a few, and most kids carried whole collections around with them. They invented games involving the scraps of waxy paper. One player would name a side of the comic, something like heads or tails. He then smacked his hand on the comic as hard as he could, then let his hand bounce back; the comic flew into the air and tumbled back to the table, fluttering and turning. Whichever side landed upright determined the winner. The child-currency of bubble-gum wrappers settled all bets.

The rage-of-the-year toy at that time was a plastic Slinky. Although flimsy as plastic forks, these Slinkies had one advantage over the old metal kind: they had all the colors of the rainbow. In fact, the toy's Russian name was Rainbow. I never saw so many people amused by such a simple toy. They swung their rainbows like jump ropes, they yo-yoed their rainbows, on stacks of books they made their rainbows do the "walks down stairs" thing. Some kids laid the rainbow Slinky out flat and stroked it, admiring the colors fusing and separating, twirling into one another. "What is the big deal?" I asked, trying to hide my amusement. A third grader named Maxim interrupted his rainbow reverie to explain: "Well . . . just look, Mr. John." He stroked the rainbow some more; pinks melted into fluorescent greens, then into yellow and back to pink. It kind of shimmered. "*Klassno*," Maxim concluded.

When I asked Tanya about it, she rolled her eyes. "I know. The kids are crazy about them. But they are kind of interesting to look at, aren't they?" Luda told me when her daughter wasn't playing with hers, she took out the rainbow in secret and made it slink back and forth.

The colorful toys were sold in every kiosk that winter. In good weather and foul, Ukrainian children *lived* at the kiosks. A row of them sprouted up in the dirty alley between our school playground and the city administration building, where the hundreds of bureaucrats who ran Zhitomir worked. Clever entrepreneurs sold goodies to please the patrons of both establishments: kids peered between the vodka bottles and pornographic magazines to admire the good chocolate, bubble-gum, colorful robots, and Barbie dolls.

On those winter afternoons, when the sun set before four, the last bell of the day sent our pupils out into cold twilight. Sometimes I had the pleasure of hearing my students dash off into the dark, still singing, "If You're Happy and You Know it, Clap Your Hands."

The little kids loved this song, mostly because they got to stamp their feet loudly—improper behavior in other classrooms. Or maybe they just liked to sing a song whose words they knew by heart. Smiling brightly, I sang along, trying to feign a cheerfulness I didn't feel. If you're not happy and you know it, singing about how happy you are sounds ridiculously ironic. Grinning, waving my arms, and singing along, I wondered what I was doing in Ukraine "being happy" with a bunch of eight-year-olds. This didn't feel like development work; it barely felt like preschool. Helping other teachers had been part of my plan. Now that I was a part of the school staff (if only an odd one), I desperately wanted to make a difference at School 23.

I saw an opportunity for more involvement when word reached me that a teacher's meeting would be held after school in the teachers' Methodology Room. Usually, teacher's meetings took place without me; when I suggested to my counterpart, Svetlana Adamovna, that as a fellow teacher I'd like to be included, she agreed immediately, but added "These meetings are never interesting. I don't imagine you would enjoy them much." Most likely, that was true. Still, I wanted the chance to behave as a member of the staff and learn more about what was expected of my colleagues. "Anyway, such meetings don't concern you," she added. "They are about salaries and other questions you don't need to hear about."

Were there secrets I wasn't to know? Or did they discuss *me* in such meetings? Paranoid as that may sound, I could not guess what the other twenty-eight English teachers really thought of me. I wanted to blend in as much as possible but also offer the school something unique: the skills a native speaker could provide. Instead, I mostly felt ignored. They probably thought they were sparing me, but I still wanted desperately to be seen as something more than guest.

On the day of the meeting, I spent a few minutes after my last lesson tidying up my desk before going to the teachers' room. All of the English teachers were plopped into chairs, looking tired after the day's lessons. They faced the front of the room, where Galina Vasilievna sat waiting.

When she saw me, she came over. "Are you ready?" she asked in Ukrainian.

Was I late? It seemed they were waiting for me before beginning.

"Yes. Ready." I answered quickly. Something felt wrong, as if I had misunderstood the time for the meeting. Galina Vasilievna welcomed the teachers and began the meeting, speaking Ukrainian in the official tone of voice she used when performing vice-principal duties.

"Thank you all for coming to this first Methodology Seminar of the new year. As you know, we all can benefit from periodic professional development. As teachers, we must always be learning, always improving our knowledge of pedagogy, always remaining up-to-date on the latest techniques and methodologies of the study of the English language.

"So I'm happy to present to you our colleague, whom you all know quite well, Mr. John."

The teachers applauded politely, turning in their chairs toward me. A spasm of jitters hit me, a wave of both anxiety and fury. I had forgotten nothing; it was some double-crossing trick.

I stood up and went to Galina Vasilievna to whisper angrily in her ear.

"Galina Vasilievna, no one told me about this."

She looked surprised. "But didn't you want to share some information with the staff? This was your idea, as I remember."

"I'm not prepared to give a lecture right this minute!" I said, getting angrier. "All of my material is at home." Glancing at the group of teachers, I saw Tatyana Ivanovna, a sour, birdlike, older teacher with a tall beehive of blond hair. She was a conservative teacher, who favored the old ways and expressed only disgust with everything since independence. She grimaced at me with something like a satisfied grin. This was my chance, and I was going to blow it.

Galina Vasilievna nervously asked, "Well, maybe you could speak for a few minutes about the differences in school systems. Since we are all here."

Everyone watched me, most of them eager to finish the day and go home. I could have bowed out and dismissed them, and they would have been happy. But I felt my credibility was on the line.

"OK, I'll speak for just a few minutes," I said.

"That would be fine," she answered, sitting down.

Giving a formal presentation would have been too awkward anyway, since I knew everyone. "Had I known I was to deliver a talk," I told them lamely, "I would have brought materials from home, and prepared lists of ideas and activities to share." I rambled into the usual talk I gave at schools and institutes about differences between American and Ukrainian schools. These teachers already knew most of the information, and looked quite bored—except for Marina and Tanya, whose expressions resembled those of parents watching their child's school play and praying he doesn't embarrass them. I talked about ways I thought we could improve English learning for all of the students (e.g., not relying on parroting, more authentic communicative activities, more real-world language skills). In my apartment lay pages of good teaching activities, as well as opportunities for grants, Fulbright study abroad, teacher exchanges. Flustered, I forgot to mention any of that. When I concluded, my audience sighed with relief, thanked me, and ran out of the room. The talk was a waste of time; I would not be asked to a meeting again.

"You did fine," Tanya said reassuringly, in the tone you'd tell your child in the school play that his falling off the stage really wasn't a big distraction. "Of course, we've heard you say a lot of this before."

Most definitely I had blown a chance. The other teachers

could dismiss me as a visiting American, off on a lark. The idea that I could do "development" work with a staff of experienced teachers seemed more unlikely than ever. Not that they wouldn't listen; they felt they already knew what I had to say.

Of course, by then it seemed to me that I had lived in Zhitomir quite a long time. To the teachers, however, I was still a newcomer. I was young and inexperienced and was not a real member of the community or the teaching staff. It would take more time to be accepted.

Socializing was a big part of being trusted, and I was never excluded from that. When the great event of Svetlana Adamovna's fiftieth birthday arrived the following month, I was recruited to help. Birthdays were big events in Ukraine, and every birthday celebration was planned weeks in advance. For Svetlana Adamovna, who knew half the people in Zhitomir, the party was opened to the entire school. The seventy people invited included teachers, friends, retired teachers, and a few special parents—all of whom had to be fed a full meal, accompanied with enough vodka and cognac to prolong the event well into the night. On the night of the party I helped Larisa and Sergey prepare the food in the teacher's lounge.

For an in-school event, the party turned somewhat wild—even by Ukrainian teachers' standards. The long, eloquent toasts initially dwindled until there remained only the humorous, or the succinct and expedient. But it was a school night, and so the party concluded sometime before midnight. I helped Sergey and Larisa unpeel the paper tablecloths, wipe up spills, and throw out the plastic cups and bowls. Our guest of honor donned her apron and, there in the third floor teacher's room, got busy rinsing forks in a pail of water brought up from the cafeteria. We scooped plates of salad back into the galvanized aluminum pail from which it had come, and after gathering up the remaining food, trundled back to her home in the cold. Our arms full of heavy packages, we stumbled happily along over the ice, laughing over the highlights of the festivities. It had been a rare party, and we rested in their apartment for a few minutes (and for another toast) before I meandered back to my dorm, very late. I felt less than shipshape the next day, but made it to school and survived the knowing grins and glares of my colleagues, who easily forgave occasional late nights of celebration. My tolerance for such socializing had increased quite a bit as well.

My own birthday came soon after. Somehow, my pupils found out about it. Like every teacher on his or her birthday, I received bundles of flowers and birthday wishes from my classes. In the middle of February, flowers (from local greenhouses) were both expensive and difficult to find, yet omitting the gesture would have been unthinkable to a Ukrainian. And what a delight! Bunches of bright-colored, delicious-smelling carnations and dahlias, as well as tulips—the word for which my fourth graders made me repeat until I pronounced the difficult soft sounds passably. The third graders gave me a picture in a plastic frame and signed it on the back. Alexey, a quiet ninth grader, gave me a jar of his father's homemade honey, earnestly wishing me "Happy birthday, dear teacher." Misha told me later (as we shared the delicious honey on toast) that it was the best kind available and would be very expensive in the bazaar if I could even find it. Sweet gifts, and an outpouring of attention for which I felt grateful but undeserving.

Over the dark, cold winter my outlook had been transformed, my goals drastically scaled back. Originally, part of why I joined Peace Corps was to bring about change through service. I had hoped that by sacrificing part of my life and the comforts of home, my labor might contribute to making one corner of the world just a little bit better. "We're proud of you," friends and relatives at home wrote me, some adding, "You're doing God's work." I wanted to tell everyone back at home they were wrong. Now that I lived and worked in Ukraine, side-by-side with the people I'd come to "help," my former perspective appeared vain and naive—and at heart ethnocentric. Ukrainian schools, after all, expected their students to perform at a much higher level than schools in the United States, especially in math, science, and foreign languages. Some students knew American literature better than the average American ninth grader.

From the richest country in the world, I had come to the land of a former enemy only to receive friendship and care from people who would never have a chance to enjoy the hopes and comforts I took for granted. That didn't feel like such a noble endeavor.

Therefore, I reconsidered my short-term goals. Inspired by Svetlana Adamovna, I determined to throw my school friends a birthday party, Ukrainian style. If I could only return some of the hospitality I had been shown, that would be something to be proud of. Gathering the makings for a birthday dinner became like a secondary project.

My invitation list was shorter—only a dozen people—and my cuisine would be all-American: pizza and hot chili. I took my liter jar to the only store in town where I had seen tomato paste, and asked the clerk to scoop out a jarful for me; I came back the next day with three more jars. I searched the stores stocking up on cheese; in the bazaar I collected ground pork, beans, red peppers, and onions. The central department store sold a Soviet version of Ritz crackers (drier and less buttery, but a bit like the real thing), and in bulk I bought four plastic bags full. To make the meal complete I conceded to fix potatoes as well. I was unconcerned that the dishes might make a weird mishmash; the first and foremost requirement was sufficient quantity.

Naturally, I made a trip to the vodka store—a short errand. Because the town distillery, a block from my dorm, had a "factory outlet" store across the street, the best vodka store within hundreds of miles was literally outside my doorstep. Its prices were even cheaper than the dollar-a-liter standard, and men walked from all over the city to buy vodka there. Some drove up in cars, which they loaded with crates full of bottles of clear liquid; back in their villages the next day, they would be far richer. Since the variances in the ridiculously low prices made no difference to me, I shopped there for the selection. I stood in the usual line, among the men reeking of sweat and foul tobacco, studying the cage that protected a display of bottles. Some were rare state brands not available elsewhere. A large, busty woman, the cashier who always worked there, handed bottles through a slot between the bars. She saw me eyeing a bottle labeled Special Edition Zhitomirska vodka. "This is the export variant," she said. "You'll like it." The vodka lady knew me by now—a rather sad commentary on my life, perhaps, except that in truth my celebrity still tended to precede me everywhere. I also asked for the traditional Ukrainian pepper vodka with the orange label, *Z Pertsem*, my favorite. One Special Edition, three Pertsovki—and then an extra two bottles of the regular brand, Russkaya, in case the first ran out—did not seem excessive. I had seen that much drunk in an evening by fewer people. At home I stashed the bottles in a cupboard. As I had learned from my hosts, I would introduce a bottle after the one on the table ran out, a practice simultaneously modest and overindulgent.

From the Peace Corps medical kit I removed all the packages of orange Gatorade we'd been given to drink in case of dehydration. The medical kit, standard from Africa to South America, also contained 15-SPF sunscreen, lip balm sunscreen, and mosquito repellent—all very useful to me from about the fifteenth of June until the fifteenth of July. At least the powdered drinks came in handy to serve at parties. The one Kool-Aid-style powder sold cheaply in the bazaar was called "Yupi"—pronounced, appropriately, "You pee." It was new to Ukraine, and everyone advised me to try it, as if it were the most marvelous time-saver invented. *"Kupi Yupi!"* they rhymed: "Buy Yupi!" Thus, I had to describe Gatorade by saying, "It's just like Yupi."

In every spare moment the week before the party I shopped and prepared food. Still I had to rush around at the last minute. My neighbors across the hall loaned me extra forks, plates, even chairs and another table. My feast had to spread out over quite a space; according to tradition the table should be so fully covered that not a corner in which to place a glass may be found.

The day of the party arrived. In my tiny kitchen, with food and dishes stacked on every flat space, I sat down and started peeling potatoes. I did not think myself much of a cook and felt nervous to be feeding so many people, all of them accustomed to fantastically thorough meals. Nevertheless, by the time Marina and Tanya arrived bringing salads, I was already having trouble finding places to set dishes down. The pizza was ready for the oven, the chili simmered away, smelling deliciously familiar. I had a moment of discomfort when Tanya informed me politely that the bottle of wine I'd bought was "church wine," normally drunk on sacramental occasions. So much of Ukrainian culture revolved around creating a memorable experience at the table. I wanted the party to reflect my appreciation of my friends—and to show them I could fend for myself.

The biggest problem had been limiting the guest list. Misha declined to come—he said he would feel uncomfortable with a group of teachers, even though he was studying to be one. Victor Ivanovich also had other plans, but I invited Svetlana Adamovna and her daughter and son-in-law. In a private moment, Larisa bemoaned, "Why did you invite my mother! Now we can't act normal. We want to relax and have a good time." Sergey added, "She won't enjoy herself either, in such a company of all young people." Other teachers and friends my age also expressed disappointment, but Marina defended me: "No, John was right to ask. She had to decline. She wasn't thinking." Actually, Svetlana Adamovna herself worried, "Why did you invite me?—it will be all young people!" But I wanted her to come. She had taken me in as a member of the family, and I had even been a part of her father's funeral. Then there was her own huge birthday celebration the week before. I replied to all of them that I had only one birthday. I also knew that if I didn't invite her, I would hurt her feelings worse than if I did and the socializing was a bit rocky.

Marina came with her husband, Igor, and their close friends Sasha and Luda. Then Tanya, Luda, and Oksana, my best teacher friends, arrived, and finally Svetlana Adamovna with Sergey and Larisa. They all wished me birthday greetings, and I urged them to sit so we could begin eating. At last, it was a pleasure to serve as host to people who had welcomed me as a guest so many times.

At the table, half the guests sat down in chairs, while the others perched awkwardly on the edge of my bed, and the dorm room that had been so large for one now looked cramped. But I was too worried about the food at the time to notice. Chili wasn't known in Ukraine, and it may have been a bad choice to serve at a big party. Russians believe Ukrainians love hot, spicy foods, but that is only in comparison to their own rather blandly seasoned food. Fresh horseradish and hot mustard in miniscule doses were common enough, but anything resembling Mexican, Thai, or Szechuan cooking would strike many Ukrainian tongues as overseasoned, so my chili had to be mild by American standards.

When I served it, an even more basic issue arose, as nobody knew what to do with it. In my hurry, I had failed to distribute bowls to every guest—actually, I had too few. Somebody suggested that my chili must be a kind of sauce. Marina, bravely wielding a large spoon as a ladle, spread chili over her plateful of boiled potatoes and asked, "Is this how you do it?" Stifling a laugh, I answered, "No, but I guess you could." While she stared at me in confusion, all the guests—greatly relieved to have the foreign cuisine decoded—repeated Marina's gesture. One by one, they each spread chili over their potatoes, and carefully picked into the mess with forks. I didn't know what to say. As I mused on the Ukrainianization of my genuine American chili, a scream erupted from Svetlana Adamovna. "*Oy!*" she hollered. "Spicy!" She waved her hand in front of her mouth until someone poured her a glassful of orange Gatorade, which she gulped down to cool her scalded tongue. I smiled at last. The extremely mild chili had come out fine after all. My guests politely praised it, except Svetlana Adamovna, who decided to eat her potatoes with butter.

A sweet-and-sour cabbage salad made from Marina's recipe delivered my proudest moment. Finely shredded cabbage with a few carrot-scrapings for color had marinated overnight in sunflower oil, vinegar, and sugar, and I must have somehow gotten the proportions just right. When Svetlana Adamovna tasted it, she asked in Russian, "Girls, who brought this? Very tasty!" Marina and Tanya smiled at their laps for a moment, savoring the joke with each other, until Marina responded, "John himself made it." Svetlana Adamovna's eyes widened, and I kept eating, pretending not to hear. After all the glorious meals and hospitable treatment I had received at her house, the exchange was a minor but deeply rewarding triumph. She registered shock, complimented the salad again (though less sincerely), and was silent.

Everyone loved the pizza. But then, they also loved the lemon slices sprinkled with shredded cheese—a weird, new dish everyone was making now that lemons were more commonly available. A plain old can of California black olives that had somehow found its way to an obscure corner of the Zhitomir bazaar proved an unusual treat—something of a surprise for everyone, including me. Tanya ate heaps of them, as if they were chocolates and she couldn't stop. In embarrassment she tried to hide the large pile of pits on her plate under some bread. I laughed, happy to be able to treat her for a change. Once everyone was eating adequately, I could relax a little.

Vague tension between Svetlana Adamovna and Marina hung over the table, making both quieter than usual. Igor's friend Sasha spoke magnanimously and entertainingly, but because only Igor knew him well, people were only genially polite. Larisa chattered about her cat and how she wanted an "Amerikanski Coaker Spanyel," rambling on about what a beautiful city St. Petersburg was and how she longed to visit it again. "Seven days isn't enough to see the Hermitage," she repeated to me again and again. "How many marvels there are to see!"

Sergey's light blue polyester suit jacket looked odd, especially with a brown striped tie, but dressing up for birthday parties was standard, and his outfit flattered me just as it was. A man serving from a man's kitchen may have confused him. Normally it was our job to sit and talk while his wife and mother-in-law completed the tasks that occupied me now. Tanya, Marina, and Oksana had tried to take over my kitchen and do such work for me—more as a helpful favor than in accordance with gender roles. Or maybe they thought I would get something wrong. But I insisted that for once they sit down and eat. I was always their guest, and I was determined for once not to accept the rules about "women's work." When I wasn't keeping track, they helped clean up in the kitchen anyway.

But we ate until the food disappeared, and after a good deal of talk and toasts with vodka, the party had warmed up. Someone suggested dancing, and several people jumped at the chance. Svetlana Adamovna looked uncomfortable, especially after Igor located a techno-dance tape Misha had left in my room and popped it into my cassette player. To a throbbing bass and the whirl of metallic synthesizers, even Svetlana Adamovna began to dance. As the music poured out of the cassette player, I felt, for once, successful. I had mastered the formula: way too much heavy food, an endless stream of evenly flowing alcohol poured out in carefully measured toasts, and then everyone up and bouncing around the room to Ace of Base at high volume. My birthday had metamorphosed into a real Ukrainian party, and there, compressed into the space where I hung laundry, prepared schoolwork, stored all my possessions, and slept and dreamed each night, eleven people were dancing madly. I had gotten something right.

Sometime after midnight, it occurred to me that I had forgotten to prepare dessert, but as usual, my friends were ahead of me. There emerged a birthday cake they had smuggled in, which was even decorated in English to read "Happy Birthday John!" We drank coffee and tea, and Tanya told me I was to watch the local Zhitomir channel on Sunday afternoon for another surprise. The show, a cross between Willard Scott and MTV, was one my pupils (along with half the town) watched every week. When I saw it later that weekend, Tanya and Oksana were on as special guests, congratulating me in English and Ukrainian by reading a happy birthday speech and then dedicating a music video to me—the Bon Jovi song "I Wish Every Day Could Be Like Christmas." I found myself singing along and smiling.

As the winter of that year continued to deepen, I realized that the darkness and cold no longer annoyed me, nor did the smoggy air tasting of metal. That tartness on my tongue had long since become natural, the blue haze in the air invisible. Even fatalism was contagious, and I caught it in the same way I caught my students' colds.

When everything in my apartment quit working, I shrugged. The Soviet-made electric heater fizzled and quit. The cassette player I bought for school ate my favorite tape and then played only a gargly murmur. The water distiller Peace Corps had provided went on the fritz, too, but I didn't worry about it; I drank boiled tap water like everybody else, despite what I had seen of the leftover sludge at the bottom of the distiller. Then my kitchen sink clogged; errant bits of potato peel, carrot shavings, or some other greasy vegetable matter had slipped down the screenless drain. The black plastic pipe underneath had to come off, and if I broke it, I could not expect to find a replacement. But my understanding of such events had altered; I had learned to expect the worst.

A shortage mentality of strict self-rationing had invaded my mind, creating in me a desire for the luxury of temporary excess. One day, when the price of cooking oil rose and the lines grew short, I took my empty bottle to the market to be filled. A full bottle of sunflower oil meant wealth to me, and abandoning my frugal habits, I fried that night's potatoes without sparing. A modest splurge, just for once, I thought: I'll treat myself to as much as I want. I wanted to squander all of what little I had, without having to worry about the consequences. There would be endless shortages, life would never get any better, and I wanted not to feel so poor, if only just for a while.

A flood of cooking oil, however, was a bad choice of product for conspicuous consumption. My fingers slippery with oil, I spilled it everywhere: all over the stove, the floor, the table. From a saturated pan, the walls became spattered, and every other pan was greasy anyway, even after many washings in cold water. Mopping up the mess, my dishrag became soaked; now I would have to boil it with precious hot water. Blessedly, the cold water at least was working, so I let the kitchen tap run while I cleaned up. So many Ukrainians let the kitchen tap run for hours—a practice I had told them was wasteful. "We don't pay for water, as you do," Misha explained. "Maybe that's why we do that." That splurging now made sense to me too. Using up my sunflower oil or letting my tap run gave me the illusion of a steady, unlimited supply of something, and a little mental boost. It somehow made me feel I wasn't living in destitution.

If the electric power had *always* been turned off—say, if I lived in a mud hut and cooked over a fire—I would have adjusted and dealt with it. But on-again, off-again was so frustrating. It wasn't the times of shortage that annoyed me, but the times when things worked. In the middle of laundry or dishes, the water would quit—and so would I. I felt at the mercy of the elements indoors as much as I did outdoors.

Some days, in a happy coincidence, I had both utilities at once. I did all of my laundry, wringing gray water from socks and scrubbing shirt collars with Brillo pads until the yellow faded. Clothes hung from the backs of chairs, from coat hangers hooked on opened doors, and from the web of clothesline crisscrossing the room. The "tap-tap-tap" of water dripping onto my rough wood floor went on like music, and my chilly room turned warm and steamy like a sauna.

Other days, for no apparent reason, the power went off and the hot water came *on* almost simultaneously. I tried to read some pattern or schedule into it all, but logic had no place in it. Sometimes I took showers in total darkness, a disorienting experience. The warm water splashing on my body gave some consolation, but for a few moments I lost track of up and down, even wondering where I was. I imagined myself floating in one of the tiny space capsules I had seen in Zhitomir's Museum of Cosmonauts, where John Maddox and I held an English Club. Outside, a nuclear reactor might be poisoning the air—the papers said the sarcophagus covering Chornobyl was cracked and leaking—or perhaps the fragile society outside the dorm had collapsed so far as to fall into outright rebellion. I could not tell, did not know how that would feel. I could imagine all kinds of fears: Nothing was dependable, nothing could be taken for granted.

I drank a lot. It seemed funny now: my secret fear before moving to Ukraine had been that I would be forced to drink pepper vodka. But there I was, having a shot by myself, then another with dinner. . . . Even Ukrainian alcoholics didn't drink alone, but usually found a partner or two. I scolded myself for getting drunk, but kept drinking. Anyway, I didn't feel I was overdoing it. "He's not an alcoholic," one Ukrainian told me. "He doesn't always finish the bottle."

When I drank vodka, every moment crystallized, every inexplicable sensation took on sharply vivid meaning. My experience melded into the liquid itself: clear, pure, intense, weighty. A shot tossed back rang in my ears, reminding me of that melancholy music, the minor-key melodies of folk songs or the wailing songs of funeral mourners. The hard edges of a difficult day ceased to scrape at my skin, and only smooth, quiet, solitude remained. My bed was a block of ice, but I fell into it like a stone into water.

As my composure went downhill, I was vaguely aware that I might be losing my mind. Strangely, I didn't care. "Normal" life—

that is, my previous existence—had no bearing on my behavior, no relation to who I had become. In fact I felt so little connection to my own country that I seriously considered never returning. Peace Corps service would end, but I could find other work, I thought, pouring myself a small glass of pepper vodka from a leftover open bottle. In the darkness outside my dormitory I saw only a few lonely porch lights of the neighborhood houses, nothing but still darkness to the invisible horizon. Really, I thought, I could stay here forever.

Chapter Thirteen

Now We Have Twenty-Eight

The living conditions I encountered in Ukraine reminded me of a joke a friend told me: "Why is the battleship Aurora (from which the Bolshevik revolution was sparked) the most powerful weapon ever invented? One shot, seventy years of destruction."

Under Soviet totalitarianism, joke-telling had thrived, perhaps as a pressure valve to release pent-up frustration. People said, however, that the practice had fizzled some by the time I arrived. "We used to have so many anecdotes," Max told me. "About Brezhnev especially, then Gorbachev too. Now it's not forbidden to poke fun at our leaders, so we don't do it as much." The collapse of communism—blamed for everything from unswept streets to bad weather—was even faulted for the decline of humor.

There were exceptions. In one, Bill Clinton and Boris Yeltsin are having a conversation on a presidential airplane. Clinton wonders, "Boris Nikolayevich, if this plane crashed, which nation do you think would cry the most?" After a moment's thought, Yeltsin answers: "The Ukrainians. Because President Kravchuk is not on board."

Ukrainians still told jokes, most of them along the lines of the blurbs in *Reader's Digest*. Many were so dry I could barely believe anyone found them funny: "First man: Did you steal that hat yourself, or did you have an accomplice? Second: Myself, of course! In such a time, how can you find anyone you can trust?" Others made sense only in the former Soviet Union: "First man: Five minutes ago, a thief stole my golden watch right off my wrist! Second: Why didn't you yell for the police? First man: I was afraid to open my mouth. I have gold teeth."

My ninth-graders had decided I was dense when I could not fathom the following joke: "Sasha, lend me 5,000 kupons." Sasha answers, "From whom?" I puzzled over it for days. They would only explain it by repeating it, slapping their heads in disbelief that it did not make me laugh. It became clearer when I learned that the same verb can mean both "to lend" and "to borrow."

Sometimes, jokes even counted as a kind of currency. One acquaintance told me how, on business in western Ukraine, he ran out of money for the return trip. He decided to hitchhike his way home on the strength of his joke-telling skills. On a piece of cardboard, he wrote "100 purely Zhitomir anecdotes." The driver who picked him up agreed to take him on the condition that any jokes he'd heard before didn't count. For three hundred miles across Ukraine, he told the driver jokes from memory—a hundred new ones and more.

People stood up at parties to recite jokes, and good new ones were always praised and admired. The kiosks at the bus station sold books of children's anecdotes—and also sexual anecdotes which definitely were not for children. Ethnic jokes, mostly about Chukchis (Siberian Eskimos) or Jews, were very common; Ukrainians (and Russians) generally do not find jokes that characterize someone because of their race offensive. If someone on a crowded bus began to tell some anecdote, every passenger craned his neck to hear it. One clown could thus soon find himself entertaining a captive busload of swaddled, red-cheeked cackling babushkas. Ukrainians didn't smile and laugh very often, but when I saw an occasional scene like this, it didn't seem to me that humor had vanished completely.

Still, some things were too hard even for dark humor. On cold mornings I cut through the old school building on the way to class. This shortcut also gave me a minute to warm up before I reached my classroom on the third floor of the new building. Just inside the doors of the old building stood ten-foot-tall plaster statues of Pioneer children wearing scarves—a girl holding books and a boy blowing a trumpet as if summoning children to war. The real children, who crashed into one another racing around the halls, always ran up to me when they saw me come in the building. They whispered, "Mr. John," and bravely shouted, "Hello" or "Good morning!" I felt so at ease in my work routine that I could not remember how the bolted-together desks, the Ukrainian alphabet, and the children's pale faces had seemed so foreign at one time; school had become my second home.

That particular morning, however, is one I'll never forget. When Luda, a third grader from my class ran up to me, I thought she wanted to say "Hello!" in English like the others.

Instead, she spoke Russian. "Mr. John, Annya Koaleko died."

"What?"

"At 1 a.m. last night."

Several kids collected in a huddle around me and repeated the news: "Did you hear, Mr. John? Annya Koaleko died." I pictured my pale, sleepy-eyed pupil with the perpetual cold. Every day she wore the uniform bought in first grade—a dark blue, ill-fitting dress with lacy pinafore—even though the school rules now permitted other clothing. I could see the sparkly white hairband that her mother used to pull back her hair. A month-long illness couldn't be that serious—kids often returned to school after ten-week absences. But by the way Luda pronounced that hour in the middle of the night I knew she was telling the truth: Annya would never come back. I looked down at the faces of her classmates. They were not smiling, not sad, but curious, staring up to see how I would take the news. There was nothing I could say. Slowly I climbed up the stairs to teach the first lesson.

Annya's class arrived for the fifth period lesson right on schedule. It happened to be my last class of the day. The remaining nine pupils rushed in as usual, and those who had not seen me told me the news again. They were still excited, not sad—the reality would sink in later that afternoon when they visited Annya's family and saw her little body laid out in a coffin in the living room of her home. My own concerns were more immediate: How can I face this class today? I couldn't ignore such a fact and go on with a normal lesson, so I probed a little to see if they wanted to talk about it. I soon sensed they didn't. Vitaliy, always the first boy to class, had a tear in his eye. But Masha, Annya's closest friend in the class, slowly and carefully pronounced her explanation.

"Well, we had thirty-two pupils in Three D until Marchenko moved away. That made thirty-one. Then two boys transferred to different schools, and there were twenty-nine. Now Annya, and we have twenty-eight."

Counting how many were left was her way of looking at her friend's death, I guess. Her recitation of the survivors helped me go ahead and have class on a day when I wanted to give up, go back to my dorm, and cry.

A book of easy word search puzzles had been sent to me from the States, and I ripped out a page for each child. They were pleased by the little drawings of airplanes and children on bicycles around the puzzle borders. They found even the words they didn't know, and I translated and praised them for completing a task not all native speakers do easily. Then we played Hangman, known there as "Field of Wonder," which they always thought was a treat. We didn't mention Annya any more. That was how I answered a question I never expected to face: What do you teach your students on the day one of their classmates dies?

The funeral would be the next day—the family had to rent an expensive bus to take friends and family out to the cemetery. My class agreed to convey my regrets to Annya's parents. I wanted to meet them and share my consolation, but what would I say? I didn't know where they lived and didn't know what I could offer if I were to see them. I had no sympathy cards (who would list such a thing on the Peace Corps packing list?) but it was the third funeral of someone I knew. This time, it was a person with whom I had spent nearly every weekday since coming to Zhitomir. It just wouldn't sink in: "one of your nine-year-old pupils got sick and died." It wouldn't process.

I had adapted to so many of the upside-down assumptions inherent in Soviet Life that most days were "normal." I wasn't living in the dingy, mysterious, romantic Eastern Europe I had once imagined; it wasn't even "the former Soviet Union," with all that implies. I lived in an apartment on Shelushkova Street and went to work every day. I taught at School 23 and rode the bus home. But Annya Koaleko's death reminded me of where I was, and how deep the disastrous ruin around me penetrated. No photographs would show Ukraine's poverty adequately, yet there were millions of people—tens of millions—from Lviv to Kharkiv, from Odessa to Kiev, tucked into boxlike apartments and suffering silently behind closed doors. Like the teachers in my school, for example, they didn't react visibly to tragedy. Perhaps they didn't know Annya, or (more likely) they were never caught off guard by bad news.

I, on the other hand, most definitely was. I had photographed that class earlier in the year and could have given the pictures of Annya to her family. But stupidly, I had mailed the negatives home. The Ukrainian post office ripped open my envelope and taped it back shut, empty. All my images of Annya had vanished along with her. I had only her notebook, filled with English homework, which she had handed in but never come back to reclaim.

Annya was nine. She would have been an infant at the time of Chornobyl, whose radiation had damaged the immune systems of everyone in the Zhitomir region. Her illness may have been related, or she may simply have lacked good medical care. Then again, the cause might have been pneumonia, influenza, or merely a high fever—any of the normal ways children die unexpectedly.

Although I didn't know whether Annya's sickliness had anything to do with Chornobyl, I couldn't help wondering. Like an invisible plague, it was blamed for everything from the past few warm winters to the coughing that probably came from too many cigarettes. Chornobyl was a poltergeist in the form of a radiation cloud, and the extent of its curse still has not been fully measured.

For much of the world, the word "Chornobyl" is a punchline, a word used only when making dark jokes about the mysteries of excessive radiation. Perhaps two-headed cows and children with horrific birth defects are so terrifying that we try to diminish them with laughter. Or perhaps radiation is just too scary to face without ironic comments about an alien-green glowing light. Maybe it's just that when a Chornobyl happens to somebody else, it doesn't seem as terrible as it really is. Chornobyl was one subject there was nothing funny about.

The people who live near Chornobyl don't glow. They get leukemia. They get thyroid cancer in overly high proportions. They have cataracts when they are in their twenties. They are more susceptible to illness in general, due to weakened immune systems. They look totally normal, yet they are sick.

Worse, the invisible sickness won't simply kill Ukrainians and Belarussians and Russians and then fade into history. Radiation damages genes: The chromosomes of anyone exposed to the Chornobyl accident may have mutated. As these people intermarry, subsequent generations will accumulate the bent and broken genes in higher proportions, with the result that the likelihood of radiation-related birth disorders may actually *increase* among the descendants of Chornobyl victims. My pupils knew this. "It's true, Mr. John," one said. "We are children of Chornobyl, but our grandchildren and great-grandchildren may even be worse off than we."

Chornobyl posed little danger to me, even though Zhitomir was the worst-hit province in Ukraine. The moment of exposure during the catastrophe (rather than lingering radiation or radioactive elements) posed the greatest risk of harm to the human body. At first Chornobyl had seemed like one of the sicknesses infecting a sick society, an item chalked up on the list of the terrible legacy of Soviet power. But the more people I met who had experienced it firsthand, the more tragic it seemed.

Nobody can really can tally fatalities with accuracy, beyond the thirty-one firemen who died as a result of the explosion. Around 10,000 died from diseases directly attributable to Chornobyl and perhaps many others where direct connections are not so easily made. The Ukrainian government states that hundreds of thousands of people are victims to some extent and that more than half a million people were exposed.

If fatalities and illnesses are in dispute, certain facts are not. On April 26, 1986, an operator at the VI Lenin Nuclear Power Plant near the then-obscure town of Chornobyl made an error during a test. As a result of his mistake, a power surge melted down the reactor core, and when the explosion ripped open the roof, a plume of radioactive debris—uranium dioxide fuel, Cesium 137, Iodine 131—shot three miles into the air. The amount released was equivalent to three hundred Hiroshimas. Soviet officials tried to hide the disaster by not reporting it, even though it was reported around the world that some nuclear catastrophe had occurred. In Kiev, sixty miles down river from Chornobyl, tens of thousands of people, many of them children, obliviously marched in the annual May Day parade, while a cloud of radioactive material descended on them.

"When we finally heard on the radio about the Chornobyl catastrophe," Tanya told me, "the government advised us to wash our windows and floors three times. I did it, even though I was sure it would do no good."

The evacuation and cleanup were handled just as callously. When 40,000 people were hospitalized, the government silently raised the legal level of acceptable radiation exposure ten times higher. Then, to reduce the effects of contaminated meat and milk, it ordered that these products be combined with untainted meat and milk from other regions and thus "diluted": one part irradiated to nine parts "clean." The resulting concoction was secretly distributed across the Soviet Union, mostly to non-ethnic Russian areas.

Later, because the Soviet government was designed to prevent exactly the kind of accountability necessary in such a situation, no solitary figure or ministry has been forced to accept the blame. The breakup of the USSR actually helped those who would avoid responsibility: Chornobyl lies in Ukraine, but very near the borders of Russia and Belarus. Belarus received by far the worst contamination; much of the marshland on its southern border is now uninhabitable, and a fifth of its farmland is extremely dangerous to human life. Cleanup must now be a trilateral international effort. The irresponsible "state" at fault no longer exists.

Chornobyl demonstrated the untrustworthiness of the authorities so convincingly that Soviet leaders were proven to be immoral, self-serving hypocrites who endangered the people they claimed to serve. In this way, Chornobyl was a kind of Soviet Watergate: It destroyed both the leadership and the public's faith in leaders. Unlike Watergate, however, Chornobyl's consequences will last not for decades, but centuries.

The thirty-kilometer exclusion zone around the reactor is referred to simply as "the Zone." Scientists go there to study the reactor, and the workers are still burying dirt, trucks, demolished buildings—everything—in super-high-contaminated areas. Everyone else is forbidden from entering the Zone, the 400,000 acres "permanently excluded from economic activity," where the soil will be lethal for centuries. Old-growth forest covers much of his area, but it has reportedly fallen completely silent. Poisoned foliage has killed everything. Even the field mice vanished.

Ten million acres of forest are polluted in some way. Land that earlier produced potatoes, grains, meat, and milk but is now located in the Zone is condemned. Factories, railways, whole towns have been lost. Just up the railway line north of Zhitomir, in the thousand-year-old town of Ovruch sits a tenth-century cathedral. The church in Ovruch is almost as old as the cathedral of Saint Sophia in Kiev, the pride of Ukraine. I never visited Ovruch, though. The trains stop at Korosten. They don't go up as far as Ovruch anymore, up that close to the Zone, at least not as often as they used to. Yet some people who want an apartment or house so badly that they are willing to risk radiation have moved back into polluted areas. There, they occupy evacuated houses, grow vegetables, and pick radioactive mushrooms.

Most amazing of all is that the Chornobyl nuclear power plant continued to operate until 2001. Energy-starved Ukraine said it could not afford a substitute for the 7 percent of the country's electric energy Chornobyl supplies. The government dragged its feet to shutdown the plant until it received Western aid for two newer reactors in Rivne and Khmelnitsky. Meanwhile, the leaking sarcophagus of concrete built over the melted hole could reportedly collapse at any moment—just up the Dnipro River from Kiev and five million people.

At a party, I once met a Chornobyl fireman named Taras. He showed me his documents to prove he had been an army reservist, called into action to help put out the reactor fire. Every soldier threw two shovelfuls of dirt into the blaze and then retreated, with more than a lifetime's dosage invisibly etched on his body. It is estimated that 750,000 people, many of them young army draftees, were exposed while working on the cleanup.

Taras had a bushy, sandy mustache and laughing blue eyes. But he didn't laugh, really; he drank more vodka at this party than any person I ever saw before or since. He choked down cupfuls at a gulp, a whole juice glass down his throat all at once. He ate spoonfuls of sour cream as chasers. He wasn't belligerent, giddy, or even visibly unhappy: he was ill, and he knew it. As for his health, he had given up; he just didn't care about it any more.

For most people in the area (though not to that extreme),

Chornobyl is a fact of their lives about which there is little to do and or say. Only meager recompense, if any, has been made. Misha's girlfriend, Natasha, and his roommate, Oleg, were both from Korosten, a town near the Zone. As victims of Chornobyl, they received a lifetime's free pass to ride trolleybuses—a privilege of which they didn't boast.

Superstitions and myths about radiation abounded, the most onerous being that vodka helped cleanse the body of it. (As if another excuse to drink were necessary.) Mushrooms actually were suspect, because radioactive elements remaining in the foot of each mushroom contaminated each time it regrew. Yet everyone collected and ate them anyway, insisting, "Oh, my mushrooms are from a special place only I know—very clean, no radiation there." Fishing in certain lakes was considered dangerous, and one person told me even walking in bare feet anywhere in the Zhitomir oblast could give you a rash on your feet. With little good information, likely-sounding (if untrue) information got passed around widely. The Ukrainian word "Chornobyl" means "wormwood," and it didn't help matters that a passage from Revelations 8 was often cited as a Biblical prediction of the catastrophe: "The third angel blew his trumpet; and a great star shot from the sky, flaming like a torch; and it fell on a third of the rivers and springs. The name of the star was Wormwood; and a third of the water turned to wormwood, and men in great numbers died of the water because it had been poisoned."

Chornobyl will never go away, and yet Ukrainians still somehow found humor in terrible straits. Larisa Petrovna, the Recertification Institute professor, once introduced me to a woman who lived near the Chornobyl zone. The woman, who was good-looking and in her thirties, had been a teacher, but her eyes smiled through a masked sadness as she told me she and her son were moving.

"To Florida," she said. "My aunt is there, and we have our visas."

She wanted to know if Florida was a nice place to live. "I

know that it's very hot, my aunt says," she confided. "And humid. I don't really like hot weather. Also, my aunt says you must drive everywhere and can't walk to shops. We will have a nice apartment, I'm happy for that. But what will I do there?" She sighed. "Our health is bad, my son is getting sick all the time. Ovruch is emptying out. I was not one of those who dreamed of moving to America someday, because I was happy here. Yet, we are going. You see how life changes?"

Then she laughed darkly. "And you, an American, have come to live here!" Larisa Petrovna joined in, and their laughter escalated into a roaring belly laugh. I stared at them both quizzically, unable to see any humor.

"John, don't be angry," she said. "You can't see how funny this is for us."

Chapter Fourteen

Falling

There came a day I went outdoors without a hat. Although slushy snow still splashed from dirty streets, the tips of my ears for once didn't feel numb. A wonderful forgotten sensation of the breeze whistling through my hair, curling in and around my ears, made me giddy. Ukrainians (for whom hat-wearing is the essence of preventive health care) yelped, "John! Why aren't you wearing a hat? Spring is weeks away! It's not yet time to put away your hat for the year!"

Sluggishly, spring edged in, though it was too early even for crocuses. The warm wind smelled wet, the dim, stale dampness of old ice melting. Dead wood poked up from under the snow, its fragrance seeping from the ground as it rotted into mulch. The path to school turned from twisted frozen ruts to squishy mud again, and I hopped between puddles until I reached the playground behind the school. A winter storm had brought down a massive tree there, and its wreckage was marvelous. The boys swung branches like swords, clashing them together and laughing when they shattered. Some saw the downed tree as a balance beam, and walked its length in parade fashion, one after another. Wobbling, they held their arms out straight like tightrope walkers and nimbly stepped over the stubs of broken-off limbs in a joyous, slow, procession, the leader of the parade jumping down and running back to walk the tree's length again.

I took the opportunity of spring holidays to leave the country. The first day of vacation I rose early, took my black carry-on bag, and walked toward the Zhitomir bus station. The bag felt immensely heavy, and I hadn't even left town yet.

Misha had kept me up the night before, drinking coffee. "You are becoming the talk of the town," he scolded. "The Vaktorsha sent us to tell you to drink less." One of the women who worked at the front desk had proclaimed herself another of my Ukrainian mothers. One too many times she had unlocked the dormitory doors after midnight to let me in, and she wasn't fooled by my shrugged apologies nor my attempt to direct my breath away from her. As a token of concern, Misha brought me a present: a circular blue pin that read, "Society for the Protection of Sobriety"—a political emblem during Gorbachev's prohibition on vodka. Misha meant it as a friendly way of looking after my well-being, but I was infuriated. Who was he to tell me how to live? "Don't worry about me," I told him. "I'll be fine. You don't have the faintest idea of what's on my mind." I should have either laughed or thrown him out, but instead had thanked him sarcastically and went to bed.

With three other Peace Corps volunteers, Mark, Mike, and Charlie, I boarded the Moscow-Budapest train in Kiev. For our overnight ride, Mike bought a whole roasted chicken, eight dinner rolls, and a two-liter bottle of Rasputin vodka with which, in our four-person cabin, we eagerly celebrated our escape from Ukraine. At the border crossing, sometime around two a.m., where we were checked at least six times by customs officials and soldiers, a fat man in a strange uniform asked who I was. Handing over my passport, I pointed to the others and in a Russian speech blurred with Rasputin vodka, said, "I'm with them," before collapsing back onto my bed. The fat official said, "You speak Russian?" I answered, "Very little," and he laughed, repeated it, and let me sleep.

I woke up in Hungary to hear Mark shouting, "Look! A gas station!" He pointed out the window to a European-looking Arco station. "A real gas station! We made it!"

In the fields, shoots of green had already begun to show. Farmland looked neat and well-kept. When we got off the train the air smelled sweet, and the train station was clean and well-lit. With instant delight, we realized we were in the West.

Budapest looked like Europe—there was nothing Soviet about it. Most of the dreadful architecture of socialist realism had been replaced or at least scrubbed and painted. Vanguards of capitalism like Dunkin Donuts, Pizza Hut, and of course the golden arches peeked around every corner. "Someone has been here ahead of us," Mike said with a grin. We couldn't get enough of it.

Coming from another direction, the commercialization of Eastern Europe might have saddened me quite a bit. But the contrast with Ukraine was so striking that Western glitz and convenience really did seem like some fantastic progress had occurred. For one thing, the grocery stores had *groceries in them*. Palpating delicious-looking fruits and vegetables I had not seen for months, I felt not only a brush with forgotten prosperity but also the presence of an old familiar logic. Here was an economy that worked. The city was full of things I had forgotten. Telephones operated, stores displayed signs, people sat at tables in sidewalk cafes—people without tracksuits or scars!—and simply ate and talked. It felt safe to assume that if I thought of something to buy I might even know where to begin looking for it. Not only the economy, but also the people seemed Western. Not being jostled on buses was a startling sensation. It reminded me of that airy sensation I felt after removing my hat after the long winter: a feeling of openness, freedom of movement, wealth of space. Even the air of dirty downtown Budapest tasted, looked, and smelled fresher. As a result, the culture shock of Hungary consisted for me mostly of the very odd feeling of reentering a place I had long ago left. Weirdly, I felt I had returned "home," as if I belonged there, in Budapest, where I did not even know the words for yes, no, and thank you. Walking through the gorgeous capital's domed palaces, its ancient streets, and its chilly museums filled with Eastern European art reminded me of where I was. But still I wasn't fooled; we were back. It soon pained me to think that such long-coveted comforts had been right here all along, an overnight train away.

My consciousness of being a Peace Corps volunteer made me want to deny those thoughts. I wished that my instincts had led me to cluck and scorn, to belittle capitalism's tasteless, inexorable march to the east. Instead, I dug out my credit card. Unused for months, it provided me a meal of goulash, green beans, and delicious Hungarian pastry at a touristy restaurant, all for an outlandish $16. That same sum bought two nights in a former castle called the Citadel atop a hill overlooking the Danube and the old city of Pest. Ukraine felt very far away indeed.

Everything about Budapest showed how eagerly it had removed itself from the "Soviet sphere of influence." We delighted in going to movies in English, something impossible even in Kiev, not to mention anyplace else in Ukraine. That spring locals flocked to watch *Schindler's List*, subtitled in Hungarian, and all but one of the showings was sold out. We managed to get in, and seeing the film there gave a different twist than what I would have experienced watching it anywhere else. At the end of the movie, when the war is over, the Jews Schindler has protected from the Nazis are free. They stand together in a crowd, unsure what to do next, as a soldier on horseback appears. "Good day," he says. "I'm a lieutenant in the Soviet Red Army, here to liberate you from the Fascists." This remark elicited from the Hungarian audience a loud, scoffing snort. They shook their heads, before an ironic chuckle rippled through the theater. To me Ukraine felt very far away, but perhaps to Hungarians it wasn't far enough.

When our train carried us back to Ukraine, we glumly watched out the window. As if heading back in time, we were returning to ugly late winter. The shoots of green grass dwindled.

The warm wind smelling of rains and the early spring sun warming my skin disappeared. Outside I saw the same gray country I had left, still burdened with dirty ice and darkness. Just inside the border we passed a barren field of winter-wheat stubble. The figure of a man caught my eye. Thirty yards from the train tracks, he lay face down in a ditch, dead still—drunk. Pointing him out to the others, I said, "We're back."

My vacation left me disheartened rather than rested. Home in Zhitomir, where nothing worked, where faces in the streets looked tense and unhappy, where people's gaits still sagged, downtrodden and tired, I felt my spirit crushed again. After so recently escaping to the "outside," I found in both my surroundings and myself nothing but bedraggled dreariness. I gritted my teeth, kept busy with school visits, and tried to be vigilant about lesson planning. But it had now occurred to me—like a sweet little pain—that I did not actually *have* to stay. Why was I stuck in sleepy gray Zhitomir, and not Budapest, or even Kiev? The dull chores of staying warm, boiling cabbage, and bathing myself with a sponge were all tasks no longer worth the energy. The simple act of rising in the morning had become a tough job—and I wasn't loving it.

Shopping, once an adventure, was demeaning and difficult. I begrudged the large chunks of time it took from me every day. To buy sugar, for instance, I first searched the market for likely looking army trucks. There, a babushka stood and poured sugar into plastic baggies as they were handed to her from the crowd. I jostled forward for position, grumbling until eventually I got a turn. I held my baggie high over my head until the babushka took it from my hand. Waving my kupons helped me get chosen sooner sometimes. The woman placed my bag on a scale, stuffed her plastic scoop into the burlap sack at her feet, and poured an even, steady stream of white granules, all the while repeating to nobody and everybody, "Sugar for 14, sugar for 14." She didn't need to say the thousand. When the needle hit three kilos she handed down my bag and took another from the crowd of outstretched hands. Sighing, stepping back, and tying a loose knot in my baggie, I sullenly headed down the row of market stalls.

A fight was breaking out in the market down at the far end where electronics, hardware, plumbing supplies, and other odds and ends were sold. Probably negotiation over, say, a carpenter's level or a bicycle inner tube had turned nasty. Suddenly one man would be shaking a fist in the other's face, and before long, both would be shouting in the slow, dizzy drawl of half-intoxicated old men. A third man would pull the first away. Once upon time I would have laughed tiredly or remarked to myself that they were acting like chimps at the zoo fussing over some grapes. But not any more. Lately, the sad antics of demoralized people had ceased to make me laugh; even as horrible absurdity, it wasn't funny.

Off to haggle with another babushka for eggs or to wait behind forty people in the bread line and then another fifteen in the milk line. Unsuccessfully, I searched again for cheese or fruit or canned tomato paste. So many little tasks scraped away at my depleted reserves of energy, taking a little here, a little there. It seemed so long ago when I had pictured myself experiencing dramatic changes every day, watching history cooked up on the spot. When I tried to remember how I had envied dynamic post-Soviet life, how I had imagined it exciting and exotic, such nonsense made me laugh. The unpredictability—a fascinating novelty for a while—was now part of the tedium. Sometimes, I even had the urge to join the man in the ditch.

When a conference for English teachers was held in Kiev that spring, all of the Peace Corps teachers were invited to make presentations or attend sessions of Ukrainian teachers. The seminars lasted a whole weekend; I went to a few and skipped the rest. With some volunteers, I spent most of Saturday drinking in a shabby cafe on Red Army Street.

All through the late winter months, my tolerance for alcohol had increased. Losing track of what I drank, I slipped into a dark night state I loved, a cruise on autopilot. Melodies hummed in my head: monkish chants, melancholy and tragic, like an ache bringing relief. When I escaped into an ocean of vodka, where everything around me swum in a grayish mirage, I felt my worries wash off, or at least my view of the ugly world became less vivid.

Later that evening was a party at a Peace Corps staffer's apartment in Kiev, where I met up with Liza, whom I had not seen in months. In my despairing mood I regretfully recalled our earlier visits, like the day we crossed the Teteriv bridge to walk through a village, enjoying the edge of autumn. That time, when we saw the old cowherd in the stubble of an autumn field, seemed so long ago. The country had since grown old and tired in front of me, and now everything I saw reminded me of decay and dying. Upon seeing Liza, though, the echoes of that day enlivened me, reminding me why I was here.

She noticed me staring. Her stare had changed as well. After too long a look, I turned away, startled by unspoken words that had passed between us.

My composure had fractured, my grip loosened. I talked with another volunteer and tried to appear normal, but it felt as though my mind were slipping gears. For a moment, I imagined how I must look through Liza's eyes: a miserable person playing a foolish role. When she put on her coat to leave, I chased after her and caught up to her in the dim hallway outside the apartment. Under a bare bulb, with a dank musty smell swirling around us, I made a ridiculous attempt to explain my strange feelings. And somehow, we kissed. Up close for the first time, I noticed how complex her eyes were. Their color intrigued me; I had thought they were brown, but now I saw a maze of colors: hazel and yellow and the green of marbles, even rifts of periwinkle—the furrows of some leftover baby blue she must once have had.

She went downstairs, and I wandered back in to the party in a trance. The charm of a magic spell had been laid on me. When I finally left the party it was very late, and I stumbled disoriented through the central streets of Kiev back to the apartment where I was staying the night. My feet wouldn't step forward properly; I weaved and swayed and meandered my way over brick streets and sidewalks, trying not to trip, focusing on my wonder at that kiss and what it meant.

The next day, one of the English teachers in our group organized a big brunch for those of us in town for the conference. Compared to our provincial towns, the Kiev markets offered a cornucopia of foodstuffs: fresh peppers, mushrooms, bananas, oranges, pineapples. With the purchase of three dozen eggs, we had the makings of a memorable breakfast. There were also boxes of orange juice and enough bargain-priced Soviet champagne to make mimosas for everybody—a thought that sickened me. Liza was at the brunch, too, but in daylight, melancholy visions and tragic choruses seemed too absurd to mention. I said hello and nothing else. The morning was spent cracking eggs, mixing green peppers, ham, cheese, and fresh mushrooms in a huge bowl, and frying up omelets while we laughed and joked. Since champagne gives me a headache, I drank orange juice with vodka.

By the time all the food was prepared, the tiny kitchen was piled high with dirty dishes. There was no place to sit in the room where the others ate, so I decided to clean up. I took sips of champagne until even the heavy pots were scoured, the long metal spoons shiny-clean, and the big frying pans scrubbed. The kitchen was sparkling, the champagne now gone, but I hadn't yet eaten. I went into the other room to pick at what was left of the omelets.

Somebody said, "Where were you, Johnny?" Suddenly I felt like I had missed the party and no one had noticed. I took a seat on the edge of Liza's chair, where she made room for me—and with a heavy thump I hit the floor.

The room erupted in laughter. Everyone had seen me slip off the edge of the chair and plop flat on my butt, which, in their festive mood, probably looked hysterical. To me, though, it was the last straw. The whole weekend was going terribly wrong. There was no way I could laugh along with everyone else. Confused and embarrassed, I stood up and walked into the spare room to collect my things. It was after four o'clock, but I could just catch a late bus back to Zhitomir. I packed my bag and left.

When I walked out of the apartment, luggage in hand, people were still laughing. "Johnny! Wait!" Mike shouted, half-giggling.

Hustling downstairs and outside into the golden afternoon light, I suddenly felt the urge to run. The metro wasn't far. I'd be at the Kiev bus station in about half an hour. Then Michael and Jeff appeared beside me.

"Johnny!" Mike said, teasing gently now. "Where you goin'?"

"Home," I said, feeling clear-headed again. "I've got to get back."

"But Johnny!" Mike giggled again. "This subway doesn't go to Columbus."

Jeff laughed then too and I almost did; instead I thanked them, told them I was fine, and headed into the dark of the Metro.

Once underground I felt a surge of fright. My vision was blurry; I could walk, but not too convincingly. I should never have left. But there was no turning around now. By the time I reached the bus station I was drowsy, but somehow found the correct line to stand in to buy tickets to Zhitomir. I stood still and tried hard not to sway, and that's the last thing I remember. I must have purchased a ticket and boarded the right bus automatically, I don't know. On the bus, I fell sound asleep.

When I awoke, in the pitch dark of evening, I was walking down Shelushkova Street in Zhitomir. Someone passed me and said, "Good evening, Mr. John." The words startled me back to life. There in the street, two blocks from my dorm, I froze in my tracks. I looked around at my neighborhood's high-rises, the familiar potholes in the road where I'd slipped on winter ice. . . . but I had no idea how I had arrived at that spot. The person who had greeted me—a student? neighbor? friend?—had disappeared into the shadows. In an instant, all the other possible outcomes of that evening occurred to me, and I was terrified. If I had boarded the wrong bus, if I had agreed to a private car ride from

Kiev, or if someone on the bus had offered to show me the way home, I might have wound up in that ditch after all—and lucky just to be sleeping.

The next morning I felt deeply chastened and guilty. It surprised me that I could now do such difficult tasks as buying a bus ticket and making the journey between cities when I was half-unconscious, but it didn't make me feel better. Even gratefulness for my good fortune didn't suffice. I thanked the guardian angel that had overseen a hundred-mile journey I could not recall. Another foolish slip like that and I might never go home.

On the third of May, a snow squall almost snapped me like a brittle twig. When low-hovering dark clouds released tiny, ugly flurries, the sight of them made me ill. May, the month of May already—and it was cold again! It was *still* cold, that is. Perhaps it had always been cold. These gray buildings, this sleety rain, this disgusting cabbage soup might be a permanent condition. Perhaps it would never warm up, never ever.

I put on my yellowing long underwear, opened the door of the electric stove, and huddled in my tiny kitchen under three layers of clothes. The town outside my window looked surly and grim, its people shabby and sullen, its skies a bruise. The way wood looks after heavy weather, Zhitomir's people appeared cracked and faded, one or two shades of liveliness scraped away by unending winter and depression that settled and stuck like factory smoke. It couldn't be laughed off or shrugged away ironically, I thought. From my too-high bathroom mirror, twelve inches wide and four inches high, stared a haggard, thin person, nearly unrecognizable. The circles under my reddened eyes looked like dark pits dug out of my face, pebbled scars left by industrial mining. You, my friend (I told the mirror), are losing it.

Visiting John Maddox's workplace on my lunch hour helped sometimes, and often I picked up his mail and mine from the post office box we shared. Seeing John, I hoped, might help me keep a grasp on what felt like my last, thin shred of sanity.

Usually the Gorispolkom, the city administration building, was jammed full of babushkas. They waited in line for interviews about openings in state-owned apartments. The number of privately owned places grew every day, and could be rented for around ten dollars a month or bought outright for $2000. But such sums were inconceivable to the pensioners, whose only income totaled an equivalent of sixty dollars a year. They had to try for housing the old-fashioned way. The official "list"—faint dot-matrix print on green-and-white computer paper, and stapled to fifty yards of wall—had little relation to the true system. Some of the names on that fifty yards of list had been posted five years ago; many names probably belonged to dead people. Yet the old folks in the hall stood stoically, waiting like the thousands before them. Everywhere I went, it was more of the same: people suffering endless futile trials, beating their heads against walls for nothing, and always standing or waiting with little or no hope for the better.

Through that unhappy bunch I threaded my way to the stairs. On the second floor, John had a high-ceilinged, chilly office with a silver metal door that looked sturdy enough to secure a battleship. He usually kept it shut, but only to retain the heat from his small electric space heater. I pounded loudly on the door. Down the long hall, a runner of garish red Soviet-era carpet stretched into the distant heart of the building. There, far down the corridor, I saw a portly man in a suit ambling away from me, a fat file tucked under his arm. I knocked again, but guessed that John wasn't there. Only a few minutes remained before I had to return to school, so I slid his mail under the door and then opened mine. Only then did I notice that one of the letters was from Liza.

I tore it open and read:

> "Why did you leave Sunday without saying goodbye?
> Are you OK?
> I wish you were here."

There was more—much more—and my legs turned weak. Her look, her long stare had not been figments of my imagination. Something incredible had happened, and suddenly a new world of possibility opened up before me. On the second floor of the Zhitomir city hall, I gave a shout of joy and burst into a crazy dance of happiness. The scarlet carpet runner wrinkled into a tangle under my feet. In that hive of bureaucrats, I had a moment of epiphany I had not permitted myself even to dream of. A moment had altered me, and the chilly spring, the depressing heaviness, and my vodka-drinking method of coping all seemed manageable.

Remembering the Ukrainian national anthem, I thought, "You're not dead yet," and then, to my surprise, laughed at myself. It was the first time I had done so in quite a long while. Although I would not have the chance to see Liza for another month, I was smiling when I went back to school to teach my third graders.

Suddenly, as if making up for lost time, Ukraine turned beautiful all at once. The sleet and darkness ended in May when rain washed the oily snow into gutters and out of sight. Grass finally sprang up through sidewalk cracks. Rough-edged dandelion leaves poked up between the sprouts of crabgrass in front of my dormitory. As the very late spring exploded into life, spring fever overtook the harried people around me. "When May weather comes, give the cow its fodder and run for the sun," the Ukrainian saying goes.

First the pussy willows blossomed. My fourth graders brought me branches as gifts. They taught me the words in Ukrainian and Russian for willow, and I told them how we compare the buds to cat paws. Their eyes widened, and they nodded to one another in surprised appreciation. "Oooh, that's true," said one girl, stroking the soft, gray buds. "They *are* like little paws."

When flowers appeared in gardens, meadows, and empty yards, my pupils delighted at loveliness free for the taking. Like their parents, giving and receiving flowers provided intense enjoyment. A plain, gut-level joy invoked by bright colors caught me off guard. Sweet, wild smells whisked away the close, sour, winter air and made the whole room fresher. I never appreciated flowers so much before. Droopy purple and white crocuses. A trio of red tulips. Bundles of pale yellow daffodils—always an odd number because even numbers of flowers were only for funerals.

Soon my pupils began to bring in lilac branches, and I learned another superstition. I told them I especially loved lilacs because the deliciously strong, musky scent sparked memories of many warm afternoons in my backyard in Ohio. After I said that, Zhenya brought bunches of them to class—some royal purple, others a dainty lavender. "Now, Mr. John," Zhenya commanded. "Pluck one of the petals and eat it." I gave him a cautious look. "It's a tradition," he added.

Vannya chimed in. "No, really, Mr. John! Seriously! You must eat one petal of the five to have good luck." Each tiny lilac blossom, I noticed for the first time, is a five-petaled flower. Smiling, I nibbled one tiny purple petal and my students' faces beamed back. Probably any fresh plant would have tasted sweet at that point, but the miniature snip of lilac petal had a fragrance and flavor that gave me an almost spiritual boost. Or maybe it was all those smiles.

In the market appeared green leaves that looked like spinach but were "bear garlic," and tasted mysteriously of lemon. Wild green onions, their stalks a foot long, as well as herbs like parsley and dill filled market stalls that for months held nothing more green than pale gray cabbage. The cawing of ravens was joined by the songs of robins and nightingales. One day I even saw a stork again, that lucky sign in Ukrainian superstition that signifies a blessed home. The heavy, grim clouds, blown off by warm wind, revealed sunshine and blue skies that lasted well into evening as the long northern days kept lengthening.

Students were put on duty cleaning up the school grounds. One odd task they performed diligently was the painting of trees.

Ivan Wilhelmovich supervised some boys in front of the school while they applied what looked like chalky whitewash to every trunk on the property. In fact, every tree trunk in Ukraine was painted white, generally to a height of about five or six feet. I had always wondered why.

When I asked the physics teacher why the trees were being painted, his blue eyes twinkled. "So they'll be more beautiful," he said.

"No, really. Why does everyone in Ukraine paint trees?"

He sighed as if I were a nagging child. "Do you know the word *Zhuk*?"

It meant beetle or bug. With pinched fingers I mimicked a flying bug and said yes, I understood. The buckets held not paint but lime mixed with some pesticide. It was applied to prevent beetles from climbing up trees, eating the leaves, and destroying them.

"We paint the trees against the 'Coloradskiy Zhuk.'" Colorado potato beetles. Grinning sideways, he added, "It's another thing we can thank your America for."

With so much outdoor work to be done, the lessons were all moved up a half hour earlier, every break was cut short, and school ended at one-fifty. That way the director (among others) could catch a bus to her half-acre kitchen garden in the country. Most of the teachers had already planted some vegetables in April; now the frost-wary tomatoes and cucumbers could go in. In their long afternoons and evenings, my colleagues were digging, fertilizing, and weeding—patiently and steadily planting food for *next* winter.

But May was also a month of holidays. May Day—when Soviet missiles were traditionally paraded through Red Square "in honor of workers everywhere"—happened to be the same Sunday as Orthodox Easter. More important, though, was May 9—Victory Day. This holiday, for any resident of the former Soviet empire, will always mean much more than a three-day weekend of barbecuing. That year was the "Fiftieth Anniversary of Liberation from the Fascists," as banners hung all over town proclaimed. Curiously, the banners were written in Ukrainian language and bore Ukrainian national symbols of independence—as if patriotism was the real issue and the colors in which it was celebrated did not matter.

"Zhitomir was bombed on the very first day of the war," Svetlana Adamovna told me. "I was only five, and we were taken away into Russia to escape. The old town was flattened as the front passed back and forth through the city." The politics of history rewriting seemed less important to most people than getting on with a more prosperous present, but even so, people felt unequivocally proud of and humbled by their wartime struggles. Information about Stalin's evil doings against his own people even while they fought the war for him was not easily digested. Rhetoric like "liberation from the fascists" remained in use, but other Soviet-era phrases like "The Great Patriotic War" were rejected by many Ukrainians, who preferred the western-sounding "Second World War." The way some people saw it, real "liberation" of Ukraine had not yet been completed.

The school assembly to commemorate the event, then, did not include much about the Soviet Union. I attended, hoping to see some of my pupils perform in the prepared songs and skits, and was fascinated by how Soviet patriotism so easily transformed into pride about Ukraine. A second-grade class sang a patriotic song, and I studied the littlest girl in the chorus. She clasped her hands behind her back, singing war songs proudly while her blue leotards sagged. It looked to me like a real live image left over from the Cold War, and I sensed the sentimental, protective machismo of Soviet power hanging in the air like smoke. Some of the parents in attendance turned teary-eyed.

Other skits, however, lauded the new mythology—the glory of Ukraine rooted in its folk traditions. Two eleventh-graders wearing Ukrainian embroidered shirts sang a duet, a Cossack love song. Another student played a piano piece by the Ukrainian composer Lysenko. Then the fourth grade performed a medley of folk songs and a rough attempt at Hopak dancing, the famous Cossack deep kneebend kicks. The dance was too difficult for all but one boy, but the effort was applauded; the students perked up at the lusty singing and dancing.

After the skits a grizzled, bemedalled veteran with a purple-veined nose gave a cantankerous speech. For the teenagers in the audience, his speech ran too long on gung-ho rhetoric, too short on recollections of bloody escapades. His tone grew shriller, as he whipped himself into a frenzy—a frightening spectacle: ".... And not *one* of us didn't believe!" he barked, his feverish battle-cry rising to its peak, "and *thanks* . . . to *that* . . . we drove Fascism *out!*"

Way in the back of the auditorium, two boys burst into cheers and brief, dying applause—a mocking gesture that lifted several vice principals from their seats, bristling with anger. They scanned the back rows for guilty faces, while the entire audience sat frozen. I was sure that the culprit had been my Vitaliy or Andriy, or maybe that ornery Yura.

"If it's not interesting," a vice principal finally bellowed, "then go home!"

Nobody was as brave as that. Even so, a blatant insult, face-to-face with a war hero—unthinkable a few years before—came off as little more sinister than boyish impertinence. Now *that* was a big change, I thought.

In a way it proved the old veteran right: The year 1944 was long gone, and so was the thrill of a community's single-minded pursuit of noble goals. The idea of everyone for himself saddened him, he said. "That's why I visit schools," he told the pupils, more calmly now. "So the memory of what we went through won't die out with me." Plainly, though, the kids wanted nothing more than to get out in the spring air, have a look at toys and candy in the kiosks, and run down to the soccer field for a pickup game.

Spring also meant the year-end national test of English for fifth and ninth graders in specialized schools for the study of English. When test day came, I was surprised to see it in the form of booklets printed on paper, one for each student, all alike. It must have cost the bankrupt state of Ukraine a fortune. In disappointment I discovered that all of the questions were multiple choice. For example, "If I had known of your good fortune, I *[answer here]* happy." The whole test was about that level of difficulty. My 9G and 9B classes had worried about the exam all year, and now I saw why. I knew that the material was beyond the level of all but my best students.

A group of about fifty pupils gathered in one of the larger classrooms, where Svetlana Adamovna, another teacher, and I were to oversee the test. "All right children," she said sternly to the fifteen-year-olds, "you may begin." I looked out at Kuzik, Serhiy, Ruslan, and the other boys. They were doomed. I thought back to what I could have done better to prepare them. Memorization and recitation wouldn't have helped; and as for grammar rules, we had worked on the most simple ones, and the pupils had learned them to some extent. But this test was just too hard.

As I watched, Ruslan stared up at the ceiling, rubbing his chin as if to ponder a question, and with a roll of his eyeballs, stole a quick glance at Oksana's paper. Kuzik leaned forward in his chair, then leaned back when he had seen Nina's answer. Glancing around the room, I comprehended the boys' sly strategy. Each had positioned himself near a girl who knew English well; not one was too isolated to view a better pupil's paper.

Svetlana Adamovna and the other teacher acted as if the class had vanished in smoke, and chatted away at a normal conversational volume, ignoring the students. The pupils didn't mind—cheating would be that much easier. I felt that I should probably ignore the cheating too, reasoning that the better my students performed, the better I would appear. But it was so blatant I had to at least raise the subject. Interrupting my colleagues as politely as possible, I asked, "Don't we want to make certain that no one copies from another person's paper?" The students looked up quickly from their writing.

Svetlana Adamovna looked at me strangely, her expression unusually sour. "Yes, of course!" she answered tersely, as if I had accused *her*. "Children! No glancing, no whispering! Anyone who does will not pass the exam." Some of my boys nodded solemnly. The teachers went back to their conversation; the kids went back to copying.

Instead of outrage or indignance I was flooded with relief: My kids would at least pass, and I could tell myself I had tried to raise the subject of honesty. For several hours they scribbled away, glancing surreptitiously around in a manner simultaneously obvious and sneaky. The second-best students checked themselves against the best, while everyone at the bottom of the class copied every answer. When the tests were collected and graded against the answer key that afternoon in Galina Vasilievna's office, my best students all received fives. The second-best students and all my weak students were clever enough to muff a few questions and receive fours. Unsuspicious, the teaching staff seemed pleased with the performance until they saw the paper of the worst hooligan in the school, a boy in my 9G class.

"Savchuk?" Galina Vasilievna shouted in startled horror. "Savchuk received a five?" The boy who could not spell his own name in English had a nearly perfect score on a test so difficult some teachers were confused by a few questions. "This is not possible," she said.

Smiling, shaking my head, I said nothing. She looked at me, and I shrugged.

"This isn't possible, is it, John?" she asked. "You know this boy's knowledge of English. Is this possible?"

"Of course not," I answered truthfully. To soften my wording with a hint of uncertainty, I added, "Maybe he was looking on someone else's paper."

"*Da, da, da, da, da,*" she said enthusiastically, in a singsong voice as if I'd discovered something. She looked over his paper again and checked it against the key. "Maybe I missed something the first time." A few flips of the red pen and his test looked much better. "Savchuk gets—a three," she pronounced.

This boy had been in trouble with the police and had been "encouraged" to pursue his education elsewhere—meaning to leave the school. After ninth grade, no more schooling was legally required, and everyone expected that he would go to work, helping his mother peddle in the bazaar. He had to be advanced to tenth grade, or else he would repeat the year—in our school. But that didn't mean he should be able to call the testing procedure into question. He would not return to our school no matter what, and we teachers should not allow him to make us look bad on the way out. That was how I understood the logic, at least.

Thus the hurdle of the state exam, a challenge I had prepared for and sweated over for months, was finessed into oblivion. All of my ninth graders passed, some on their own merits, some not. I learned that most of my own pupils were moving on to vocational schools or technical colleges, where they would study no more English anyway. The end of the school year was a little disappointing, to think that all of my effort would amount to so little. But by then I was not likely to be disillusioned by much. I was so relieved that my students passed, I hardly minded.

Chapter Fifteen

A Summer Day Is Like a Year

When the school year ended, I went back to Kiev for mid-service training. Being with Americans again was a strange feeling. The warm June evenings were light until nine, and we spent them outdoors. Some volunteers had aluminum bats and softballs for their school sent to Ukraine, and in a field outside our labor union hotel, we played a game in the newly cut grass that smelled of summer.

Earlier that day, a man using a scythe with a long wooden handle had cut the grass. In graceful rhythm, he swung the scythe high above his head, then down to precisely the right height for cutting grass with a sweeping follow-through high above his head again. He loped around the field as if preoccupied, not even paying attention as he swung the tool downward, turned it, and swept it up again. Eventually he piled the dry bundles into the trunk of his car. The hostel didn't mind, he told us, if he came into Kiev and cut grass for his cow in the village.

Liza had learned to play guitar over the dark winter months. Her practice paid off with golden summer evenings on a balcony of our hostel, as she picked out James Taylor songs. There was something new between us, an unacknowledged spark. But I didn't know how to approach her—she was strong and independent and didn't need me; I was afraid to make a wrong move. I thought about that connection in the spring, our kiss, her letter, and I longed to prove myself worthy of her. I kept saying stupid things around her, in an effort to capture that gaze which had taken possession of my senses. I thought, "I have to make her laugh" or "I have to get her attention." The color of her eyes was like a spell whose charm entranced me. I was falling in love. I wanted her beside me, I wanted to see her grow old. When I met her I secretly imagined how she would look at age fifty-five. I could picture her features aging, could add wrinkles and lines to her face, and see how the bright sparkle of her eyes would only be that much brighter.

On the last day of mid-service training, my inner world changed for good. Liza and I sat in a sandy play area, next to a paint-chipped jungle gym made of bent steel bars. Some nearby half-buried tires looked like the many backs of a long sea monster surfacing and diving into the sea. A rusty slide looked as slick as sandpaper. Somebody had made a campfire, and the burned ring full of ashes and broken bottles looked like a burnhole or the remains of tiny missile strike. The whole lot was surrounded by cinder-block wall. There, on that dismal playground, we kissed again, and differently than before—my scourge of vodka played no part. It was hot and sunny for a few minutes, and I found words to tell Liza what she meant to me. When it began to rain, her eyes told me a new relationship had been born. My heart welled up with joy, and my dream of being with Liza seemed to have come true. We arranged to meet in Vinnitsa, in her town, the following week.

It was a lucky stroke that the Zhitomir-Vinnitsa bus stopped on the edge of town, leaving me on the outskirts of Vinnitsa. The neighborhood was not the greatest, except that it was where Liza lived. All around were rows of aging apartment buildings, some of which were factory worker dormitories like those in my own neighborhood. All of them looked so much alike that at first I wasn't sure which one was Liza's.

I crossed a courtyard with a well and several benches where old women in scarves and housecoats sat gossiping. The previous fall I had visited once, and remembered how her second-story balcony looked out on children playing below. I located building 162B and went around back. The entryway was shabby and musty with the smell of old urine, perhaps left by one of the many stray dogs orbiting the dumpsters outside, or perhaps not.

On the second floor I rang the bell. No one answered. I knocked, lightly. The hallway was totally dark. There were muffled shouts from behind another door, like a quarrel between a man and a woman. I knocked harder.

Maybe she's out buying bread, I thought. She knew what time my bus would arrive, but perhaps she needed a few last-minute supplies. I went back out into the late morning light and noticed how warm the day had become. After hollering up to her balcony a few times, I headed back to the courtyard, passing the old women again and stopping in at the nearest bread store. She wasn't there. Hungry already, I bought a loaf of black bread myself. Errands often took longer than expected, I reminded myself. She had no telephone and could have been called away. Or kept too long at an acquaintance's. I didn't mind waiting awhile.

After half an hour I returned and knocked again. Still, nobody home.

The day was balmy, so I left the dirty hallway and went for a walk. Nearby was a veterans cemetery, where a tall black marble monolith listed the names of a company of Vinnitsa's dead soldiers. The huge red star embedded in the top of the monument was well-polished; grass grew tall around the few graves, most marked by crosses made of aluminum pipe. I sat on a bench in the small cemetery and wrote Liza a note.

Maybe she had misunderstood me. Maybe she didn't believe how serious I was, or that I had come to her town hoping for the chance to be alone and talk for hours. Then a horrible thought occurred to me.

Maybe she did realize all of that.

My heart started to pound faster. It was now two hours since my bus arrived, on time, as expected. She must have left, gone somewhere, traveled to another city . . . she must have run away rather than have to tell me I was not for her. My hands started to shake; this was premature, I decided. I had to go back and try her apartment again.

Still no one answered.

By then I was beginning to wonder where I would spend the night. Liza and I had made plans to visit our friend Sherry the next day in Fastiv, a four-hour electric train ride away. Maybe Liza was already there? But I was sure we had agreed on Saturday at her house. It had to be what I most feared: She had decided she couldn't face me.

I went back to the cemetery and wrote a longer note, beginning with that line from the Ukrainian song about the days of the week: "I arrived, you weren't there. You deceived me, let me down. You're driving me crazy." I went on to say something like "All along I wondered if we could make it work, and now before it's even started, you're gone somewhere for the weekend, and left me here. I guess I'm not even angry at you—I just wish that our lives could have come together and resembled a dream I was holding onto." I don't remember what all I wrote, but it was heavy with resignation.

I went back, knocked again, and waited. One last chance. . . . Nobody came to the door. I folded the letter, slipped it under the door, and went back outside.

It was mid-afternoon, the summer haze at its thickest, the sky above Vinnitsa a dirty orange. Over the brick wall behind Liza's building, the idle smokestacks of the reinforced-concrete factory leaned against the horizon. A stray dog eyed me nervously to see if I wanted the strip of sausage skin hanging from his jowls. Unbearable loneliness hit me like a blow, and my throat tightened to hold back the deepest sense of sorrow I have ever felt.

Far from Zhitomir, far from anyplace where anyone knew me,

I had a smothering sensation of being lost in time and abandoned to danger. There was nobody to call, nobody to turn to. But instead of fear I felt a stoic calm, like flat bedrock into which I could fall no deeper. I had taken a hard landing at the bottom of a well and wanted to lie quietly, eyes closed, and count my broken bones. I could get on the bus back to Zhitomir (if there were any). Or take an electric train (if there were any) to Fastiv. I didn't know and didn't care. It didn't matter what happened to me, and I was miserable enough to sleep the night away there by the dumpsters.

In fact, that was the perfect answer. I wanted nothing else, deserved no better, had no reason to hope for anything more. Through a hole in the cinderblock wall I slipped myself and my bag into a kind of alley. An aboveground heating pipe, swaddled in aluminum-colored shiny foam, stretched the length of the wall. The alley was secluded and could be accessed only through that hole in the wall. The ground was soft.

Uncorking the bottle of white wine I had brought, I sat back and took a deep, heavy swallow. It was cheap and disgustingly sour. I drank some more. Perfect, in fact, yes. This was perfect.

How many hours did I sit in that alley thinking, talking to myself, and cursing? I'd been hurt before, but not quite like this, and never so badly. I was stupid for believing I could convince Liza to love me. Why did I ever think she might be interested? The closeness I felt in the spring, the look in her eyes, had all been my imagination, phantom stars in a black sky. There was no point to it. There was no reason I was even born. Sure, I would keep living, I thought between gulps, but life would never be the same. I would go back to Zhitomir, keep teaching, maybe stay in Ukraine forever. Why not?

It began to get dark. The wine made me feel more relaxed, but the idea of sleeping in that alley had come to seem unwise. I crawled back through the hole and caught a trolleybus to the center of town. A babushka told me how to get to the train station by changing buses, and soon I was in line for tickets to Fastiv. A train left at six that evening and would arrive before midnight. I would find Sherry, I decided, but not tell her anything.

Hungry again, I ate a greasy roll from a vendor in the train station. Along with the terrible wine, it made me feel ill, and I went outside for fresh air. On the platform I set down my bag and sat on it, head in my hands, my spirit beaten. No one questioned me; no one wondered why I looked so unhappy; I blended in better than I ever had. For a minute, I laughed to think that I had turned Ukrainian—not because I was hopeless or miserable, but because I was abandoned. I felt left alone and forgotten, and illogically, that seemed fitting and just. When I boarded the electric train there were empty seats—a rare phenomenon about which I felt only dull surprise. Exhausted, I flopped over on a bench and went to sleep.

When I woke up with a start and looked out the train window, I knew immediately that I had missed my stop. It was after midnight, the train was almost empty, and Fastiv was behind me. In the pitch darkness outside I saw no roads, no towns, only a few solitary lights from isolated houses coasting by now and then as the train swayed gently along. My eyes ached. The muck of grogginess fell away when I realized we would arrive in Kiev soon. Well, change of plan, I thought. Then I corrected myself: There is no plan.

Kiev's train station was no rose garden even in daylight, but at midnight, a lurid fluorescent bulb lit the shuffling figures who were stuck there and made it look like a nightmarish graveyard. I had a premonition that a violent crime was about to be committed. Walking from my train, I tried to look purposeful, though I had no idea where I was headed. I had acquaintances in Kiev, knew of apartments where I might stay, but it was so late. What would I say? A family of gypsy women and very young children sat on the floor inside the ticketing hall. I had a strong urge to walk over, set down my bag, and join them. Instead I went to the sleepy cashier.

"Any trains for Fastiv?"

"Last one tonight in three minutes."

I bought a return ticket for the direction I had come from and boarded the train just before it pulled away. This time I stayed awake, waiting for Fastiv, and watched the bright moon out the window. I was clear-headed now; luck seemed on my side. The urge to walk out into a field and go to sleep was gone, but I still felt a listless blank at my center, an emptiness never to be filled in a way I had so vividly imagined.

In Fastiv I went to Sherry's friend Galla's house, where Sherry often stayed overnight. Liza and I together would have met her there the next day. But it *was* the next day—four in the morning of the next day, that is. I stood across the street from Galla's cozy-looking, small-town house, which resembled Misha's. Somehow I couldn't knock, couldn't go in. I had no way to describe the fall my heart had taken and have it make sense.

There was a big walnut tree and some high grass across the street from Galla's. A wooden fence protecting her neighbor's yard made the clump of weeds look secluded and safe. I set down my bag and curled up on it. At first I couldn't sleep but soon dropped off, dreaming fitfully, a few times starting awake and bumping my head on the tree trunk.

The June night was chilly, and I shivered alone under the tree, huddled in that clump of weeds. Galla's house looked warm and welcoming, but it still seemed ridiculous to knock and ask to go in. Then something slithered by my leg. Jumping upright to my feet, I yelped in fright, thinking it was a rat come to feed on the forlorn shell of myself. But now it wasn't moving. A rat would run away, I thought, peering closer, at a ruffled little ball, dead still.

"Yozhik!" I said out loud to no one. A hedgehog. I had never seen a real live hedgehog before. He looked like the hedgehogs I had seen in pictures: a round hump of a body, covered in blunt spikes, and a cute little face. He looked so harmless, like some hybrid that was half-shrew, half-possum. Hedgehogs, I remembered, were the butt of Ukrainian jokes for being so dumb. My students had giggled at the anecdote about a hedgehog who walks around a barrel saying, "When will I get to the end of this fence?" The joke made me laugh when I thought of it. The Yozhik was like me—curled up at the first sight of danger, and too dumb and shortsighted to tell a fence from a barrel. Liza or no, I would have to get my act together and shape up.

I stroked the poor, frightened guy. His spikiness felt soft, and he cooed like a dove, which was actually a hedgehog sound for terror. When I left him alone for a while, my Yozhik got up and left.

Some men came strolling down the street then, carrying fishing poles. Crouching in the weeds, freezing stiff as the hedgehog, I prayed they wouldn't stop and ask me my business. They didn't see me in the weeds and headed on down to the river. It was almost light.

Galla answered my sheepish knock quickly, for having to get out of bed at six. When she saw my face, she greeted me with a sigh. "Go sleep on the couch. You can explain in the morning."

The next morning Sherry told me I was crazy. When I tried to explain everything to her, she said, "That doesn't sound like Liza." My body felt like it had run a marathon the day before, and I didn't argue. My resolve had collapsed, and I felt like a deflated balloon.

We left Galla's to go back to Sherry's apartment, and when we got there, found a note. Sherry read it quickly, before handing it to me.

In Liza's handwriting, I read:

> Sherry—
>   I'm here!! I have no idea what happened yesterday—
> I was home all day, waiting for John!
>   Anyway, I'm at Galla's. See you soon!
>
>   Love, Liza

"You," Sherry said, "are a dumb ass."

On the way back to Galla's my heart fluttered, my mind raced. What had gone wrong? She was home all day? And now she was here in Fastiv! I wanted to run all the way to Galla's. The few blocks' walk took forever.

She could not have understood the hug I gave her when I fell into her arms at first sight. She kissed me on the cheek and said, "What *happened* to you?"

How could I tell her how crushed I had felt? The mental torture I had put myself through now seemed childish and ridiculous. Last night's roller-coaster emotions had been for nothing. Now that we were together again, I felt myself resurrected. Laughing in wonder, speaking to her after such a horrible night was like a miracle. "I knocked and knocked," I said, "and you never came to the door!"

"I sat in my apartment all day, playing guitar and wishing you would arrive," she said. "The whole day! Waiting, staring out the window at the old women on the bench...."

"Wait!" I interrupted. "Your apartment doesn't face the courtyard. It's the one . . ."

She groaned, and punched me gently.

I still wonder what the Ukrainians in the other apartment thought of my note.

Like the hedgehog who discovers his fence is a barrel, I stopped circling in a bad pattern. With summer's arrival and my new relationship with Liza, I crossed into a new phase of my life. Before, I had always wanted to leave Ukraine, yet tried pretend that I was happy. Now I couldn't imagine how it felt to live elsewhere. I hadn't been home in over a year; in some ways I felt I had a new home.

The chore of shopping was much easier performed by two. With Liza in Vinnitsa's market named "Harvest," one of us haggled, while the other hefted the bags of cabbages and potatoes. We bought armfuls of vegetables and fruit. One day, despite the market's amalgam of smells, an isolated fragrance, sweet as perfume, drifted to my nose. The magnificent scent, both familiar and forgotten, led me to the end of a counter and a fragrant mound of ripe strawberries.

We bought a plastic bagful and headed back to Liza's apartment. The afternoon turned warm, and we took the footpath along Vinnitsa's main river, the Yuzhniy Booh. She told me the local legend of a Cossack battle that had occurred in the middle of the river when it was frozen solid. On such a sunny day especially, that time seemed long ago and far away. We found a grassy spot on the bank and ate the strawberries, which had been crushed together in the bag. They were a delicious, crimson mess. Liza reminded me of the Ukrainian joke so many of our friends had told us: "When is the first strawberry in Ukraine? The first week of July. When is the first strawberry in America? Six in the morning, when the stores open." We didn't even try to explain all-night supermarkets—how you could buy a strawberry any time of night all year. The anecdote's contrast was already pro-American enough. Ukrainians only had strawberries a few weeks out of the year, but oh, how those strawberries tasted! Carefully chosen and picked from someone's well-cared-for garden, they were the sweetest, juiciest, most delicious fruit I ever had. It was as if I had never eaten strawberries before. Sitting on the riverbank, we ate the whole bag, licking our sticky, red fingers to savor every last bit of the fruit.

I discovered so many new things about Liza that delighted me. I already loved how, when she hurried, her gait turned to a little trot, bouncing on heels and toes. I found out she liked candles. Her apartment was not entirely neat. She had stacks of mini-cassettes her parents sent her, which she listened to when she got lonely. She liked to cook a fried-potato pie that we pretended was quiche. On her wall, a handwritten card read "Yes!" She told me it was a leftover scrap of material from some lesson, but I thought of it as a reminder to be positive in circumstances that so easily made me cynical.

After a big meal and some luscious red Crimean wine, we made tea, adding honey from a jar I bought from an old man at the bazaar. On her balcony, cluttered with her landlord's spare car parts, lumber, and tools, we listened to kids playing in the courtyard. Children from several apartment buildings gravitated to the central yard, where a slide and a sandbox formed the community playground. All of them—some as young as four and three—ran and played, unattended. As summer's late twilight approached, women's voices called down from surrounding buildings, their calls like evening chimes.

"Va-a-a-a-sya! Come in!"
"Ka-a-a-a-tya! Hurry up!"
"Irichka! Your soup's getting cold!"

The kids kept digging in the sand, racing their toy trucks or playing with dolls, calling back, "Coming, Ma! Just a minute!"

We heard the squeak-splash! squeak-splash! of someone pumping water from the courtyard well into a galvanized tin bucket. Probably someone's babushka, drawing water to bathe a grubby, tired child. We couldn't tell; we could hardly see through all the gorgeous, rustling leaves on the courtyard trees. I pulled Liza to me and whispered in her ear how wonderful and beautiful she was. I wanted to be alert to her every move, to reach and curl myself around her; to touch her until beams of her bright, sparkling inner self spilled out for me. With her, Ukraine transformed into a land of warm showers, radiant sunsets, easy laughter, and music.

When I went back to Zhitomir, the school building, now empty of children, echoed like an empty theater. I asked Galina Vasilievna what kinds of things should be done during summer. She said, "What work in summer? You will have a rest. Maybe you will go to Svetlana's dacha. No one is here at school! What would you do?"

I gave a few more presentations at the teacher colleges, organized the nearly two hundred books donated by people back home, and recorded a few language tapes. But I didn't go out of my way to find extra things to do. Instead, I grew my beard out. Some of my teacher friends told me I looked like a "Zek"—slang for prisoner. Everyone knew some prison slang; maybe everyone had known someone in prison too. It made me look older, but then, a year of living in Ukraine the way I had was like two years of the easy life back home.

However, there was plenty of easy living in Ukraine, too, if I knew how to look for it. Svetlana Adamovna's family had been seeing less and less of me all spring. She still thought of herself as my "Ukrainian mama," and I enjoyed the time I spent with her and her family. When she insisted that I visit their dacha for a week, I agreed. I owed them some help in their garden, and I wanted to see more of the countryside.

For some people, a "dacha" can be a piece of land no bigger than an acre used as a garden and with no buildings except a toolshed. For others—the former elite, the newly rich—a dacha can be a massive house far bigger than the city apartment. Even a provincial town like Zhitomir had its own elites. Factory owners, top army officers, and even small businessmen who did little more than speculate on gasoline built country houses, some of them three stories tall with twelve and fifteen rooms. Such folks, if they have *blat*, or influence, have bricks and lumber delivered to their doors, a simple matter of traded favors. A bad move can wreck the project, though. Outside Zhitomir I had seen a huge hole in the ground where a country mansion had been constructed, then torn down. "An army colonel forced his soldiers to build his dacha, since they had nothing to do anyway," Tanya explained, "but he was reported and arrested, and his house taken apart."

What Svetlana Adamovna's family had called a "dacha" was the cottage and yard she had inherited from her father, the man whose funeral I attended the year before. He had been principal of a country school in a village outside the city. From his garden they reaped the potatoes they ate all winter, tomatoes and cucumbers for canning, fresh squash and zucchini in summer, raspberries for jam, and grapes for making homemade wine.

Svetlana Adamovna and her husband were going to the dacha later in the week, so I went to Kornin with Sergey, Larisa, and Betty, their golden Persian cat, who was making her first visit to the dacha as well. The poor cat meowed throughout the hot, two-hour electric train ride. The slow-moving train stopped every ten or fifteen minutes to let off passengers carrying hoes, burlap sacks, and young trees. We hopped off at a deserted road intersection where a weathered sign read "Kornin." Other than a little brick hut and a couple of benches, I saw only forest and a huge sweep of golden wheat extending to the horizon, where a grain silo or some sort of farm building stood.

"Don't worry," Sergey said. "It's not far. Couple kilometers."

We walked down the road past the collective farm's wheat field. Betty squirmed in Larisa's arms, but couldn't escape the firm grip on her scruff. She wasn't an outside cat, and Larisa was afraid she would bolt into the forest. Other than Betty's mewing, the countryside was silent. The wheat field had no visible rows, only random tufts and bunches, swirling in the breeze like miles of wavy blond hair. Between the strands, I could see the soil, truly black and fertile-looking, dark as a deliciously rich brownie.

After forty-five minutes or so, we passed the farm building I had seen, which was actually a decrepit beet-sugar refinery. At least it looked a wreck to me.

"Oh, no, it works," Sergey said. "In the fall, at harvest time, it will go round the clock."

The cottage was between the factory and the school, but both were abandoned and silent. It was cool inside the cottage, and larger than it had seemed from outside. "Here you go, Betty," Larisa said, finally releasing her. The cat sniffed around the two large rooms, examining each piece of Larisa's grandfather's furniture.

I wanted to see the town "center," so Sergey and I walked on a couple of kilometers. We looked at the cows along the road, the clumps of trees, and the little creeks and pastures. When a women several hundred yards ahead of us crossed the road with a bucket, Sergey abruptly said, "Stop!" I paused, thinking he knew her and didn't want to have to speak. After a few minutes, when she had finished pumping and her bucket was full, she went back across the road. "All right. Let's go," Sergey said, and began walking again. I looked confused. "If a woman carrying an empty bucket crosses the road, it's bad luck," he explained. "You have to wait until she returns with it full." I smiled at his superstition but said nothing.

Kornin made Baranivka look like a metropolis. Sergey laughed at the "department store," which had only one department and nothing but a dozen frumpy dresses for sale. The only food store was empty except for huge jars of birch juice and boxes of loose tea leaves. A Lenin statue stood outside, holding his proletarian cap in front of him. I told Sergey how I wanted to make a photo album of Lenin in all his different poses. Sergey laughed. "Well, this is a good one. You see, here he's covering his testicles."

It was Saturday afternoon, so there was a "bazaar," at which Sergey shook his head in disbelief: on the hood of a single automobile a stereo system was for sale, next to the omnipresent cigarettes and Snickers. A few boys in dirty tracksuits milled around, and Sergey asked if there were any other stores or places to buy anything. They shook their heads but didn't speak. After visiting Kornin, I understood how people could remark on Zhitomir's "city life."

I marveled that people in such a small village could have enough to eat. "Ach—this is nothing!" Sergey remarked. "You should see the *small* villages. Some of them you could hardly find. The bus goes there only once a week, and the mayor comes into a bigger town like Kornin to buy sausage for his whole village." We followed the road back to the cottage, eating mulberries from trees on the edge of the thick pine woods. The road was empty of cars, although at one point six huge red combines roared past us, leaving behind them remarkable silence broken only by the sound of the wind in the wheat.

Instead of doing chores, I spent the week sleeping in the sun. The heat on my skin felt nice, and I absorbed it deeply, even enjoying my slight sunburn. I concentrated on memorizing the feel of the sun's warmth, in hopes I could recreate the sensation during cold winter nights in my dorm. For an hour I watched green apples fall from a tree across the lane until a wandering goat tried to eat them. Sergey and I shooed him away and collected the best-looking ones from the ground. I watered Larisa's marigolds and watched Betty tiptoe through tall grass for the first time. I helped Larisa cook, and marinated meat and onions with Sergey for a barbecue by the fire. The only excitement was when a drunk wiped out his bicycle coming around the corner. He crashed into the fence pretty hard, but got up silently, dusted off his clothes, and walked the bike on down the lane. The only other person I talked to was a neighbor woman who approached when she saw me picking cucumbers and weeding the potato patch. When she learned I was a "foreigner," she confided that the terrible economic times made her fearful that Germany was about to invade again, "any day now." Despite the isolation and scarcities, I could see what might have appealed to all those invading armies over the centuries, who only passed through Ukraine on the way to somewhere busier and richer.

Back in Zhitomir that summer Max and Tanya arranged a picnic, partly so they could meet the new person in my life. They had become my best friends in Zhitomir, and I wanted to introduce Liza to them. Happily for me, they took to her immediately, complimenting her Russian and repeating "Without an accent!" many times. We took two small rowboats to a spot on the other side of the Teteriv. We took turns rowing, gliding quietly across the dark green water. Along the bank, among the pine trees were a few cottages and, far downriver, the sanatorium and hotel where factory workers used to take vacations in Soviet days. The hotel, sloped on one side like a terraced pyramid, had balconies on three sides overlooking the Teteriv.

We spread our blankets on a grassy area on the shore, then laid out jars of pickles and metal canisters of egg salad. Soon a smoking campfire was roasting our shishkabobs of marinated meat and onions. Max removed the cap of the first bottle of vodka. "It's nice to finally meet you," Max said to Liza, proposing the first toast. "We want only the best for our John, and we can see immediately that he has found it."

We ate and drank and laid in the sun, listening to the breeze in the pines behind us. The day was so pleasant I felt a little guilty. Max scolded me for mentioning work.

"You have time for that later! Do you know the folk saying, 'A summer day is like a year'? No, you do not. You Americans think differently than we do, it seems to me. You've lost your peasant souls. The peasant is attuned to the seasons. He doesn't think in terms of hours or weeks." He gazed across the river. "For centuries, we have left our huts and looked at the sky. 'Will it rain? Will we work today?' Time is vast, and we are caught in its flow, like leaves in this river. You want to make time obey you. That is nothing but . . ." He paused to ask Tanya to help him remember the word he wanted.

"Folly," she said.

"Ah. Folly," Max said. "It is okay to say this?" I laughed and said yes, it was okay. "As for me," he went on, "I try never to rush to complete something. Give me your glass."

Tanya turned to Liza. "Max loves to philosophize," she smiled, "but it is all an excuse for a toast." Even so, his words struck a chord in me. I felt ready to let this picnic, my time in Ukraine, and even my whole life be swept away on whatever current it might. With the familiar feel of vodka warm in my veins, Max's declamations of Slavic stoicism made a great deal of sense. I tried to picture my own peasant soul, and laid back to relax in the sun.

Chapter Sixteen

The Spy Corps

The Holiday of the First Bell was not the same the second year. Anatoly Fedorovich, the gym teacher (a man I now knew), still stood sternly with the microphone, his chest puffed out, his teacherly glare scanning the crowd. Ivan Wilhelmovich again peeked out from behind the loudspeaker system with which he fiddled. The children looked radiant, even in their dark uniforms, because of the bundles of bouquets they carried, just as they had on my very first Holiday of the First Bell. But for me, the event was just not the same.

Naturally, the year before, bedazzled by all the flowers, I had marveled at a boy who shouted out the very first "Hello" from the pupils of School 23. My workplace had looked exotic. Now, a year later, although I had first-day-of-school excitement, I stood outside the building to watch the Day of Knowledge ceremony with Tanya, Oksana, and Luda—my friends.

"The children look beautiful," Tanya said flatly, without emotion. "Don't they?"

"Beautiful," Oksana echoed.

The march played, a few students read heroic Ukrainian poetry, and the director welcomed parents and children to the new school year. The triumphant march music crackling over the dilapidated sound system rang tinny and hollow. An eleventh-grade boy carried a first-grade girl on his shoulder as she rang the handbell, her two tiny hands swinging it back and forth with all her might. The boy—a "school-leaver," in Ukrainian English—whom I remembered seeing in the halls the year before now sported a wisp of mustache, barely visible from across the schoolyard. Like him, I was about to start my final year at School 23; now I was a school-leaver too.

Svetlana Adamovna must have seen that eleventh-grade boy enter the school as a first grader. This realization gave me a glimpse of the larger cycle I was part of, but it also made me feel rather small. I had been self-righteous to think I was performing noble service by teaching English; now I began to wonder if I might even be paving the way for some of the Western influences I had wanted to escape.

Marina quit teaching. Price Waterhouse, the multinational accounting firm, was working with the government on the sluggish privatization initiative. When the company set up offices in the provinces, it needed administrative staff who spoke fluent English. Marina got the job and told me that her year of practicing and listening to American speech with me had helped. The job paid a monthly salary twenty times higher than the school's. This left me feeling torn; I felt glad to have contributed to my friend's success, but assisting younger teachers to stop teaching English wasn't exactly why I had come to School 23.

The year before I had begged for older pupils; now I wasn't so sure. I knew my young children so well, and they were accustomed to my odd (for them) style of teaching. And it was common for one English teacher to stay with the same group for several years, working with them as they progressed sometimes all the way from the first form to the eleventh and last. So when Galina Vasilievna gave me my schedule, I was pleased to find new groups of ninth graders but the same groups of younger pupils.

"You will have the same children as last year: from classes 5G and 5D.

"Don't you mean 5G and 4D?" I asked.

"No," she said, waving a finger. "There is no fourth grade." This puzzled me a little since I had taught fourth grade the year before.

Seeing the kids on the first day felt like a happy reunion. Some were brown-skinned from summer vacations in camps on the Black Sea, around Odessa, or in Crimea. Others were sunburned from working in their grandmothers' gardens. Most scratched at peeling noses and forearms. I was startled to see how much they had grown; they were startled by changes in me as well.

"Mr. John, you grew a beard!" Natasha said, half in horror.

"You're right!" I exclaimed back. "Good thing you told me."

Timur said, "Mr. John, your Ukrainian has gotten a lot better over the summer!" Before the compliment could sink in, I shuddered to think what Timur thought of my Ukrainian to begin with.

My pupils of 3D had become pupils of 5D, and so I asked them how they had bypassed fourth grade over the summer.

"There is no fourth grade, Mr. John," Vova explained.

"But how is that possible?" I asked. "I taught fourth grade last year!"

"Oh . . ." Vova said, frowning. "Well yes, that's possible."

"*How* is it possible?" I exclaimed, half-feigning frustration. "My 4G pupils became 5G and you became 5D. Your group jumped over one year! Maybe it's because you are so clever?"

"Exactly!" shouted Sasha. "We're geniuses!" He guffawed like a donkey.

"All this time in Ukraine, and I still don't understand your system," I moaned, teasing them. They were always entertained to learn what Mr. John didn't know.

Masha broke in. "Da, da, da," she said, nodding wisely. "I know why this is."

"Mashka," I pleaded. "Please make this clear to me."

Masha stood up from her chair. "Here it is. We started the

first form when we were seven years old. Other kids started when they were six. So last year we all studied the same material. Now we're all in the fifth form." Her tone implied that the inherent logic should be obvious. "It's because of when our birthdays fall, and because of how they changed the rules a few years back."

"So, next year you all will skip to the seventh form, correct?"

"Nooo!" they shouted in surprise, then laughed when they saw I was joking.

"Mr. John," Vova said gravely, "We're clever, but not that clever."

Tanya now had no classroom of her own, which meant that meeting during breaks was more difficult—no more "snack bar." My room, across the hall from the vice principal's office, was not so convenient: at any moment we might be called upon to do some extra task. Losing the socializing time meant fewer chances to practice English informally, the only unofficial part of my job and yet (or therefore?) my most useful function. As the school's expert native speaker, I was frequently visited by teachers with questions about English, sometimes on pronunciation and sometimes on grammar points so obscure I had to look them up. But despite the extra tasks and school visits I took on, my actual contribution seemed meager.

Other volunteers were leaving their mark. Charlie Cochran, for example, wrote and published the first existing English-Ukrainian Dictionary of Computer Terms. Sherry Baer helped plan construction to install indoor toilets in her school, which was still serviced by just one decrepit outhouse. Contractual squabbles with workers and local licensing authorities submarined the project, but thanks to Sherry, her school at least *began* to pursue development it would never have attempted in the past. Another volunteer, Maggie Berg, through an agency called Counterpart, acquired nearly a million dollars in donated military surplus—hospital beds, refrigerators, TVs, and miscellaneous furniture—for orphanages and hospitals in Odessa.

Then there was Lisa Muldoon. When she told her students they were going to raise enough money in bake sales, car washes, and other fundraisers to go on a class trip to Prague nobody believed her; the idea of earning enough money to visit *Kiev* would have been laughed at. Her goal was to show a few normal kids without special privileges what a former communist country *could* look like. The class raised more than $10,000 and, along with the school principal, made the trip of a lifetime.

Though I was proud of my work at School 23, I had no visible, lasting accomplishment of that kind to show for it. Galina Vasilievna expressed surprise one day when I mentioned that my typewriter, my teaching materials, and all of the children's books that had been sent over would stay at School 23 when I left. Her gratitude made me feel sad; had she expected me to make all those audiotapes, visual aids, written-out song lyrics, and rules for language games and then take them home? Other teachers thought of them as "my" materials and occasionally agreed out of politeness to try out some book or poster, but after so many years they naturally preferred methods, materials, and a curriculum they knew by heart. A roomful of strange, foreign books was a solution to a problem that didn't exist. I envied the volunteers who left their host countries with some solid, tangible evidence of their presence—a well in the desert, a medical clinic, a soccer field or community center.

Liza had reassured me, reminding me of a story of a volunteer who noticed villagers walking several miles and back to get water from a well. After a year of sweat and toil, the volunteer and the villagers constructed a supply pipe and a freshwater tap just outside the village. He was horrified, then, to see that with running water close by, village women still made the long walk to the faraway well. "We appreciate what you did," they told him, "but the hike for water is our only time all day to talk with one another."

Still, my nagging feeling remained. What did I have to show for my efforts? "Oh, John," Tanya chided me. "What do you think you can do for us? Pay our salaries? Bring back a good economy?

It is enough that you're here and we can talk to you. You've given us an opportunity we never had before." I told Tanya not to schmooze—a word I had taught her and which she loved—but even so her flattery made me feel better.

"Besides," she teased, "the school put up a monument to you across the street."

I had seen the workers installing a granite pedestal, and for a half-second didn't know she was kidding. The bust, with its rock-jawed look of fury, wasn't Lenin or Marx but Lyatoshinsky, the Ukrainian composer for whom School 23's street was named. Just like in the bad old days, the government efficiently installed monuments (albeit to new heroes) instead of tending to its energy crisis. It seemed like not much was changing.

However, if one looked more closely, signs of openings to the West were appearing. By that time I knew every kiosk and shop in town, so when anything new arrived, I found out quickly. On the second floor of the downtown central department store, a Western Union office was installed. Its new paint and bright decals on the teller windows stood in stark contrast to the otherwise gray drabness of the store. Dim, yellowish light shone through a few high windows, still painted in flat colors with blockish Soviet-era advertisements for categories of products: "Radios," "Women's Clothes," and "Cosmetics." The store sold shapkas, heavy wool coats, and poor-quality shoes, but now also Gillette razors, TDK audiocassettes, and Western cosmetics and perfume of all kinds.

I stood in line to exchange money, and when my turn came the young woman cashier raised her eyebrows slightly when I exchanged dollars for kupons—the rate that day (and most days) suggested the reverse. Instead of handling telegrams or money transfers, the Western Union women in the black-and-yellow booth traded dollars for kupons all day to men who popped in from the bazaar. I noticed the woman's stylish eyeglasses—frames like that were impossible to buy in Zhitomir. Taking my twenty dollar bill, she counted out 500,000s and 100,000s in a big stack, until I had three million. The man behind me nudged forward, and I pocketed the wad of bills and went down the wide, stone staircase.

A group of kids stood around the counter where videogames were sold, watching a young man behind the counter play Gran Prix racing. He ignored them, focused intensely on winning. The kids stood silently and observed as his race car swerved around a corner, narrowly missing a jagged computer-graphic tree. For hours the clerk played the game while the children watched, spellbound. He was not offering turns.

I went to the other side of the store to buy lightbulbs, still feeling lucky to find them for sale. The clerk took the bulbs from their paper packages, and one at a time screwed each one into a socket installed on the countertop. The bulbs that did not work she placed in the half-full trashcan beneath the counter.

The four working bulbs and my fresh bottle of "Hello!" laundry detergent cost me a few hundred thousand of my kupons, a little over a dollar. On my way out I looked over a display case full of watch batteries, shiny barrettes, and plastic earrings and perfume labeled "*Dragon* Noir" and "*Channel* No. 5." The naming of Western goods fascinated me, especially how words and ideas "found their interpretation" (as Tanya liked to say).

The dreary, monochrome products of the communist economy looked so depressing because of their lack of variety. Soap, for example, was the same everywhere: a puce-colored, oversized brick that felt grainy and coarse when rubbed on skin. It looked like some relic from a general store in the 1930s, not because of its poor quality but its lack of packaging. Fundamental to my worldview had been the choice of differently packaged, differently named soaps, which, I saw now, were in essence identical. The scarcity of names, not of products, gave the impression of impoverishment. At home, I could buy Lever 2000, Irish Spring, Zest, Buoy, Coast, Dove, Ivory, each with its own distinguishing scent, color, shape, and commercial. One soap draws a "Z" on the shower door, one is an "eye-opener," one 99.9% pure. All are produced by the same few companies, but I had grown up with market niches and the illusion of luxury that choice gives. Now, such an amazing differentiation of products seemed surreally artificial in the Soviet Union, where there was often *no* soap. That economic failure actually contributed to the disintegration of the USSR; a shortage of soap that drove Siberian miners to strike became a catalyst for the fall of the government.

Then, again, Ukrainians had names for varieties of things I never knew existed. I never would have guessed there could be thirty-seven kinds of state-produced sausage or eighty different varieties of potatoes.

The afternoon was overcast and cold, but I needed to do some more shopping before going home. I walked the few blocks to House of Radios to see if anything new or useful had appeared on the shelves. At that time there were few hard currency stores in provincial towns in Ukraine and none in Zhitomir. House of Radios was the closest thing, the best store in town for what I thought of as Western-style shopping: seeking something you need, rather than accepting whatever you find. House of Radios would take kupons (at a bad exchange rate), but most people brought dollars or Deutschmarks. John Maddox once left a note in our shared mailbox recommending this store to me. The note read: "John! House of Radios has canned ravioli!" I ran to the store—less for love of Chef Boyardee than for the luxurious ease of preparation of a meal-in-a-can. But I was too late—the canned ravioli had already sold out.

Today, I hoped for something better. When the midday break ended at five after three, a woman inside the store unlocked the padlock on the thick chain that held the doors shut. Merging with the crowd, I shuffled in to see what was for sale.

House of Radios had been the state outlet for Soviet-made electronic equipment. The faded orange walls were painted with pictures of old models of radios and televisions no longer sold there (or maybe anywhere). House of Radios sold no electronics now. Under a mural displaying a squarish 1970s Hi-Fi hung wool coats, shoes, sweaters, and leather purses, each priced in dollars. In the section of the store labeled "Televisions," women fondled pairs of red pumps and satiny miniskirts, talking in low admiring tones. All of the clothing, most of it junky and cheap, had been hauled in from Poland, Slovakia, Bulgaria, Romania, or Russia, countries with liberalized privatization, more foreign investment, and more foreign goods than Ukraine. Prices for everything were much higher than in the States. A package of Huggies (labeled in German) cost twenty dollars for 30 diapers, which meant that all but the very richest Ukrainian mothers would continue to wash their babies' cloth diapers by hand.

To me, the pickings looked slim indeed, yet some of the shoppers acted as if the store was filled with exotic marvels. From beneath a glass-topped counter glared a GI Joe in an Italian package—"Pronto!" and "Signore!" his speech balloons barked. Two young men in shapkas and winter coats admired the colorful box, unable to determine that GI Joe was, in fact, a doll.

"What are these?" one said. "Books?"

The other thought long and hard. "No," he answered. "It's from Israel." His tone of voice implied that he had explained the otherness of Western goods once and for all.

Two women near me complained, "Why don't they label these things? How are we to know what they are?" She wanted to buy Western goods, even when she did not know their uses or purpose. It reminded me of how, the autumn before, I had bought tea biscuits, not knowing what was in the package because I couldn't read it.

I moved down the long store, past displays of bathroom fixtures, floor tiles, and complete furniture suites, until I was at the last counter. There in a jumble of expensive teasets, plastic flowers, and lipstick I spotted Haribo candy in a big tub. Expecting Gummi-bears, I saw Gummi-worms, a concept apparently too complicated to explain to Ukrainian buyers—the large tub was labeled "Pommes Frites." Working the potato angle, I figured. To promote sales of these Gummi-French-Fries, a tub had been divvied up into smaller, more affordable portions, each plastic baggie labeled "Caramels—with the Taste of Lemon."

A funny image struck me: somewhere, wandering around Germany in his tracksuit, a pea-brained Ukrainian mobster sampled and tasted unfamiliar products, invented descriptive Russian names, and loaded up his truck full of them. The tastes of this generation of Ukrainians cannot help being dominated by the choices preferred by the mob. Leopard-skin tights, leather jackets, aviator sunglasses, and platinum-blonde hair rinse—all the accoutrements of mafia chic—look less silly when it is *everyone* with money who parades in them.

To many Ukrainians' disappointment, imported goods were often of even *worse* quality than Soviet-made ones. Only the West's cheapest, worst-quality junk finds its way that far east. And goods from China (labeled in weird versions of English and which "looked" Western) were affordable but of the flimsiest construction. For some people, a shoddy import resulted in customer satisfaction anyway; it was a relief and a vindication to have objective evidence of the West's shortcomings. For example, after trying a package of powdered chicken-and-noodle soup, Tanya told me, "Americans eat not-very-tasty soups." Being able to dismiss all American soup probably made her feel better about all the time and effort she had to put into making her own.

That propensity to generalize could be frustrating though. After tasting imported Hungarian sausage, Liza's friend said, "I don't like *your* sausage. It's not tasty." Liza said that although Hungary was west of Ukraine, it hardly represented "The West," but her friend replied, "Well, you know what I mean." The Soviet-era comparison of Ours versus Anything Else still applied—and not only to soups and sausages. Tanya once told me she had visited Germany on a school trip, and when I registered surprise she added with a half-smile, "Well, before the wall fell. I'm talking about *our* Germany." It was not always clear whether a thing fell into the category of foreign or familiar.

In the borderlands between the Soviet and Western economies, Ukraine's jumbled mix of products confused me too. I had gone to House of Radios this time because John Maddox had reported a sighting of Reynolds Wrap. This time John's tip paid off; I struck gold—or actually, an element more useful in the kitchen, aluminum. From under a glass counter, like a silver bracelet or Rolex watch, gleamed a gorgeous shiny box.

The last time I had seen aluminum foil was in Budapest, where I bought some in a grocery store. It was almost confiscated by Ukrainian border guards when I reentered the country. Opening the package and unwrapping the roll, the customs officer leered, "What is *this*?" as if he had caught me smuggling contraband. Not knowing its Russian name, I said, "Uhh... like paper, but for the kitchen." He could see that it was metal, and perhaps thought it had secret military uses. I was about to give him some so that I could keep the rest, when his supervisor arrived. "*I* know what that is," he growled. "It's *nothing*." My whole roll of foil survived the crossing, and I later learned the word for it in case I wanted more. It hadn't lasted long; when Misha saw it in my kitchen he said, "Hey! Where did you get this? This is great stuff! Let me have a piece or two!"

So I was delighted to find it in House of Radios, along with plastic wrap and wax paper. Tiny, typed Russian placards were placed next to the products to identify them: wax paper was labeled "paper for sandwiches"; Saran wrap, "plastic sheets to keep food fresh." My knowledge of the dictionary's word for foil was wasted; its label read "paper to protect while cooking." What I had told the border guard had been correct after all.

Apparently, the purpose of the small sandwich bags had been unascertainable by the pea-brained mobster. When the thug's imagination ran dry, he went with whatever was printed on the box—in this case, "Toppie," the name of the German discount brand.

Finding "Toppie" in Zhitomir could be taken as some indicator of Ukrainian economic progress, though rather a sad one. Ukrainians would soon have Ziploc, Band-Aids, Kleenex, Glad bags—all the disposable items the capitalist world consumes every day by the millions. To the counter clerk at House of Radios,

I said—with utter seriousness in my voice—"Two packages of 'Toppie' please, and one 'paper to protect while cooking.'"

Despite Misha's appreciation of the magic of aluminum foil, he often scolded me for my wastefulness. He frequented the market's busiest kiosk, a thriving business named "Refilling Disposable Cigarette Lighters." Ukrainians punched holes in the bottoms, added butane, and plugged the hole: a full lighter, good as new. The kiosk replaced flints and other tiny plastic pieces as well. In contrast, I threw out my empty lighters.

"That's so stupid!" Misha said. "A lighter costs fifty thousand coupons, but to refill it costs only 20,000."

"I'd have to stand in another line," I told him. Misha rolled his eyes and frowned. "Besides, for me it's so cheap it's not worth it." He saved everything and found uses for all kinds of junk I would discard. To my amazement, he once fixed an annoying broken knob on my stove with a sliver of toothpick.

"Everything your country makes is for one time use only," he said. "You don't put ink refills in your ballpoint pens. You make plastic liter bottles that you don't reuse. You drink tea from a paper bag which you throw away. This is not so economical."

"Convenient, though," I said quietly.

"Yes," Misha answered, his voice growing distant, as if straining to be polite. "John, don't be hurt, but it seems to me not everything about America is good."

Misha's reluctance to criticize America was typical; people often teased each other with the saying, "If you're so smart, why are you not rich?" Toward America an attitude of love-hate, or maybe admiring disdain, prevails, but people hesitated to express it. In fact, they usually voiced the opposite. Praise for the West, no longer forbidden, was offered categorically and unthinkingly.

One an afternoon in Vinnitsa Liza and I were sitting around drinking tea with her teacher friend Larisa. A friend of Larisa's was there, a woman named Luda, who made forays into Poland to sell Ukrainian embroidery and buy goods to sell in Vinnitsa's bazaar. The conversation turned to the United States. "Tell me, Liza," the woman challenged, "isn't it true that everything in America is better than here?" When Liza quickly disagreed, Luda asked her to come up with anything in Ukraine that was superior to the United States.

"Well, your bread is much better than ours," Liza began.

"Bread," the woman said, rolling her eyes. "Big deal."

"It's good that you have such frequent public transportation."

"But in America you all have your own cars, right? Don't you like that better than our awful, crowded trolleybuses?"

"Still," Liza persisted. "There are so many things. Our lives are dominated by machines...."

"Microwaves? Answering machines? We watch your movies, we know how it is. Machines do your work for you, and you have time to relax."

Lisa persisted. "It's not that simple. Our pace of life is much more rushed. People are always anxious..." She glossed over this idea—Ukrainians were anxious too, because they weren't being paid their salaries. "You don't understand. Here, you relate to each other differently. People help one another and support each other and depend on each other."

"That's only because we are so poor and we wouldn't survive otherwise."

The self-image of Ukraine as an inferior, poor nation was reinforced by messages that streets in the West were paved with gold. When I remarked that my apartment had as many cockroaches as my last apartment in the U.S., a teacher asked in genuine shock if America really had cockroaches too. Our weather, some folks imagined, was always a perfect June day, nationwide. Even some who ridiculed American life imagined it as an endless bask in a tropical paradise. "As for me, I don't want to move to America," the physics teacher Ivan Wilhelmovich once told me after a few shots of vodka. "You must understand, Johnik, that there is more to life than sitting around drinking pineapple juice and eating coconuts."

One teacher expressed amazement that I was staying a second year. She had been told that I would leave in the spring, and she bought me a going-away present a year early. My presence in Ukraine was universally seen as odd—and even, perhaps, suspicious.

Before I joined, I guess I wasn't aware how much Soviet people already "knew" about the Peace Corps. I had no idea how thoroughly it had been characterized as the "Spy Corps," nothing more than a front for the CIA. Among American organizations, only the CIA had more defamatory articles written about it than the Peace Corps. The communist regime had fallen, but no doubt some people still believed I had been sent to make Ukraine safe for capitalism.

In a moment of candor, Misha once asked, "Did you do something bad in America?" He wondered if I was working off some kind of punishment. My answer resounded with confidence and pride: "Nope! I'm a volunteer!" Later, I learned that Stalin had used the term 'volunteer' to describe people who had been assigned to quite involuntary hard labor.

The image of the Peace Corps as the vanguard of capitalism was not totally fabricated by the Soviet propaganda machine. In fact, an ideological slant really had been part of the organization from its inception. During Kennedy's presidency, Congress feared the prospect of American young people sent overseas on a lark, and imagined that a Peace Corps might even damage our country's national interest. To avoid the possibility of the first Peace Corps volunteers being "corrupted," Congress required that a portion of Peace Corps training "include instruction in the philosophy, strategy, tactics, and menace of communism." According to the official Peace Corps Handbook of 1961, "The training course includes the study of Communism as an ideology and as an organizational weapon, as well as a study of the history, teachings, and special vocabulary of communism in the area of the assignment. . . . We know that Communists are against the Peace Corps and its program. In trying to discredit us, they call us spies and agents of imperialism. It will be very important to be prepared to deal with Communist attempts to provoke you or to deflect you from your goals." In their post-service evaluations, early volunteers advocated to have this material dropped from training; it proved completely irrelevant to the true challenges they faced. Anticommunist lectures during Peace Corps trainings throughout the 1960s were scaled back, but remained a component until the '70s.

The Soviet Union portrayed the Peace Corps as a kind of Hitler Youth of the CIA. Every citizen had heard of the organization, and the newspapers described its activities as one more component of the West's attempt to derail their country and its projects. But so much old propaganda had been debunked that I had assumed the Peace Corps agenda was now clear. After all, the Peace Corps had to be "invited" to work in a country. Hungary, the first former communist satellite to do so, flabbergasted Peace Corps officials by asking for 10,000 volunteers. (Worldwide, the entire Peace Corps numbers about 6000.) Officials in Soviet republics invited volunteers even before their independence had been finalized. Kazakhstan's president, Nursultan Nazarbayev, said "A hundred volunteers is not enough. I would like to see thousands here." So, proudly, Peace Corps marched east to Moscow, sending people like me to places that had been restricted from foreigner contact only a few years before. Perhaps that very eagerness made some people skeptical. The majority of Westerners in their country were businesspeople or missionaries; if Peace Corps didn't want to buy factories or people's souls, why, they must have wondered, had we *really* come?

That autumn, at Max and Tanya's house for dinner one evening, I realized how many occasions I had spent with them talking, eating, drinking, laughing. As usual, the company that night was happily noisy. I stared at their living room wall, which was decorated with a mural of a Russian forest scene. Birch trees in a meadow extended into the distance, reminding me of the summer's picnics. Across from me stood the built-in bookshelves, filled with English dictionaries, novels by Irving Stone and Theodore Dreiser, and Steven King novels in Russian ("Max loves terrible books") Tanya had said, and laughed when I corrected her. I felt nostalgic for those early evenings when we knew so little about each other. How many times had I left my shoes in the hallway to enter the one apartment where I could leave behind my public persona—"Mr. John, Third Wonder of Zhitomir"—and go back to feeling like a normal person.

I went out on the balcony; the others, deep in conversation, did not notice. All those evenings we had talked late into the night, we always went out to watch sleepy Zhitomir from their balcony. From that fourth-story perch I could almost see the central square and the enormous, granite Grandpa Lenin. At that moment, I thought of him as a gatekeeper or gargoyle, some symbol of the forces that meant to prevent me from being there. And yet within his gaze stood my bank, my favorite milk store, the post office, School 23. It felt like I had lived there for years.

When I came in from the balcony, Max was involved in heavy discussion with his friend Andrew about the weakness of Ukraine's military. Andrew bemoaned that "General Frost" and the vastness of Russian land had defeated Napoleon and Hitler, but that they could no longer be counted on; renewed spending on military industry was necessary, especially now that Ukraine's independence had left so much in ruins. Max waved off Andrew's concern.

"As for Russia, it seems not a likely possibility that we will go to war. And as for with the West, impossible. Don't forget our greatest advantage, even greater than weather: the tenacity of our natives in defending the soil of their motherland. With no more than a bite of bread and a sip of drink—even without weapons—we would defend our own ground with such fierceness that no one can conquer us." He saw me enter from the balcony. "Not even the Americans," he smiled.

Andrew laughed and smiled too. I felt so at home, so relaxed. Maybe it was the wine, but I felt like playing a joke. "You know, guys," I said, turning serious. "It's hard for me to say this, but—well, I can tell you now, because you'll understand. I have to admit it to someone. I'm a spy."

Andrew and Max stopped laughing. Tanya set down her glass. There was an awkward silence that was taking far too long. I stopped smiling too and felt a burning pain, wishing I had never said those words even in jest.

"Well. . . ." Tanya said at last. "John, we have seen into your character. You have an open heart. You are a citizen of the world. If this really is true, then that's all right with us."

Max looked uncomfortable, but agreed. "It's nothing!" he said, much too heartily. "Don't even think of it. We don't mind."

I was crestfallen. After everything I had shared with them! They knew all my frustrations and pains of crossing cultures. I had talked about missing home, had talked about how I liked Zhitomir, had described how important my teaching was, how I only wanted to be useful and cared about nothing else. All along, they had suspected I might be insincere, even deceiving them.

"Ha ha!" I laughed, trying not to sound strained. "I gotcha! I was just kidding, you guys. Come on! What did you think?"

Max laughed slightly; Andrew smiled again. Tanya still looked solemn. "Well, John, we just want you to know, that even if you were a spy, we would still like you."

I felt stunned by this confession. It eventually came out that they had discussed the question and decided my friendship was worth that risk—a compliment in a twisted way. They had trusted me a great deal even when somewhere deep down they believed I might not be trustworthy. Yet it was an eerie feeling—they had taken it for granted that I might not be what I seemed.

Another horrible realization came to me, when I remembered a conversation I had had with Svetlana Adamovna after returning from a trip to Kiev, a trip in which I had spent over a week away from Zhitomir. I had called Svetlana Adamovna, my "Ukrainian mama," from the phone in the lobby of dorm to tell her that I was home safe.

"John! Where have you been!" she admonished me.
"I went back to Kiev for a few days. Why?"
"You must not leave without . . . without telling me. I was unable to explain where you were, and they have been asking about you."

I assumed she meant the principal, or someone else at school, so I attempted to make a joke. "Who do you mean, 'they'?" I laughed. "The KGB?"

The phone line was silent a moment. "Well, they're not called that now," she said at last.

An adrenaline rush hit me; I was being watched. Oddly, it was not only annoyingly, unnervingly intrusive, but somehow flattering. I tried to imagine who they might send to keep track of me and felt sorry that Svetlana Adamovna had been put in the awkward position of having to account for my whereabouts. I apologized to her, and she changed the subject.

But after Tanya's remarks I now understood. I had imagined some shrunken slug of a man slinking around back alleys taking grainy photographs of me buying cabbage. I watched to see if I were being followed, like in the movies. Now I saw how naive I had been. I wasn't being tailed by some Neanderthal putz from the KGB; my guardian was one of my closest friends—my colleague and counterpart. My "Ukrainian mama."

That her playing the part of a second mother had been heartfelt and genuine dismayed me most of all. I had been treated like a son: fed endlessly at their table, shown around town, taken on vacation, assisted in living there. We had made friends. However, I reasoned, if some authority figure had asked Svetlana Adamovna to occasionally report updates on my habits and lifestyle, she was not the kind of person who would easily have said no. She had been a favored under the old system, which did not necessarily make her a bad person, but certainly did not lead her to doubt its motives. Perhaps it even flattered her, that my counterpart was officially responsible for keeping an eye on me. Perhaps it was even flattering to me.

Mostly, I realized that I had counted myself "in" far too hastily. I had been there a year and felt quite at home. Yet once again, I felt acutely my essential "strangerness." Zhitomir, of course, was not where I belonged at all.

Chapter Seventeen

Borderland

After a year and a half, I sometimes felt I knew less about Ukraine than I had a month after my arrival. I understood the language; I knew fairly intuitively how Ukrainians acted, reasoned, and felt about the world. Often I was even mistaken for a local. Visitors to Zhitomir would ask for directions to the bazaar or some particular street, which I told them; most didn't remark on my accent and probably never knew they were speaking to an American.

But being taken for a Ukrainian didn't mean I had fully adopted Ukrainian ways of thinking—or even understood them. One day, walking home from school past the Central Department Store, I was stopped by a policeman. Without explaining, he called me over and asked me to follow him down an alley beside the store. If we had not been at the busiest corner of town I might have worried. In the alley was a makeshift shed where another policeman sat at a desk. I followed the officer in.

Near a sad-looking babushka I took a seat and listened as the officer at the desk began to explain. Calling me "citizen," he reported that the babushka had been apprehended selling goods on the street without a license and was going to be fined. All they needed for me to do was sign the protocol, witnessing that the woman was guilty as charged. Before I could answer, he went on to explain that I had been merely chosen at random, that my signing would not reflect on me, and that I could be assured they had followed careful, fully legal procedures in arresting the woman, who sat dejectedly, appearing not even to listen.

"Um, excuse me . . ." I finally interrupted. "Probably I should tell you that I'm not Ukrainian. I'm an American citizen."

The woman was alert now. Both policemen turned to each other, then to me—then to each other again, like vaudeville actors mimicking shock. I handed over my documents and told them I was an English teacher. At last the first policeman laughed.

"Well, you can go then," he said, handing my green card back. The old woman asked if that meant she was free too, but the policeman turned stern again, merely knitting his thick brows by way of an answer.

He stepped outside with me, and I headed back to Kievska Street feeling very relieved—first that I was not in trouble, and second that I did not have to testify against anyone about a violation I knew nothing about. "Imagine that," the policeman said, as we went in separate directions. "First guy we stop is an American. Imagine that."

As for me, I could only wonder at how the weird logic of justice operated. In matters of guilt and innocence, an altogether different set of assumptions was in operation from that in the United States. Friends later told me the procedure was perfectly normal and that a typical Ukrainian would maybe ask a few questions, then likely just sign the witness form and go about his daily business. I couldn't pressure anyone to explain the reasoning behind this—they were too busy laughing at the spectacle of me being chosen to perform the duty.

I got no closer to understanding certain of these cultural behaviors and attitudes, many of which were admittedly the leftovers of Soviet-led society. Another two years in Zhitomir might have helped me to understand my host country and its people better, but the longer I stayed, the less often my experiences had the power to surprise me. With gradual acculturation, that first openness—my "fresh eyes"—had disappeared. I now knew what

I could expect from work and life, which seemed less like an adventure.

But despite my feeling at ease where once I had felt bewildered, I still could not pinpoint what made Ukrainians unique—or, more to the point, what made them distinct from Russians. The cultures—even the two languages—seemed so intermingled that any bold line drawn between the two tended to misrepresent reality. My friend Olena's parents, one Russian, one Ukrainian, when arguing would revert to their native tongues—each shouting in his or her own language, the fuss perfectly comprehensible to both. Many Ukrainians barely spoke Ukrainian and did not like to, and not always because their passports labeled their nationality as Russian. Everyone shared the Soviet legacy, which made Ukrainians seem more similar to Russians than they might have a hundred years before. No doubt, a difference had always existed, but I was unable to put my finger on it precisely.

Certain generalizations could be made. Some in the United States had dubbed Ukrainians the "Texans" of the Soviet Union, because a stereotype of stubbornness and independent-mindedness coupled with warm hearts and generous hospitality made the comparison seem apt. True, Ukrainians were exceptionally generous, as a rule, but the characterization inadequately described the people I knew. Russian stereotypes were limited to the peculiar Ukrainian fondness for "salo." But love of raw pigfat didn't make for much of a cultural distinction.

So I asked everyone I knew: "What's the difference between a Ukrainian and a Russian?" It sounded like the lead-in to a joke, but nobody could quite fill in the punchline. One evening at Max and Tanya's, some of my best Ukrainian friends tried to explain.

"We're very different from Russians," Tanya said.
"How?"
"We have a different history, our own language . . ."

"Sure, sure," I interrupted. "But outside the obvious. How about character? Could an outsider tell a Ukrainian from a Russian?"

Indecisively, she answered, "Well . . . Russians drink more."

By then, after dozens of evening meals and discussions, Tanya, Max, and I had consumed so many bottles of vodka, cognac, champagne, sweet Crimean muscatel—I rolled my eyes in disbelief.

"No, really," she said. "You should see life in their villages, John. Horrible. They live in their *izbas* in Siberia, and are poor, dirty, and always cold. A Ukrainian house is always neater and cleaner than a Russian's. And their villages are full of drunks stumbling around all day."

"Wouldn't a Russian tell me that Ukrainians drink a lot?"

"Well, we do take pride in that," she said.

"The difference is Moscow," Max told me. "Moscow is another country. It is not even in Russia, as far as culture and the people are concerned. We have Kiev, but it is like a provincial town in comparison with Moscow and St. Petersburg. Great Ukrainian ballerinas, hockey players, musicians and singers, artists—as soon as they have become someone important, they all go to Moscow. Ever since independence, the center of our culture is in another country."

That was interesting, but still I persisted, pressing them to compare national characters. They explained that Ukrainian peasants, in their relatively warmer climate, had traditionally worked harder, on their *own* land, while Russians had formed themselves into communal structures in order to fight off harsher winters. Tanya added that the Ukrainian *sertse*, or "heart," contrasted with the Russian *dusha*, or "soul," and this I could believe to an extent. But that heavy "deep-souledness" seemed inherent in everyone I knew in Ukraine, and it could not be called strictly Russian. Something more concrete made Ukrainians different. I told them about how, after visiting Moscow during the summer, I had waited for my train a few hours in Kiev Station and had instantly recognized every person around me as distinctively Ukrainian.

"Did they look like peasants who had come to sell things?" Max smiled.

They wore poor clothing, had plain faces, and surrounded themselves with bundles and packages piled on the ground, it was true. Of course, I had also recognized the familiar, soft sing-songy language which I felt so overjoyed to hear again, there in the heart of Moscow, where the jabber was harsh and sour. The Ukrainian language sounded to me like warbling in contrast. Still, it was something about the people themselves that looked different.

"I will tell you what it was," Luda proclaimed. "I am the only one who has a right to note this distinction." Luda's family roots were Polish, and her father had been an army colonel. Growing up, she had lived all over the Soviet Union—in Magadan, Minsk, and the city of Grozny in Chechnya, which was to fall under siege within a few months.

"I am a Polish woman, a *Polyachka*," Luda said, "and I have lived in Zhitomir long enough to tell you the most important character distinction of Ukrainians. It is cleverness. Ukrainians are more *khitree*."

The word meant "sly or cunning," but didn't necessarily have negative connotations. If you tricked a person, he might lightly scold you by wagging a finger and saying admirably, "*Akh ti khitree!*" It meant clever in the sense of good at getting around the rules—in a country where all rules were both touted with great superficial noise and spectacle, and then simultaneously bent, avoided, or broken by all. A cunning person got what he wanted despite all obstacles, through deception or other means. In a land of scarcity, such a quality was something of a talent. Or maybe a necessity—with a salary of only ten dollars that doesn't arrive for six months anyway, cunning might also be called knack for survival.

On the scale of character qualities, however, a talent for

cunning spoke as little about the culture as did love of pigfat. Perhaps I was foolish to seek stereotypes such as "Italians love wine and good food" or "Germans value efficiency." But if Ukrainians were not essentially different from Russians, what was the big deal about being an independent country? The world so often thinks of Ukraine as someplace "in Russia"—so why shouldn't it? If nothing more special than excessive slyness made them different, what was to prevent Ukraine from rejoining its richer, more powerful "Great Russian" cousin? I asked the art teacher at school, whom I knew to be something of a Ukrainian nationalist.

"*Muscali*," he told me, using the derogatory Ukrainian word for Russians. "They are always thinking of empire. Solzhenitsyn is one of the worst—such a hero in Russia, yet he wants us to come back into the fold." He made a spitting gesture, then put his arm around my shoulder. "John, you haven't been here so long. If you studied our history, you would see. One of our famous writers said, 'The Russian democrat is no democrat at all on the Ukrainian question.'"

The art teacher launched into a description of Ukraine's resistance against all foreign powers throughout the centuries. The piece of land now called Ukraine is both extremely large (800 miles across) and poorly protected by natural boundaries. In fact, the name *Ukraine* means "borderland." From this borderland, other nations chipped away pieces or took large portions of it under their own control so frequently and disastrously that the longstanding historical concept of an independent Ukrainian state has never actually been a physical reality. Ukrainians have lost to their enemies so often that the only legacy to which they can point is the valiant fight they put up while being conquered. Ukrainians were forced to fall into step under so many invading societies that they often define themselves more by who they are *not* rather than who they are. So instead of explaining Ukrainian identity, the art teacher told me who the Ukrainians had fought. This list—which included Turks, Poles,

Russians, Romanians, Swedes, Tatars, and Germans—was an answer in itself.

A great tradition of freedom was killed off during the *kozak* era, the teacher explained. For Westerners, the word "cossack" usually denotes a wild marauder, but for Ukrainians, the *kozak* represents a brave, independent warrior-frontiersman who would fight anyone in defense of his country. In the eighteenth century and earlier, the *kozaks* of Zaporizhya ruled themselves in a virtual nation-state which—the art teacher emphasized—had democratic traditions: On any question facing the community, a vote was taken in the fortress's central compound and the group that bellowed loudest was the winning side. This community lived on an island surrounded by a great rapids down the Dnipro River from Kiev. From that home base, the *kozaks* raided all the neighboring countries on horseback—except for the Turks, whom they attacked by ship. Istanbul was savaged so many times by *kozaks* crossing the Black Sea that the sultan ordered a huge chain to be stretched across the Bosphorus Strait to wreck the *kozak* ships. Thanks to such fierceness, the Ukrainian peasantry idolized the *kozaks* as their protectors and champions.

In 1775, Catherine the Great extended the Russian empire by defeating the *kozaks* and even forbidding citizens to pronounce the name of the Zaporizhian camp. The American and French revolutions, the growth of successful popular uprisings, and the birth of modern democracy were right around the historical corner, but an independent nation of Ukraine was not to be born. After the oppressions of the Russian empire were replaced by those of the Soviet Union, Ukrainian nationalism was crushed again. In the 1930s, for example, not by coincidence Stalin ordered a dam built at Zaporizhya, and both the rapids and the historic island they had protected were submerged. Also not by coincidence, Stalin's 1933 terror famine was fiercest not only in the most independence-minded provinces of Ukraine but in the areas around the delta of the Don River and the Kuban—historically *kozak* strongholds. *Kozak* generals like Petro Sahaidachny, Bohdan

Khmelnytsky, and Ivan Mazepa are Ukraine's George Washingtons—except that all died without seeing their revolutions meet with success.

Some Ukrainians can proudly trace their ancestry back to *kozak* blood, and the legendary noble warrior is now a national icon. Almost all the Ukrainian folk songs I learned involved a brave *kozak* trying to win the love of a young maiden. However, these women were supposed to be as feisty and strong-minded as *kozak* men. One song ends with the young woman refusing to marry the *kozak* until he can provide a house of his own. These historical images, though, did not provide much of an antidote to post-Soviet reality. The art teacher told me he did not expect to see great changes in his lifetime. But on his scale of perspective, the fight for a strong Ukrainian nation had been happening for centuries and in all likelihood would continue. "It will be many, many years before we shake the Soviet yoke these Russians have put on us," he said.

His stories reminded me of a joke that my friend Mike, a volunteer in Poltava and a former high school history teacher, had told me. I recited it for the art teacher.

A *kozak* finds a lamp, and when he rubs it a genie appears and offers the *kozak* three wishes in gratitude for his release. The *kozak* thinks a moment, then says, "All right. I wish the Mongol army would attack Norway." The genie shrugs, but waves his wand, and the Mongol army rushes across Asia, attacks Norway, and retreats. "For my next wish," the *kozak* says, "I wish the Mongol army to attack Sweden." The genie frowns, but waves his wand. The Mongols pour into Sweden, destroy it, and retreat. The genie, wondering if his bargain was understood, reminds the Cossack: "This is your last wish. Remember, now, you can have anything: a palace, riches, women . . ." The *kozak* nods and says he understands. "For my last wish," he proclaims, "I wish the Mongol army to attack . . . Finland!" The genie waves his wand, the Mongols rush into Finland, wreck it, and go home. The *kozak* sits down, smiles, and smokes his pipe. "I don't understand," the genie says in exasperation. "You could have had anything, and you wished for the Mongol army to attack Norway, Sweden, and Finland?"

"Ah yes!" the *kozak* said, rubbing his hands with glee. "And every time, they went through Russia."

Not everyone, perhaps, laughed at this joke so heartily as did the art teacher. Most of the people I knew did not harbor bitter grudges or historical grievances, and for many fervent nationalism was down their list of priorities somewhere after a good pair of shoes. In fact, some people blamed Ukraine's economic troubles on the very same loud-mouthed angry nationalists who had advocated most strongly for independence. They feared that just talking in such a way had the potential to make things even worse.

Dividing up the Soviet Union raised the terrible problem of when to stop dividing. Who gets to draw the lines between groups? How many shades of a color can be discerned? In Yugoslavia, the question of how to divide and whom to call "other" resulted in war. The same had already occurred in many parts of the former Soviet Union: Chechnya, Abkhazia, Nagorno-Karabakh, Tajikistan, and the TransDniester region of Moldova. Ukrainians watched these conflicts on their televisions; unlike ourselves, they could picture all too clearly an identical horror occurring on the streets outside their apartments.

The state of Ukraine includes a variety of heritages, not all of which have blended together well. Crimea, for example, was "given" to Ukraine by Khrushchev in 1954 to commemorate the 300th anniversary of the ceding of the territory of Ukraine to Russia. Crimea's people, mostly ethnic Russians and Tatars, want little to do with Ukrainian language, symbols, or even laws. To associate itself with Russia, in 1994 Crimea actually switched time zones—it fell back to Moscow time after daylight savings ended and never returned to the Ukrainian clock. A vacationer from, say, Donetsk, who visits Yalta travels west but the time becomes later. When I asked my ninth graders if they thought

Crimea would secede, a boy named Andriy said: "Not to worry, Mr. John. They are attached to us by land. We can always turn off their water, electricity, and gas."

Geographically and culturally, of course, Crimea is an exception. But even the city of Odessa explored the possibility of leaving the nation of Ukraine. With a special character of its own, neither Ukrainian nor purely Russian, some Odessans suggested declaring the city a free-trade zone, not subject to either the Ukrainian *or* Russian government. Other regions, such as the industrial region of Donetsk and the Donbass, look to Russia; if its depleted mines were not such a used-up, polluted liability, Russia might look to it too. Much of western Ukraine was part of Poland before 1940, and its disdain for everything Russian is so strong that speaking Russian in some cities there can bring jeers and spitting. "We will definitely have a civil war," Sergey told me more than once. "I am sure of it."

Thus to some extent, advocating nationalism and Ukrainian culture was a radical idea, even though, oddly enough, the entrenched government run by former communists was doing so. The view of Ukrainian culture as distinct and different from Russian—but not "inferior" or "lesser"—was held by everyone in Ukraine. The Russians had great history, great science, a great space program, the greatest artists on the planet when it came to ballet or chess. Russian hockey was better, Russian TV was far better—and most important of all, the Russian ruble was steadier and worth more. Given the numerous examples of the greatness of their big brother, no wonder so many Ukrainians did not arrive at a belief in Ukraine's greatness so easily.

To counteract such feelings, those who deeply loved Ukrainian culture promoted it incessantly. To anyone who had waited years for independence, such moments must have been glorious. But craving a culture separate from Russia's was not the pastime of most Ukrainians for the past forty years. Even those who despised Russification must have eventually tired of the flagwaving television productions, the music, writing, and theatre, all of which monochromatically glorified folk culture along the same few themes: *kozaks*, milkmaids, animal tales, painted Easter eggs. My friends rolled their eyes, and changed channels. They valued their symbols as we do, but who wants every day to be the Fourth of July?

I always walked to school in the morning down First of May Street, past Fire Station Number Two where, in the early, still-dawning light stood a fire engine that would have looked old-fashioned in the United States (although it might have been new—it gleamed from many washings). Water trickled into the gutter down the rough cracked asphalt outside the garage doors. The firemen already at work stood around in black rubber boots laughing, and I could tell from the sidewalk that they smoked the cheap, unfiltered Kosmos cigarettes that smell like meadow grass burning, sour and acrid.

There I met Zoya Ivanovna, a fellow teacher with whom I fell into stride on the way to work. She shuffled along, not hunched like so many older women here, though showing the beginnings of a stoop. Her hair was white, her face worn, and her gait a kind of bruised, tired trudge far heavier than mine. She looked close to seventy, but was only fifty-eight, a few years older than my mother. I had liked her at first simply because of her name: Zoya Ivanovna. It sounded gentle and thoughtful, yet exotic—even daring. When I said so to Marina, she laughed. "Zoya," she said with disgust. "That's a village girl name. Zoya is a name for a cow," she added, wrinkling her eyebrows. "Zoya" sounded to her like "Bessie" or "Gertie" sounds to me: quaint, rural, perhaps implying chubbiness. To tell the truth, the woman I walked to school with was not exactly slender and cosmopolitan. But in my perception Zoya Ivanovna will always remains the thoughtful— even daring—figure her name first implied.

We always began our conversation the same way: "Are we late?" Sometimes we spoke Russian, sometimes English, each of us slow and stilted in the other's tongue. Until I arrived she had taught English more than twenty-five years without ever speaking with a native speaker.

We always noted the bad weather and how many lessons each of us had that day, some days never venturing beyond small talk. Usually we wound up on the subject of Zoya Ivanovna's back trouble. Walking, standing, even sitting, she was in constant pain. The doctors had told her she really needed surgery, but it was too expensive and too dangerous. She couldn't even afford painkillers—not that aspirin or much of anything else was available in the pharmacies. "But I talk too much about myself," she said.

Her grandchildren had the "grippe," she told me. Four of them lived with her, her daughter and son-in-law, who shared one small three-bedroom apartment. After teaching school all day, Zoya Ivanovna was responsible for shopping, cooking, cleaning up after them, and babysitting when their parents were at work. She never got any rest, she said. Had she done nothing but complain, I wouldn't have blamed her. But she was kind and bright, and in her way, Zoya Ivanovna attempted to be positive.

The new currency was supposed to be released any day now, and she voiced a predictable disgust with the political maneuvering on the subject. "*Hryvnia*," she muttered, blurting the new currency's name as if it were a curse. "Doesn't that sound unpleasant? Rubles, kopecks—those are words. Words with *good* sounds." As with her own name, I had no idea which words sounded inherently pleasant to a native speaker. I guessed she was mainly nostalgic for the good old days of cheap sausage. Then she added, "Why must everything go back to the past?"

This I didn't understand at first. How could newly independent Ukraine or its currency—the signs of democracy, market reform, and freedom—be a throwback to the past? Then I remembered that *hryvnia* was a word borrowed from one of Ukraine's small windows of independence. After the Russian civil war between the Whites and Reds, Ukraine spent a few months under its own blue-and-yellow flag, with its own parliament and currency, trappings of nationalism that were erased when the Bolsheviks took over. Modern politicians had borrowed the name *hryvnia* to harken back to that earlier period of sovereignty.

Zoya Ivanovna must have seen the Soviet era as a climax, a high point, I thought. Her whole life she had believed in government of the proletariat, and in the idea that all nations are evolving towards an equal and just communal paradise. I recalled how another well-educated, intelligent Ukrainian friend of mine once insisted to me that despite the fall of the Soviet Union, one day all nations would join together in revolutions empowering the common person—if not in a hundred years, then certainly within a thousand. It was government, not Marxist ideology that had been flawed, and true government of the proletariat was inevitable—someday. When I scoffed at my friend's view, she looked a little hurt and never mentioned the subject again.

Zoya Ivanovna and I were almost to school, and she didn't want to talk about contemporary politics any more either. She noted massive puddles spreading across the intersection of Lyatoshinsky and Moscow streets, one of the central intersections of Zhitomir, at the entrance to the bazaar. We were in the heart of the old city, though now only Soviet construction existed. When the front lines of World War II passed through Zhitomir then fell back, passed through and fell back, again and again, the entire city was razed. A few repaired churches hinted at its prewar grandeur, but otherwise it differed little from the instant cities that have sprung up across the Soviet Union since 1945: rows of blocky tenements, each identically ugly.

The street there had been paved over many times, Zoya Ivanovna told me, its crown raised again and again. No one could engineer a lasting run-off, and water continued to collect despite everyone's best efforts.

"Here was once a—how do you say . . . *bolota?*"

Swamp, I told her. A swamp.

"Yes. There was once a swamp here. A very long time ago."

Suddenly I felt a strange sense of timelessness. She meant a *very* long time ago. I tried to picture that spot as it might have looked in the year 884, the time of Zhitomir's first official mention in written history. Nearby would have been camps of pagan Slavs, their *khati*, or thatched-roof huts, in a circle around a common area. A hundred years before St. Volodymyr of Kiev created the Eastern Orthodox church, people lived here on this hilltop above the Teteriv and Kamenka rivers, and even then it was called Zhitomir. Before the Renaissance, before the Middle Ages, before the Mongol empire was anyone's bad dream, there lived in this very place a people who named this town "Harvest of Peace": "*Zhito*" and "*Mir*." Castles, cathedrals, and homes had come and gone hundreds of times over eleven centuries. Once a swamp, now a main intersection, and someday perhaps—who can imagine a thousand years?—a swamp again.

I loved this side of Zoya Ivanovna, the woman who could make me see beyond the surface. Only rarely did she confide in me her true opinions of other teachers, of Ukrainian life, and of the way she believed the world works, drawing on her wise, wide, historical perspective.

"By the way," she went on, "where is your hat?"

Disheartened by the conversation's turn for the mundane, I mumbled that I liked the cool, light mist.

"You need an umbrella or a hat," she said, "because your hair will absorb the extra radiation and fall out."

She hadn't intended to make a pun of "fall out" but I laughed anyway. Wear a hat to avoid radiation—I wondered who thought that one up. Zoya Ivanovna frowned, and I stopped laughing. If the rain really was radioactive, I doubted any hat would help me much.

We finally reached the school building, meandering our way between puddles to the front door. Her classroom was here in the old building, built right after the war; mine was in the new building, the homelier bureaucratic addition of the 1970s. I held open the door, but Zoya Ivanovna didn't enter.

"Thank you," she said. "I won't go to school today."

Confused, I asked why not. "I must go to *Gorispolkom*." She was on her way to the city administration building where John Maddox worked, right around the corner. For once, we weren't going in together to teach. I was puzzled what business she had with the mayor and the "city fathers," who didn't meet with average people too often. Zoya Ivanovna noticed my curiosity. Her face turned sadder than I had ever seen it.

"I received this letter," she told me, pulling from her satchel an official-looking sheet of stationery with a blue-and-yellow trident symbol in the upper corner, large and glaring. I read slowly, noting that it had come from Kiev.

"Are you in trouble?" I asked, wondering if her pension had been reduced for some reason.

"It's about my father."

I tried to read between the lines of bureaucratic doublespeak, seeking a plain, familiar word. A date in the text stood out: 1938.

"I never told you about my history," Zoya Ivanovna began, her voice trembling. "My uncle and aunt brought me up because my mother died when I was born. I loved them all my life like parents. They took me in and were good to me. So I never missed my father."

She paused, and I noticed tears forming in the corners of her eyes. The bell must have rung by now, I thought. My students are sitting upstairs in class, waiting for me, and I'm late. But there was no way I was going to hurry her.

"I barely remember him. I was three when he left. My uncle always told me he ran away. That he didn't want me." She was crying now. "Only now, after all this time," she said, regaining her indignation and turning angry, "do I learn the truth."

A few of the words I had read now fell into place. Labor camp. Victim. Disappear.

"In 1938 he was taken from us. I will never know where he went. Maybe he was killed right away, maybe he died in the *lager*." The *lager*, or Stalinist labor camp, was the final home of millions of Ukrainians and other Soviet citizens imprisoned throughout the 1930s and 1940s. Ten million? Fifteen million? Twenty million? Nobody counted and nobody knows. During the 1930s the Communist government starved, shot, or deported one in every five Ukrainians—over ten million people.

"Of course I don't know where he is buried," Zoya Ivanovna said. "Maybe even Siberia. I will never visit his grave." She took back her letter, which was a formal notification that the newly independent government was now making old records public. As a victim of the Stalinist terror, she was entitled to restitution.

"Now this," she went on, becoming angrier. "Now this. They will give me one million kupons." The equivalent of eight dollars, not even a month's salary. "And all is . . . done." She searched for words in English, sputtering with bitterness. "Repay! How can they repay for this?"

I listened, nodded, kept silent—she asked no more from me than my sympathy, and I would have listened to her for hours if need be. Speaking English made Zoya Ivanovna open up, as if to shape the contours of her hurt in a foreign language was not to touch the most painful part. Furthermore, she wanted me, an outsider, to understand.

"Worst of all is that I was deceived. I grew up proud to be a member of the Party. I was a loyal Komsomolka. I believed in the Party. I became a teacher, and for so many years told my students how good is our life. After school in my free time I went door to door during elections." Soviet schools asked teachers to campaign for local candidates, even when there was only one. Like in the United States, teachers performed all kinds of extra work—except that Zoya Ivanovna's effort supported only the Party's corrupt officials. "When I think of that . . ." she began again, then stopped, her face twisted. She couldn't go on.

On the cusp of her retirement, all the energy she'd expended over all those years was nullified, made pointless. She felt duped. She was tricked by a state that used her up while she preached its superiority. She had boasted of its fairness in comparison with others. Her life's work in support of her ideals turned out to have been more like a cruel joke. First they took her father's life; then they took hers.

"You are late for class," she said. "Your pupils are waiting." Tears had formed in my eyes, and through them I saw by my watch that my ninth-graders had been there already ten minutes. "Go to your lesson," Zoya Ivanovna said.

After such an outpouring I wanted to do something to show I cared. Had I known her better, I might have hugged her. Instead I leaned towards her slightly, looking straight into her clear, pale blue eyes. She would return to school later and teach her lessons, as always. With her bad back, she would raise her arm slowly, not all the way up, to point to the words on the blackboard that read, "Have you the time, Mr. Jones?" She would spend the rest of her days teaching English to children who would grow up in the same town she had, but a town in a nation with a different name. Beyond that, she would never be involved in any school function, any extra work, ever again, she told me. That was her silent protest, her chosen way of finally telling the system, "No." If I couldn't put my arms around her I wanted to say I was sorry—but that wasn't right either. I touched her on the elbow, and I hope she read in my eyes what I meant to say.

"Thank you," said Zoya Ivanovna. "Thank you for listening."

I should have thanked her for solving my mystery. Ukrainians of every kind shared one thing in common: They grew up in a country that exiled, Russified, Sovietized, jailed, or even killed them for asserting their identity as Ukrainians. No wonder the national anthem's chorus proclaimed: "Our foes will perish like dew in the sun. We, brother, will rule our own country." With the melody of that song in my head I went upstairs to my classroom of Ukrainian children.

Chapter Eighteen

Stayers, Leavers

My older pupils became young adults right about the time when Lenin monuments were being replaced by Pepsi billboards proclaiming them (in Ukrainian) the "New Generation" and "New Russians" were seen driving Jeep Cherokees and sporting gold jewelry. They understood quite well the qualities their new society rewarded. The younger pupils, that generation of children now growing up, will barely remember the Soviet Union. They are being raised on bubble gum, Arnold Schwarzenegger, and Madonna albums—components of childhood for much of the world. Whether coveted or hated, Pepsi, Jeeps, and bubble gum are the American Way. Someday, those pupils are likely to question the myth of America as a paradise, but in the meantime they watch MTV.

That year a video by the Pet Shop Boys played endlessly, urging: "Go West, in the open air. Go West, life is peaceful there. Go West, where the skies are blue. Go West, this is what we're gonna do." The eminently hummable melody (based on the USSR's national anthem) was accompanied by images of granite Lenins who waved one open hand invitingly. With obvious irony, the song seemed to say, "So that's what Grandpa Lenin's gesture meant all those years!" Along with the simple, meaningless freedom to choose Pepsi came real dilemmas, the most serious one of all being the freedom to emigrate.

My young pupils considered this question—one not raised in their parents' lifetimes—quite earnestly. So many of their acquaintances, neighbors, and friends had left Ukraine, and not only Jews emigrating to Israel. Thousands of Ukrainians moved to Canada and to every large city in the United States, or to Germany, France, Argentina, Cyprus, the United Arab Emirates. Each destination—first as a source of commerce, next as a place to which to escape—formed a subject of discussion among my friends. Luda told me she heard that Australia accepts Ukrainians who could show they had a relative who emigrated there. As for the United States, if a Ukrainian had no family in our country it was common to come on a temporary visa and simply stay. Finding some kind of work in the United States was not as challenging as earning survival wages in Ukraine. For the less brave, even Russia was a destination for emigration or at least migrant work.

Like a sinking ship, Ukraine was being abandoned. Economic chaos, corruption and lawlessness, pollution, resurgence of disease, and other social problems are not specific to the former Soviet Union; however, with the average person not free to travel in the past, the opportunity to do so now often turns into the possibility to start a better, safer life somewhere else. That quality as much as anything else made Ukraine feel like an abnormal place. In most countries not at war, it is uncommon for everyone to have a relative or acquaintance who has left for good.

Those who left Ukraine found that streets in the West were definitely paved more smoothly than their own pocked, shredded blacktop—but not with gold. Plenty of emigres sent back positive reports. However, according to my Ukrainian friends, a great many others wrote to say, "It's not how I expected." "People here are not like us." "I miss my native soil."

People keep leaving anyway.

As a special project in my second year of teaching, I worked with Galina Vasilievna and Svetlana Adamovna to arrange a special after-school "English club." I originally intended it to be an informal group that would meet just to practice speaking, without the pressures of grades or regular homework assignments. On top of my regular lessons, it meant extra work for me, but it turned out to be one of the most rewarding activities I performed at School 23.

At first, on Wednesday afternoons as soon as school ended, sixth and seventh graders timidly filed into my room and took chairs, as if preparing to hear a lecture in English. We got to know each other after the first few weeks, and before long the group had surpassed all my expectations. Most were the brightest, most gifted students in the school, specially selected by their Ukrainian teachers to join my English Club. When other kids attended, I always welcomed them too, and they joined right in with the excellent speakers. All had an arsenal of stocked-up vocabulary and extensive grammar, and now they had a practical reason to speak: in discussion and conversation in "Mr. John's special class." Once they became comfortable, English burst forth from them in amazingly complex, creative sentences. When they saw that I cared more about *what* they wanted to say than how correctly they said it, they began to speak without fear.

On an early December day when we had grown tired of more structured conversation exercises, I told them we would have a discussion session. Liza told me about a question she had used with her ninth graders, a topic that turned out to be intensely thought-provoking: "If you and your family had the opportunity to leave your country, on the condition that you would never be able to return to your home, even to visit, would you do so?"

We split into "leavers" and "stayers," and I watched with great interest to see which pupils would take which side. I had prepared them the week before by giving them the topic in advance, and they had all thought about it for some time. Most of the girls (and a few boys) uncomfortably shifted to the side of the room where the leavers were to sit. About a third of the class, mostly boys, remained on the other side of the room. Wondering for a moment if drawing lines was a bad idea, I saw edgy looks in their eyes. Was I promoting discord rather than English practice? I took a breath and began anyway.

"So," I said. "Does this mean that those of you in the 'leavers' group, if given the chance, would go away forever? Let's see if we can discuss this issue."

A few half-articulated reasons came out. One girl named Dasha said, "I would stay with my family no matter what; if they weren't leaving, I would never go to a foreign country." Others in the group nervously assented. "My family is all I need. If I can be with them where there is economic opportunity, I could be happy."

Andrey, a rather popular, outspoken boy on the other side of the room, said, "Then why are you not on our side of the room? Your family is here, and you can make something of yourself in your homeland. Why would you leave?"

"I . . . want to see another country," Dasha said.

"But to leave forever?" Andrey said indignantly. I could see that the question had touched some nerves. On the stayers' side, boys were nodding, gelling into a uniformly opinionated group.

The other side, however, felt strongly too. "I want my children to have a good education, to have opportunities," a girl named Yaroslava said. "Right now, in this country, it's not possible."

"What are you saying?" Andrey shouted. "In our school you learn biology, physics, chemistry, mathematics. You know in the West such subjects are not taught so well. It is rather ungrateful of you to say you have had a bad education!" The boys harrumphed, and it looked like the discussion was headed for full-blown argument. People began to murmur to each other.

"I just mean. . . ." Yaroslava paused. In Ukrainian she said, "Well, I can explain, Mr. John, but in a foreign language it's too difficult."

"Wait!" I broke in. "No Ukrainian! Not a word! That's our rule, right? Just try it in English. I know it's not easy."

Yaroslava took a deep breath. "I love my country . . ." she began. The boys groaned, but I cut them off abruptly. "I love my country," she repeated, "but right now it is not safe to live here, not healthy, and I want my children to be . . . civilized."

The boys all burst out in argument at once. Tersely I reminded them that not everyone could speak at once, and we would need to raise hands. Ten hands shot up, and I called out names. "Okay, Andrey, you first, then Oksana, then Yaroslava." The loudest were heard first, but as the conversation progressed, I called on the shyer ones, who spoke too. Amidst the waving hands and hurriedly formed questions and challenges, I scribbled notes, phrases, ideas, and opposing viewpoints on the chalkboard. They supplied them so fast I could barely keep up.

Eventually, some of the more outspoken boys fell back on patriotism, suggesting that the leavers were selfish. "We are the younger generation," Andrey pronounced, "and it is up to us to rebuild our country. If you leave your motherland you are—" He stared up at the ceiling a second, searching for a word. "You are *shirking* your motherland and your duty to make it better."

A boy named Ilya nodded vigorously, and I found myself surprised to find him one of the most fervent stayers. I had noticed Ilya the year before—he stood out in a crowd of students, partly because he had a slight disability. His left eye tilted back in its socket, and he moved with the tenderness of an invalid. "He is not well," Svetlana Adamovna had told me. Although Ilya's physical health might not have been perfect, he was one of the brightest students in the school and had told me he dreamed of visiting England. Interested in vampires, he had spent the summer reading Bram Stoker's *Dracula* in English. He wore a wide smile and pronounced carefully thought-out phrases with a stammer. A Ukrainian school was a hard place to be a misfit, and the year before I once found him doubled over in the hallway, crying. Some bigger boys had punched him until he crumpled in a corner. Helping him up, I got angry, and asked him bitterly if he was hurt.

"Mr. John, I'm all right," he said, still wincing and holding his stomach with both hands. "You don't understand. Our Ukrainian boys can be very . . . cruel."

Now that he was in seventh grade, though, the soft baby down on Ilya's cheeks had worn thin. With fierce pride, he lectured the English Club on love of country. "This is our motherland. Motherland! Mr. John, excuse my language please, but one does not *spit* on this! You girls are thinking you will go away and become rich. This is like a treason." The young child I had known the year before had changed into a passionate adolescent. The girls, however, were unmoved by his speech. Ilya was still awkward, and they giggled behind his back.

Zhenya, Ilya's good friend, chimed in to answer the girls' giggles. "And you . . . don't maybe rich." Ilya corrected him, and Zhenya repeated Ilya's sentence. "Maybe you won't be rich." Red-haired, loyal Zhenya was not as sharp as Ilya, but the two had bonded, and looked out for one another. Slowly, cautiously, he went on, using his own words. "I think . . . in America . . . you will work . . . like donkeys."

When I finished laughing, agreeing he might be right, I called on one of the leavers who wanted to respond, a precocious black-haired girl named Nina. "Well then," she said, "I will have the chance for a rich husband. He will see that I am nice and will marry me." Nina's friend Oksana nodded, and the two of them gave each other very coy, knowing looks, far beyond their years. It startled me a little; they weren't children any more either.

Ilya stood up, and awkwardly but firmly asserted, "Girls, let me say this: Rockefellers and Fords are not on every doorstep."

Nina wanted to correct herself. "It doesn't matter if he's rich. The man I will marry must be my one true love. So, your question, Mr. John—it depends on this. Without love, I wouldn't go. But if I found love, what else is there?"

The boys rolled their eyes. As seventh graders, finding their one true love was apparently not their foremost concern. Irina, one of the few girls on the stayer side, had been very quiet while the boys talked of patriotism, but now she spoke up, challenging Nina. "Do your friends here mean nothing to you?" She went on, getting angry, and I feared the discussion might turn difficult again. "You are very cold, if you think you could go to another country forever, and never see your friends. This tells me that you do not have any close friends." Nina and Oksana were sitting so close to each other they looked attached. "Well," one said, "We could find new friends." The other agreed.

I called on Seryozha, a very small boy with large ears. He almost never spoke because he was so shy; I was thrilled that he had something to say. Brokenly, but with quiet urgency, he said, "If—I—were live in USA . . . what to tell children why I came?"

The group paused in their argument, as if considering what Seryozha said. I could see them trying to visualize living somewhere else. The question, so personal to them, drew them out and enabled them to speak English without self-consciously worrying about impressing anyone. They were speaking their own thoughts for the purpose of being understood, and it was thrilling, exhilarating to watch. More moderator than teacher, I gently directed the conversation just enough to keep it balanced and moving forward, speaking as little as possible except to prevent the shyer ones from being interrupted or shouted down. I could feel the rarest of teaching moments, real thought provoking more real thought, in the most heartfelt, authentic communication I had experienced in a foreign-language classroom. It was the moment I had been dreaming of.

A second Oksana, another quiet girl who had not yet spoken, raised her hand. When I called on her, she spoke in almost a whisper: "We should stay because we are the future."

Yaroslava agreed. "It's my motherland. It's a part of me, and I'm a part of it."

"Mr. John," Andrey said, turning away from the opposing side of the class, "how would you answer this question?"

"Yes, Mr. John," Nina said. "What do you think is right?"

The others chimed in, begging me to express my own views. They wanted me to validate one point of view, to resolve the question with a definitive answer. "It's not for me to say," I said. "Each person must decide. All I can tell you is that it is sad to see the most intelligent people in a country leave the others behind."

The hour had long since passed, and although both sides continued to shout—in English!—as they elaborated their points of view, I let them go. Andrey left the room still arguing with Dasha, and Zhenya paused at the doorway long enough to say, "Mr. John, thank you for the lesson!" It pained me to think that if I were a better teacher maybe I could have made every day—or at least more of the days—this genuine, relevant, and productive. One thought comforted me: I had found my purpose at the school. Helping my English Club students practice their speaking skills was a task I was better equipped to perform than any soul within a hundred miles.

Nina and Oksana were the last to leave. They put on their warm coats, took up their heavy bookbags full of homework, and came to the front of the class to tell me they had reconsidered. Nina admitted that leaving a friend forever would be painful, and Oksana agreed wholeheartedly. "If we had to leave," she said, "certainly it would be very sad. But we could remember our past, together." Nina stared at me intensely, as if intending some deeper meaning.

"That's true," I said, meeting her gaze.

"Well, goodbye, Mr. John," she said. They both headed for the door. Oksana called back, "Thank you for the interesting lesson."

Nina took one final look, to make sure she had seen in my eyes what we both felt—how transient and fragile the moment was. In that classroom in my after-school English Club, I was storing up moments soon to vanish, and it pained me to think that Ukraine would soon be only a memory for me. I was most definitely a leaver. All the people I knew in Zhitomir—Max and Tanya, Marina and Igor, Misha, Luda, Julia, Nina Volodimirivna, Svetlana Adamovna and her family, and my dozens of students—would be unreachable to me. Even if I were to visit again someday, I could never recreate the relationships we had when I lived and worked in their community. When the day came to get on the bus leaving town, I would be torn from the cucumbers and the old Ladas, the scarved babushkas and boys in felt boots, the balconies flying laundry boldly as flags, children tromping through the halls shouting, "Hello Mr. John, hello Mr. John"—everything that was my present life.

The afternoon light in the classroom faded, and outside the early winter dark approached—so early. Far, far too early.

The following spring, when the school year ended, there were the usual big parties, with lots of food brought to the classes, with singing and dancing in the classroom on the last day of school. I said goodbye to my fifth graders in disbelief; the little kids had grown up in two years and would be sixth graders in the fall. My after-school English Club went so well that we produced a class newspaper, xeroxed it at the newly opened copies store, and sold it throughout the school in the last week of May. Against my wishes, the kids named the paper "Mr. John and his Johnovtsi."

Svetlana Adamovna arranged a goodbye party for me in the Teacher's Methodology Room, where I had first met with the principal so long ago. A big group of teachers ate homemade food and made toasts, and of course I toasted them as well, trying not to reveal my sadness.

Then some of the teachers gathered to sing. They had written original lyrics in English to a familiar tune in honor of the occasion. Often, they made such performances to honor someone's birthday, and this event was like a birthday—a celebration of my coming, and the marking of a period of time passing. Tanya, Luda, and even Svetlana Alexandrovna, whom I had displaced from her classroom, stood at the head of the table. When they faltered and stumbled over the words, I only smiled; I had performed in similar events and knew for certain that my friends had first seen the words only ten minutes earlier. They knew that I knew, and it couldn't have mattered less. To the tune of "Oh, Susanna," they sang:

You came from Columbus city
With your knowledge in your head,
You are going to Ohio
And don't forget that we have met.

O-oh, Johnny, oh don't cry for us.
We'll remember you forever
And you mustn't forget us.

We had a dream the other night
When everything was gray,
We thought we saw that Johnny came
Descending down the plane.

The nice sweet smile was on your face
The tear was in your eye,
You said: "I'll come to you some day,
My dear girls, don't you cry."

O-oh, Johnny, oh don't cry for us.
We'll remember you forever
And you mustn't forget us.

In June, right before it was time for me to leave Ukraine, Misha stopped by my dorm while I was packing. Books, clothes, photographs, and souvenirs were strewn all over the place. It had been ninety-degree weather all week, and sweat dripped from my forehead as I separated clothes into separate piles.

"How are you going to get all this stuff home?" he asked, eyeing my Ohio State t-shirt.

"I'm not," I said, tossing him the shirt.

"*Klass!*" he said, holding it up against himself and tossing back his hair. "What about all this other stuff?" Misha asked.

"The typewriter, cassette player, and books go to School 23, kitchen things to my teacher friends . . . let's see, neckties. . . ."

"For me," Misha said, grinning. In packing for Peace Corps I took ten nice silk ties and had worn them frequently. I kept three for job interviews in America; the rest were his. While I spent the afternoon stuffing my luggage, Misha tried on ties and admired himself in my mirror. I was thinking about Liza and the trip we had planned. Together, we would travel throughout Eastern Europe over the end of the summer, working our way south to the warm Greek islands in the Aegean Sea. We were heading back to the United States a couple—my dream come true.

"Look at this," I said, pulling a box from the closet. From inside the box I removed a piece of paper with instructions, printed in tiny Russian. Misha came over and asked what it was for.

"First thing I ever bought here," I told him. "It's a brand new lamp, never been used." The July week I arrived in Zhitomir two years ago—before I could communicate at all—all I could think about was finding the word for writing desk and a lamp to go with it. When the Komandant had tried to tell me about a television set that I didn't want, I had set off on my very first spree alone, ready to prowl the town and practice my reconnaissance shopping. In a store full of junk, I found the tulip-shaped lamp with a curved neck and a round base and spent ten bucks on it. Only when I returned to the dorm did I realize that it was a wall lamp, hopelessly unbalanced, and would never sit on a desk. It turned out to be impossible to hang as well, and there was no place to plug it in. It reminded me of how confused I had been at first, how eager to prove myself—unaware of how foolish I must have looked in school, in town, and in people's homes. Wandering around like a zombie, I had been welcomed, reassured, even pampered. The useless lamp that sat in my closet unused for two years recreated that time so vividly I thought for a moment I might cry. My two years were over, and when I moved out of the dorm, the stupid lamp would stay and I would leave. Probably the Komandant would discover it and figure out how to hook it up in his office.

Misha returned to the mirror, intent on carefully adjusting

and readjusting the tight triangular knot in one of his new ties. "By the way," he said offhandedly, "did you take a shower this week?"

"Umm, no," I said, not sure what he was suggesting. "Why?"

"Just thought you'd be happy about the hot water coming on."

I yelped like a wounded dog and shoved past him into the bathroom. Turning the squeaky tap as fast as I could caused a cinnamon-colored muck to spatter into the sink; the thick gush turned from brown to clear, and in seconds steamy water raced around a sink basin that had known only cold for what, a year now? No, *over* a year. Way back in October, eight months ago, I had given up on hot water and had quit touching the left tap. The first winter I had longed for hot running water, but by the second I had grown accustomed to never having it. Still, for two long winters of cold, dark evenings in this apartment, I had dreamed of a luxurious bath. Hot, running water, flowing copiously—in July. It was a sick joke.

"It's the middle of summer!" I shouted. "What do we need hot water for now?" In horror, I realized that my words echoed exactly those with which the Komandant had answered my complaints about cold showers one hot August week so long ago when I moved in this place.

"Oh, I don't know," Misha said, still more interested in his tie. "I think the Institute got some bonus credit or state subsidy or something. The girls downstairs have been lined up taking showers for days."

"Days?" I screeched. "You mean I had hot water and didn't know?" I put my hand under the faucet, and though it nearly scalded me, I held it there a long time. Hot, very hot, running water.

"Don't feel bad," Misha said. "Rumor has it that it will quit any day now." Turning to me, his necktie knotted perfectly, he smiled and added, "Maybe tomorrow."

For the rest of the week I could hardly keep from laughing.

In my final month, after school had let out, I agreed to a few last school visits. Performing as an English-speaking celebrity had grown old and tiresome, but one of the things I had learned about myself in Ukraine was that I often had a hard time saying no. When the Pedagogical High School in Korostyshiv invited me to attend its English Festival, I agreed.

On a hot, hazy afternoon I found myself in a gymnasium filled with teenagers, most of whom had (like me) been wheedled into attending. The school was a special one for training future teachers; the best graduates were assured of places in Zhitomir's Teacher Training College. In addition to heavy training in math and science, the high schoolers took intensive foreign language classes, both English and German. The "festival" was more like an assembly to show off talents, and as one of my last starring performances as "The American Teacher Mr. John," I was made an official judge of the event.

Imitating a popular television game show, the brightest pupils had divided themselves into two competing teams. Each team collaborated to answer questions about "Famous People," and I dutifully scored both the correctness and the grammar and pronunciation of the answer on a little chart handed me by the head teacher. By now, assigning fives and fours with the wanton imperiousness of a tyrant had become second nature.

The poetry readings were especially difficult to score. The students' talent for memorizing was universal, though they spoke from memory and not from understanding of the sounds they made. Still, I gave Victoria's "So We'll Go No More a 'Roving" a five, and Svitlana's "I Want to Live" a four, smiling and nodding even when some lines were incomprehensible. Soviet teachers' books listed Scottish pronunciation as extra-difficult and therefore good memorization material. One of the students blubbered out: "O My Luve's like a red, red, rose, That's newly sprung in June . . ." but faltered on "Till a' the seas gang dry, my dear, And the rocks melt wi' the sun." Slavic Scottish, hilarious at first, was now old hat too. I gave her a four for effort.

We moved into the "Who knows more proverbs" section of the contest, which had to be called off after both teams and the audience combined to recite more than forty, with no end in sight. The students had to perform an impromptu "Interview-and-Answer," and then another called "What would you say to your darling?" I was impressed with the Pedagogical High School's English teacher—her English, though stilted and archaic, was confident and sure. She was plainly a fantastic teacher who motivated kids not only to memorize grammar rules and poetry, but forced them to use the language to speak. That teacher would have gotten fives from me in every category.

Then came the inevitable.

"Now, Mr. John," a bright-eyed teenager pronounced in precise elocution. "We would like to sing for you one of our favorite new songs in English."

They were going to sing "Yesterday"—I just knew it. Of all the songs I had sung and had heard over and over, this was one I could not bear to hear again. I wondered if its tiresome lyrics and sappy melancholy just might drive me out of the room.

The group assembled in front of me, mostly teenage girls, and faced the judges' table and the audience. My stomach fell. Smiling tightly, I waited for the first screechy note. Of all the moments in Ukraine, listening to renditions of "Yesterday" were not the ones I was going to miss.

But I was wrong. The song was another one. Cheerfully, the girls sang:

> There was a farmer had a dog,
> And Bingo was his name-O.
> Bee! Eye! En-gee-oh!
> Bee! Eye! En-gee-oh!
> Bee! Eye! En-gee-oh!
> And Bingo was his name-O.

I looked in bewilderment at the English teacher—it had to

be a joke being played on me. But she smiled obliviously at her well-trained pupils, never winking or glancing at me as if to hint at any secret, shared knowledge. Now the kids were clapping the letters that dropped out, and the audience quickly caught on and joined in.

    [Clap! Clap!] En-gee-oh!
    [Clap! Clap!] En-gee-oh!
    [Clap! Clap!] En-gee-oh!

    A whole gymnasium full of kids, parents, and teachers—none of whom I had ever met—whacked their hands together in delight to a song I had taught half a dozen times at the Teacher Recertification Institute. I knew that it was mine—no teacher I ever met in Ukraine already knew the song. The wonderful Korostyshiv teacher must have been at one of my sessions, or perhaps she had been to some subsequent session without me. In my last month in Ukraine, a bit of flotsam I had tossed into the country's ocean washed back up on the shore in front of me. Here was a fragment of knowledge with which I had amused my own pupils on a long-ago overwrought afternoon. Now, I imagined, perhaps children all over the oblast were singing it.

    Best of all, the tune in which the kids in Korostyshiv sang "Bingo" sounded completely original. I had probably squawked off-key every time I sang it to a teacher's group, and the teachers always scribbled the words as quickly as possible. They must have pieced together melodies of their own later. Every school in the oblast probably sang "Bingo" a different way. Thus, what I heard at that English Festival were the oddest sounds—unmistakably the same song, yet filtered through Slavic ears and returning to me in a sadly introspective melody.

    [Clap! Clap! Clap-clap] OH!
    [Clap! Clap! Clap-clap] OH!
    [Clap! Clap! Clap-clap] OH!
    And Bingo was his name-O!

The final words, as if to match the melancholy sound of an accordion, dropped to their minor-key conclusion. When the gymnasium burst into thunderous clapping, my hands together made the loudest sound of all. That one ridiculous moment was for me a watershed: the culmination of my Peace Corps work. I actually got to experience my legacy.

Some Peace Corps volunteers can take pride the moment water pours through a newly built pipe into an inaccessible village. Others might point out children who did not die of curable diseases, thanks to the volunteer's aid or training. Some Peace Corps volunteers organize construction of a brand-new school building. My greatest accomplishment? In a few schools in rural central Ukraine, children learning English can now sing "Bingo"—to their very own tune.

I can live with that.

Epilogue

One of Liza's favorite illustrative anecdotes about life in Ukraine was what Volodymyr, a Peace Corps Ukraine administrator told her when they were discussing the frequent electricity outages in central Ukraine.

"It is difficult for us when the electricity goes out," Volodymyr said with a sly grin. "How can we hear over the radio that our life is getting better and better?"

* * *

It would be wonderful today, in 2002, to report that life in Ukraine is getting better. Surely someone there is announcing that over the radio at this very minute. Whether the majority of Ukrainians agree is another question.

The period of 1993-1995, described in this book, was one of uncharacteristic hyperinflation, destroying wages and reducing the country to the barter economy. Since the 1998 introduction of the national currency—the ugly-sounding *Hryvny*—hyperinflation has been checked and some limited economic stability has come. But the country has been rocked by scandal, with several politicians at the highest level accused of corruption and murder. One absconded overseas with millions from the treasury. The sitting president, Leonid Kuchma, was captured on an audiotape threatening to get rid of a young outspoken journalist who was later found beheaded in the woods. Most

Ukrainians were so accustomed to abuse of power that the scandal did not unseat him. Protests around the incident flared briefly but fizzled, since most people have no time to care about such matters, when keeping food on the table is still such a challenge.

Liza and I returned to Kiev, Zhitomir, and Vinnitsa for a visit in the summer of 1999 and were overjoyed to reunite with the stayers—old friends like Tanya, Svetlana Adamovna, and even Misha. Other friends are gone. Some of them have left for good.

Less than a year after my Peace Corps service ended, I telephoned Svetlana Adamovna to find out that her husband, Victor Ivanovich Mesyats, had died within months after at last reaching retirement. His wiry frame with which he liked to show off judo moves was more fragile than it seemed. Smoking two packs of unfiltered tobacco since the age of 14 finished him in his early '60s. Svetlana Adamovna still has Sergey and Larisa to help make trips to the dacha for tomatoes, potatoes, and berries for jam, but his sudden loss hurt her deeply.

Leaving Ukraine for better opportunities wasn't necessarily a safe route either. A friend, Sasha, the friend who attended my birthday party and with whom I played basketball after school, emigrated with his wife and new baby to Germany. To earn money, he bought used cars and transported them back into Ukraine to sell—a very dangerous business, given how lawlessness and corruption still ruled the country. Tanya informed me that on one return trip he had simply disappeared. Given the business he was in, the worst was automatically assumed. He was never found.

Even Max, Tanya's great big bear of a husband, whose English was perfect and who had impressed me with his ability to make do in such a disastrous economy by starting a small coat-manufacturing business, had decided to leave and work outside Ukraine. Tanya stayed at School 23 and continued teaching—even winning a prestigious Teacher of the Year award in the Zhitomir region and then receiving recognition on the national level. Despite his skills and successes as an entrepreneur, foreign language teacher, and charismatic, great human being,

Max felt he had to leave Ukraine to succeed. He moved to London and took a job as a construction worker. He sent home money to Tanya but stayed in the UK for years, noting at one point that he even feared possible retribution from authorities if he showed his face in Zhitomir again; recriminations of that kind had happened in nearby Belarus to those who worked abroad and returned. Tanya applied for a visa to visit him in England—it was her dream to travel, though she intended to go for a summer and then come back to teach. But twice she was denied a visa when attempting to "Go West" legally.

The urge to leave has now grown so strong that even the most horrifying, life-threatening risks imaginable are being taken. With aid from the unscrupulous, many Ukrainian women without Tanya's abilities and prospects have chosen to slip over the border to take jobs as "waitresses" or "dancers," and—usually unwittingly—have been enslaved as sex workers and prevented from returning to Ukraine. The International Organization for Migration estimates that between 1991 and 1998, 500,000 Ukrainian women had been trafficked to the West, with 100,000 of them literally enslaved in the sex industry. Popular destination countries for women from Ukraine include: Turkey, Greece, Cyprus, Italy, Spain, Yugoslavia, Bosnia and Herzegovina, Hungary, Czech Republic, Croatia, Germany, United Arab Emirates, Syria, China, the Netherlands, Canada and Japan.

> Ukrainian women are the largest group of foreign women in prostitution in Turkey and the second largest group of foreign women in prostitution outside the U.S. military bases in Korea. In Israel and Turkey, women from Ukraine, Russia and other former Soviet republics are so prevalent that prostitutes are called "Natashas."
>
> Levels of violence and discrimination directed against women trafficked into prostitution are extreme. Trafficked women get little sympathy or assistance once they are under the control of traffickers and pimps, either

from the general public or social service agencies. In receiving countries, they are treated as criminals, either as prostitutes or illegal immigrants. When they are discovered, often in police raids, they are arrested or jailed pending deportation. Almost no services exist that address the needs of victims of trafficking who are suffering from trauma, poor health, and physical injuries.

The International Organization for Migration (IOM) conducted a survey of 1,189 women and girls, aged 15 to 35, in ten urban regions of Ukraine. The purpose was to assess women's attitudes and intentions toward migration. The IOM concluded that 40 percent of the women in Ukraine are at risk of becoming victims of trafficking mainly due to their interest in emigrating or seeking employment abroad. Although many young women are eager to travel to seek jobs, prostitution was viewed as absolutely unacceptable. When asked if "a job in the sex industry" was an "acceptable job abroad," none of the women and girls in any age group (ages 15-17, 18-19, 20-24, 25-35) said yes. When asked if being a "dancer" or "stripper" was an "acceptable job abroad," however, all of the girls aged 15-17 indicated that it was, while none of the older women said yes.

The "Natasha" Trade—The Transnational Shadow Market of Trafficking in Women, Donna M. Hughes, University of Rhode Island "In the Shadows: Promoting Prosperity or Undermining Stability?" Journal of International Affairs, Spring 2000

The risks to stayers are high, but mostly known; the risks to leavers are mostly unknown—and can be suppressed and rationalized with high hopes.

For Max, it seems, hope was not enough. In the summer of

2001, after Tanya had just failed to receive permission to visit him for the second time, Max was killed in a fall from his balcony. Interpol could not tell her for certain whether he had been pushed out of the window, fell while drinking, or jumped.

The pictures of Max that Tanya showed me when Liza and I visited were of a thinner, sadder man than the one I knew in 1994. Max had always compensated for a melancholy temperament with wry remarks, anecdotal jokes, and big meals and heavy drinking. It was hard for me to imagine Max—robust, sensitive, witty, as hearty a person as I ever met—carrying bricks or pushing wheelbarrows on a construction site, laughing and joking with his unknowing British co-workers while, far from home, he tried to forget a life that none of them could never understand without having lived it. I received Tanya's news by email, an invention that would have changed my Peace Corps experience dramatically, I think, had it been available to me in 1993. Stunned, I left my office and wandered around in the rain crying, grateful that no one could see my tears.

I thought back to a song Max had loved—one that all Ukraine knew by heart, to my astonishment. Freddie Mercury, the tragically deceased singer of the band Queen, was unbelievably popular—even among people whose tastes ran to Metallica. Like the Beatles, Queen's music had inexplicably come to Ukraine when other groups were still banned, and Freddie Mercury is probably even today more popular in Ukraine than anywhere in Western Europe. Somehow its earnest corniness was infectious, and I joined in celebrating its campy sentimentality until I was moved by lyrics that would have made me roll my eyes before I knew so many people who took them seriously.

One Queen song that spoke to Max and so many others was "The Show Must Go On":

> Empty spaces, what are we living for?
> Abandoned places, I guess we know the score
> On and on, does anybody know what we are living for?

Another hero, another mind is crying
Behind the curtain, in the pantomime
Oh, the light, does anybody want to take it any more?

The show must go on. The show must go on.
Inside my heart is breaking, my makeup may be flaking
But my smile still stays on.

*   *   *

At School 23, the show goes on. Other Peace Corps volunteers took my place and, I sincerely hope, performed far better as teachers than I did. School 23 Principal Nina Volodymirivna and Vice Principal for English Galina Vasilievna each traveled to the US with assistance from a teachers' group near Seattle called Accent on Understanding. Later, other teachers took similar opportunities to come to my homeland. In 2001, in gratitude for all my "Ukrainian Mama" did for me, I was proud to have the chance to help pay part of Svetlana Adamovna's travel expenses so that she could spend a month here learning about US schools and teaching Americans about schools and life in Ukraine. I heard afterward that she was a big hit—she became the group's leader (no surprise there) and, so I was told, a charming guest everywhere she went. I didn't have the chance to see her here but I know she is well and can be proud of her amazing career, in which for thirty-some years she taught thousands of Ukrainian children to speak, read, write, and of course sing in English. I hope she feels that "the show" was worth it. I hope Tanya and my other friends at school think so too. Like good teachers everywhere, they have touched more lives than they will ever know.

Today Misha is a teacher too. He reluctantly returned to Baranivka, where his mother lives and where his brother teaches art and history. Misha travels by bus every day out to a much smaller village, where teachers are scarce—and paid even more poorly and rarely than in cities like Zhitomir. When Liza and I visited Zhitomir, I did not expect to see him, as we were only in town a few days and I doubted I could even reach him. A call from the rustic old local telephone station, which hadn't changed at all (our hotel had no phones through which I could reach him), connected me suddenly and somehow unexpectedly with Misha's old granddad—the one who thought it unlikely that Poland produced orange soda since he had been to Poland, and no oranges grew there.

A gravelly voice barked, "Yeah?"

"Hello?" I said. "Misha? Is Misha there?"

"No, he's at work," the voice said. Work, I thought. Misha sure has changed!

"This is John!" I shouted. "It's John, from America! I'm in Zhitomir!"

"Who?" he said. The connection was bad, his hearing had always been terrible, and even in person it took some time to make him understand most things.

"Dedushka!" I yelled. "This is John! Misha's American friend from his dormitory. Remember I visited your house five years ago? I'm in Zhitomir right now. I'll be here for five days."

"You're coming to Zhitomir?"

"I'm here, I'm here already," I said, realizing now my attempt to contact Misha would be futile. "Please tell Misha he can reach me at this number." I slowly read out Svetlana Adamovna's telephone number, or slowly yelled it out one number at a time, actually. It seemed as though he was trying to take it down. "Please tell Misha I was in Zhitomir and I said hello."

"All right," his granddad answered. When I hung up I sighed. At least I had tried.

But the next day Misha was with us in a happy reunion. Miraculously, he sat with Liza and me, as we drank beer together on a cliff overlooking the little creek called the Kamenka. The banks far below us were peppered with goats grazing by the little mushroom-like houses plastered bright white. From the muddy lane below, the sound of dogs idly barking at each other floated up to us as if from a quaint, pastoral scene from the distant past.

"I dropped everything I was doing and came as soon as I got the message," Misha was telling me. I had underestimated Dedushka's mental faculties and long years of experience conveying crucial information over staticky telephone wires. "Dedushka gave me the number and when your teacher friend told me you were here I told my principal to find a sub for the rest of the week." Misha had jumped on a bus and raced into town the very next day. I was touched, glad to see him, and worried about his job.

"I can get a teaching job anytime," he said. "You're only visiting just this once."

Tanya arranged a picnic in the woods of the Park of Relaxation and Culture, down by the reservoir's beach outside of town. Along with some of her friends whom I became acquainted with, Larisa and Sergey came, as well as Misha. Over a fire we roasted shashlyk, ate fresh vegetables and farmers' cheese, drank more than a few toasts of vodka, and laid in the rare, warm August sun, talking. One of Tanya's teacher friends was talking to Misha about his teaching job in the village, encouraging him to think of the country's future and all he was doing to raise Ukrainian children who will, she hoped, be the kind of stayers who rebuild the country into a safer, happier, perhaps even a lighter place. It was a rare, summer sunny day like many of memory. Unlike when I left Peace Corps, I parted from Misha this time feeling that I would surely see him again someday.

As for me, I look back on Ukraine with fondness and take every chance I can get to tell stories about the place I spent two years changing. . . . myself. I would love to say I made the world a better place, but what I really did was make myself better: more open-minded, more experienced in overcoming real and daunting challenges, and, I think, more able to evaluate what matters and what is truly worth worrying about—my wife, Liza, and our new baby.

    I do still worry about Ukraine and hunt the headlines for good news. Chernobyl, at long last, was shut down with financial assistance from the West, though dangerous, dirty, expensive nuclear power remains a government priority in a country where electric efficiency is still so poor. Public investment has newly made the center of Kiev a shining city of gold-domed cathedrals, a tribute to its thousand years of history, though crime and poverty around the perimeter where most people live remain abhorrently high. Access to all manner of Western goods continues to increase as it did during my time there (Peace Corps volunteers can pick up "BeegMaks" at McDonald's drive-thrus all over Kiev if, somehow, they wish). Yet public health continues to decline. My youngest third and fourth grade students are in college now, and—unlike the vanishing generation of the aged who supported and sustained the Soviet Union all their lives—they have grown up with fewer illusions, fewer resources, and less of a naïve, generous openness about what the West has to offer. They know Europe sees them as its unwashed eastern cousins, and while Russia may not present the most attractive offer to fervent nationalists, Ukrainians looking for jobs see a move to Moscow as more sensible than the romantic urge to seek one's fortune in the West. Ukraine will likely be invited into NATO any day now; NATO troops are at the borders of the former USSR now that Poland, Hungary, and Slovakia are all members. If only Ukraine's people will remember how ill-served their country has been by military solutions in the twentieth century. Perhaps, knowing war both hot and cold, they can find better alternatives. Maybe the mirage of peace and prosperity they sought by voting for Ukrainian independence in 1991 is on the horizon. Maybe tomorrow.

    In the meantime, you can be sure that Ukrainians are ever singing, if still with a heavy heart. On lazy warm spring afternoons here in the US, I often glance at my watch and count forward seven hours, wondering what my Ukrainian friends are up to at that moment. While the sun's soft rays warm my bare skin, I realize it is night in Zhitomir, where spring has yet to come. Snow still covers the ground, the bitter wind whips around the corners of the crumbling high rises, and tomorrow promises another challenging struggle to keep spirits lifted. But there, where the end of the day has arrived, an occasion is likely to have come up. The bottles of crystal-clear solace have appeared as if from nowhere. Someone in a cozy apartment stacked to the ceiling with three-liter jars of pickled cucumbers and tomatoes has reached for a guitar, an accordion, a small glass, and a piece of bread. The kettle is on. Its steam, fogging the windows, shutting out the darkness outside, offers an indescribably strong comfort. Someone, impossibly, is beaming her beautiful, sad smile. If I hold still and listen, I can hear the song beginning.

Related websites,

as of February 2002

My website:

http://www.deever.com

Peace Corps

http://www.peacecorps.gov/countries/ukraine/index.cfm
http://peacecorpswriters.org/
http://peacecorpsonline.org
http://pages.prodigy.net/l.hodges/peacorps.htm
http://fox.co.net/ukraine

US assistance

http://www.ednannia.kiev.ua
http://www.usukraine.org
http://www.usaid.kiev.ua
http://www.eurasia.kiev.ua

Culture and Travel

http://www.brama.com
http://www.lavra.kiev.ua
http://www.1plus1.tv (Ukraine's Channel One; click on Webcam for live views of Independence Square and the statue that replaced the giant Lenin.)

Photos

http://www.tiffi.com/ukraine
http://www.uazone.net/gallery

Chornobyl

http://www.ic-chernobyl.kiev.ua/e.htm
http://www.childrenofchornobyl.org
http://www.belarusguide.com/chernobyl1/chlist.htm
http://www.ase.org
http://www.battelle.org/bclscrpt/bookstore99/nuclearlegacy.cfm